AF660774

ISLAM AND SOCEITY

By the same editor

- Higher Education in India: Concept, History, Problems and Suggestions
- Higher Education: An International Perspective
- Islam and Society
- Pedagogy of Islam

The Editor

Dr. Mujibul Hasan Siddiqui, M.A (Economics), M.Ed., M.Phil. (Education), Ph.D.(Education), PGDHE, PGDDE, MADE, CCCA, CCPALA is working as Associate Professor in the Department of Education, Aligarh Muslim University, Aligarh-202002, Uttar Pradesh, India. He has also worked as Acting Chairperson in the Department of Education, Aligarh Muslim University, Aligarh. He has authored and edited many books, encyclopaedias in the area of education, research and innovative teaching, published more than fifty research papers, reviewed eighty national and international research papers. He has attended several national and international seminars, workshops, conferences in India. He is a member of Scientific Advisory Committee of International Conferences, USA IISTE Journal of Education and Practice, IISTE International Institute of Science Technology and Education, Accelerating Global Knowledge, Creation and Sharing IISTE USA P.O. Box 5934, New York, NY 10016 USA and Institute of Knowledge, Sri Lanka and India. He is a member of editorial board of several national and international journals of research. He is the foreign examiner of Ph.D. research scholars and M.Ed. Students and evaluated Ph.D. theses and Dissertations in Faculty of Education of the University of South Africa (UNISA) and University of Zululand, South Africa. He has received several academic and research excellence awards in India like Life Time Education Achievement Award, Bharat Gaurav Ratan Award, Best Educationist Award, Bharat Shiksha Ratan Award, Eminent Educationist Award, Rashtriya Vidya Saraswati Puraskar. He has visited Lootah Groups of Companies as Educational Adviser Dubai, UAE. Member in the International Pannel of the Board of Research Advisers North Carolina, U.S.A. Vice-President of Commonwealth Association for Educational Administration and Management, Uttar Pradesh.

Islam and Society

Edited by
Mujibul Hasan Siddiqui

CONCEPT PUBLISHING COMPANY PVT. LTD.
NEW DELHI-110059

© Editor

All rights reserved. No part of this work may be reproduced, stored, adapted, or transmitted in any form or by any means, electronic, mechanical, photocopying, micro-filming recording or otherwise, or translated in any language, without the prior written permission of the copyright owner and the publisher. The book is sold subject to the condition that it shall not, by way of trade or otherwise, be lent, resold, hired out, or otherwise circulated without the publisher's prior written consent in any form of binding or cover other than that in which it is published.

The views and opinions expressed in this book are author(s)'s own and the facts reported by him/her have been verified to the extent possible, and the publishers are not in anyway liable for the same.

ISBN-13: 978-93-88937-60-3

First Published 2020

Published and Printed by

Concept
Since 1974

Concept Publishing Company Pvt. Ltd.
A/15-16, Commercial Block, Mohan Garden,
New Delhi-110059 (INDIA)
T : 91 11 25351460, 91 11 25351794
E : publishing@conceptpub.com; *W* : www.conceptpub.com

Cataloging in Publication Data--Courtesy: D.K. Agencies (P) Ltd. <docinfo@dkagencies.com>

Islam and society / edited by Mujibul Hasan Siddiqui.
pages cm
Contributed articles.
Includes bibliographical references and index.
ISBN 9789388937603

1. Islam—Social aspects. 2. Islamic education. 3. Women in Islam. 4. Islam and politics. I. Siddiqui, Mujibul Hasan, editor.

LCC BP50.I85 2020 | DDC 297.09 23

Preface

Islam is the religious faith of Muslims, based on the words and religious system founded by the prophet Muhammad and taught by the Holy Quran, the basic principle of which is absolute submission to a unique and personal God, Allah. Islam is the whole body of Muslim believers in Allah. Islam is excellent religion in world affecting the behaviour of human beings for the upliftment of society in general. For the sake of this advancement of society there would be well coordination between Islam and society in respect of implementation and application. This book entitled *Islam and Society* constitutes fifteen chapters.

The first chapter "Islam: A True Religion of Peace, Tranquillity & Intellect" describes meaning, definition, and purpose of Islam. This chapter also highlights about mercy and forgiveness, trustworthiness, social peace, peace between labour and capital, international peace, peace between the ruler and the ruled, peace in the family, peace among individuals, reform, and virtuous deeds. This chapter further describes that Islam prohibits violence and promotes peace and justice and historical evidences favouring the peace-loving attitude of Muslims.

The second chapter "Two Streams of Education in South Asia: A Brief Study" covers relation of knowledge to Islam, academic debacle after 1857. The eighteenth century South Asia produced three Muslim geniuses. Syed Ahmad was a Mughal title-holder who could visualize the imminent collapse of a degenerate political system; farmer's son cultivates future and conflicts of a poet's views. On the Opposite sides of the Raj, practical problems for Syed Ahmad, Maulana Nanautawi was moving slowly and he was sure of every small step. He displayed stability of intellect. This chapter again makes emphasis on Islamic concept of education, efforts to merge two systems, Maulana Nanautawi's viewpoint, divergent views of contemporary society, no-bargain attitude of Europe, choice between attitude and education, Hakim ul Islam's plans impeded, fatwa against Syed Ahmad, Deoband's contribution to Aligarh, issues dividing the academia.

The third chapter describes about "Impact of Religious Factors on Development of Education System". It includes looking to the past, Islam, Christianity, Buddhism, Hinduism, Judaism, Religion in Education.

The fourth chapter entitled "The Need of Islamic Reform: An Analysis of Justification" describes the history of reform in Islam, the words of many scholars about Islam from India and the world. Islam and Islamic learning need to be democratised. As Maulana Azad said: "Our history is replete with the doings of ulemas who have brought humiliation and disgrace to Islam in every age." We have to acknowledge deep problems in classical Islamic thought, educate about the formation of Sharia, reform traditional Sharia, promote and protect freedoms, accept the equality of humanity, hope and patience, and avoid false reformists.

Chapter fifth states about "Boko Haram Islamist Insurgency in Nigeria: Its Global Jihadist Connections."

The sixth chapter describes "Islamic Education and Politics: Readings in the History of Madrasah System in India". This chapter highlights the concepts of promoted Islamic education, objectives of Madrasah education, concept and meaning of Islamic education, Madrasah educational institution, the Madrasah educational system, curriculum in Madrasah, curriculum addressing the needs of globalized era, development of Islamic education: Phase I—The Advent of Islam, Phase II—Islamic Conquests and the Development of the Muslim State, Phase III–Creativity.

This chapter further states about the evolution in the educational system of Madrasah, reformation of Madrasah, Madrasah in India: an outline of history and curriculum, Madrasa education in colonial India, tracing the Islamic education in India. We need to observe and categorize the impacts of policies applied by British Company on the Indian Muslim society during British India. In relation to its educational policies the Company's activities can be divided into four periods: 1. The first period (1600-1700), 2. Second Period (1700-1813), 3. Third Period (1813-1835), 4. Fourth Period (1835-1947). This chapter puts light on the post-independence status of Madrasah education in India, the state-madrasah relationships in India after Independence, the area intensive and Madrasa modernization programme.

The seventh chapter addresses the crucial issue, viz., "Dower (*Mahr*) in Islam: A Criti Analysis". Mahr in the Holy Qur'an, Mahr in Sunnah, The Methods of Mahr Payment, The Philosophy of Mahr.

The eighth chapter states about "Women in the Light of Islam: As Child and as Daughter, As Sister and As Wife". This chapter gives more emphasis on equality of men and women in Islam and their complementary nature to one another.

The ninth chapter states about "Islamic Education under the Great Mughals (1526-1857 A.D.)".

The tenth chapter, "Islamic Education through Modern Teaching Methods in Jordan" describes about the Trends of Islamic Education Teachers towards the use of modern strategies in Jordan.

The eleventh chapter states about "Women, Quranic Injunctions and Indian Nation-State". It consists of Quranic perspective, concept of equality in the society, education and work, an independent legal personality with full equal rights, equality in political matters, human rights of Muslim women in India with constitutional provision.

The twelfth chapter states about "Basic Notion of Islamic State and Politics." This chapter gives attention on the concept of Islamic state, the primary structure of the Islamic state, the Key features of an Islamic state, executive and legislature in the Islamic state, the Purpose of an Islamic state, fundamental rights in Islamic state, non-Muslim rights in Islamic state, the law of the Islamic state, sources of the Islamic law of Shariah, Objectives of the Shariah law, implementation of Sharia law, the political dimension of Islam, principles of Islamic political system and justice and equality which includes (*al-Adlwa al-Musawat*): 1. God's Sovereignty (*Hakimiyyat Allah*), 2. Caliphate or Imamate Government (*Hukumat al-Khilafawa al-Imama*), 3. Consultative Government : (*Hukumat al-Shura*), 4. Pledge of Allegiance (*Bay'a*), 5. Obedience (*Täah*), 6. Justice and Equality: (*al-`Adlwa al-Musawat*). This chapter also provides due emphasis on the concept of democracy in Islam, Islamic democracy and Western democracy.

The thirteenth chapter "Significance of Seeking Education in Islam: With Special Reference to Women's Education," postures concept of education from Islamic perspective, acquisition of knowledge as highlighted by Quran, standards for Islamic education, the goal of education in Islam, Islamic views on girls' education as rights. The scholars have divided the knowledge that a woman should seek into two types of obligations: 1. Individual obligation 2.Collective obligation. The following common barriers to girls' education: (1) Poverty in India, (2) Cultural environment, (3) Inadequate State strategies and policies, (4) School atmosphere, (5) Lack of proper religious knowledge, (6) Lack of political will.

The fourteenth chapter illustrates the "Human Rights in the Light of Islam" which contains the right to life, the right to the safety of life, respect for the chastity of women, the right to a basic standard of life, individual's right to freedom, the right to justice, equality of human beings, the right to co-operate and not to co-operate.

The fifteenth chapter entitled, "*Tajdid* (Islamic revival) of Snah Wali Allah Dehlawi: Political Dimension" focuses on Mughal Empire in the post-Aurangazeb era, Nadir Shah's invasion and its impact, the third battle of Panipat and its impact, Shah Wali Allah's *Tajdid* in the prevalent political situation.

Contents

List of Contributors

Ahmad Mahmoud Ali Al Ghzawi, Research Scholar, Department of Education, Aligarh Muslim University, Aligarh.
Email: *ali0781473197@gmail.com*

Dr. Firdous Ahmad Sofal, Assistant Professor, School of Education, Central University of Kashmir, Academic Campus-I, Nowgam, Srinagar, 190015 J&K, India
Email: *sofaleducation@cukashmir.ac.in, sofaleducation@gmail.com*

Dr. Gulshana Wani, Assistant Professor, University of Kashmir, Campus I, Hazratbal, Nowgam, Srinagar.
Email: *drgulshanwani@yahoo.com*

Hussein Ahmed Abdo Rajhy, Lecturer, College of Education-Abs, Hajjah University, Yemen & Ph.D. Researcher, Department of Education, Dr. Babasaheb Ambedkar Marathwada University, Aurangabad, Maharashtra, India. **Email**: *husseinrajhy@gmail.com, shmiase@gmail.com*

Dr. Iftekhar Ahmed Ansari, Associate Professor, Department of Political Science, N.R.E.C. College, Khurja
Email: *politicsnrec@gmail.com*

Dr. Ismail Thamarasseri, Assistant Professor, Department of Education, Central University of Kashmir, Wanabal, Nowgam Bypass, Srinagar-190015, Jammu & Kashmir, India.
E-mail: *ismailktkl@gmail.com*

Dr. Khan Gulnaz Begum Md. Ishaque, Assistant Professor, Pratibha Niketan College, Nanded, Maharashtra.

Dr. Meraj Ahmad Meraj, Assistant Professor, Department of Arabic, Aliah University, Kolkata.
Email: *merajjnu@gmail.com*

Dr. Mohammad Hanif Ahmad, Assistant Professor (Education and Training), College of Teacher Education, Sambhal, Uttar Pradesh (A Constituent College of Maulana Azad National Urdu University, Hyderabad).
Email: *hanifm69@gmail.com*

Muhammad Tariq Ghazi, Director, Umam Studies House (USH), Toronto, Canada
Email: *m.tariqghazi@gmail.com*

Dr. Mujibul Hasan Siddiqui, Associate Professor, Department of Education, Aligarh Muslim University, Aligarh.
Email: *mhsiddiqui50@gmail.com*

Dr. Shah Raziq Khalid, Associate Professor, Department of Law, S.V. College, Aligarh.
Email: *srksvc70@gmail.com*

Dr. Md. Tarique Anwer, Guest Faculty, Department of Political Science, S.P.M. College for Women (SOL), University of Delhi, Delhi.

Thanveer T., Ph.D. Research Scholar, School of Humanities and Social Sciences, Hamdard University, New Delhi.
Email: *tanveerkpm@gmail.com*

Usma Nazir, Research Scholar, Aligarh Muslim University, Aligarh
Email: *usma.amu@gmail.com*

Zaffar Ahmad Nadaf, Guest Faculty, School of Education, Central University of Kashmir, Campus I, Nowgam, Srinagar.
Email: *zanadaf.amu@gmail.com*

Zayon O. Nzegbulam, Chief Lecturer (Associate Prof.), The School of General Studies, Abia State Polytechnic, Aba and a Ph.D. Research Scholar, Department of Defence and Strategic Studies, Punjabi University, Patiala, India. **Email**: *dearhumble1@gmail.com*

1
Islam: A True Religion of Peace, Tranquillity and Intellect

Mujibul Hasan Siddiqui and *Zaffar Ahmad Nadaf*

Introduction

In the current era, many people regard Islam as a religion that promotes violence and terrorism, the misconception that is in contrast to the teachings of Islam. Indeed, 'peace' as Islamic philosophy can be explicitly inferred from the meaning of the word "Islam itself." Islam is in fact a religion that promotes peace and understanding among people of all faiths in all fields of human relationship. Terrorism has surfaced as the biggest menace of the current times, particularly in past few decades. Unfortunately and unjustly, Islam and Muslims are deemed by most of the world population to be the root cause of this upsurge of terrorism all across the world.

There is no doubt that this is far from accurate. However, a considerable majority of the world's population still blames Islam and Muslims. This is mostly because of the "bad press" deliberately being created against Muslims by the big guns of world media.

The best way to authenticate or reject this claim for a common person is to see what the actual teachings of Islam are. Is it really a religion that promotes violence and terrorism, or is the reality totally opposite to this misconception? One convenient way of observing and analyzing all this is to learn what the Holy Qur'an, the religious Scripture of Muslims, has to say about this.

Meanings of "Islam"

Let us start our conversation with the fact that the word "Islam" is derived from "salaam", a word meaning peace. It also relates a person submitting himself to the will of The Mightiest in order to seek eternal peace and tranquillity. The crux of this observation is that the very origins of Islam are inclined towards peace and harmony.

The Definition of Islam

The root of the word Islam, refers to "making peace, being in a mutually peaceful environment, greetings, rescue, safety, being secure, finding peace, reaching salvation and well-being or being far from danger, attaining goodness, comfort and favour, keeping away from troubles and disasters, submitting the self and obeying, respect, being far from wrong."

The "submitting the self and obeying" here means, "submitting to justice and righteousness in order to reach peace and safety and being in a peaceful environment by one's free will." In fact, salaam and salaamat, means, "to reach salvation," and their rubai form (with four radical letters) aslama means "submitted, became Muslim, and made peace." "Islam" as either a noun or a verb with these meanings is mentioned in many verses in the Qur'an.

From this perspective, Islam is "submission to God, accepting His authority as well as obeying His orders"; "one's total submission to God and serving only Him"; "embracing the messages of the Prophet Muhammad (peace be upon him) and abiding by them." In this sense, a Muslim is one who is under the peaceful and safe shade of Islam. God wants a Muslim to live in a safe and peaceful environment and to make efforts for the spread and continuity of peace.

Since Islam means living in a peaceful environment that emerges as a result of submission to God, the Qur'an asks that all humanity should embrace Islam, that is, peace, and reminds us to avoid following Satan. As stated in the verse, "O you who believe! Come in full submission to God, all of you, (without allowing any discord among you due to worldly reasons), and do not follow in the footsteps of Satan, for indeed he is a manifest enemy to you (seeking to seduce you to rebel against God, with glittering promises)" (Qur'an, 2:208). Satan is the enemy of peace. This verse is followed by a reminder of God's All-Glorious with irresistible might if believers "stumble and fall back" from following God's way to realize peace and agreement.

The Purpose of Islam

In order to be able portray a fair image of Islam; we have to consider its divinely inspired purposes, which yield, as a result, a just worldly order. By applying preventive measures to ensure security of wealth, life, mind, religion, and reproduction, Islam aims to build a society in peace, serenity, friendship, collaboration, altruism, justice, and virtue.

According to the Qur'an, all Muslims are brothers and sisters to each other and if a disagreement appears among them they make peace and correct it (Qur'an, 49:10). They help each other to avoid what God forbids and to observe their religious awareness at every stage in their life (Qur'an, 5:2); they carry out important tasks after shura, that is, consultation (Qur'an, 3:159; 42:38); and they always witness truthfully and are just even if it is against their close relatives (Qur'an, 4:135).

Again, as mentioned in the Qur'an, a true Muslim follows the straight path. That means that he or she is faithful, honest, and just, is calm, lives to perfectly observe his or her religion and in guidance of reason. Pursuing the straight path can be understood as being absolutely truthful and honest in all circumstances, as well as embracing a moderate way of life that encourages good relations with everyone.

Living on the straight path is the most significant desire for any Muslim. Upon the revelation of the verse, Pursue, then, what is exactly right (in every matter of the Religion), as you are commanded (by God), and those who, along with you, have turned (to God with faith, repenting their former ways, let them do likewise); and do not rebel against the bounds of the Straight Path (O believers)! He indeed sees well all that you do (Qur'an, 11:112), the Prophet Muhammad (peace be upon him) said, "The chapter Hud has made me older." In this sense, the Companions commented on the verse, "There was no verse revealed to the Prophet Muhammad that is more powerful than this." Such a verse that so powerfully enjoins "what is right" should have the power to eradicate all kinds of violence and oppression, which are obviously not the right path to follow in social relations.

Mercy and Forgiveness

Divine compassion and Prophetic mercy assign special importance to forgiveness and tolerance. As God the Most Gracious is merciful to all people, His Prophet Muhammad (peace be upon him) is merciful and compassionate to all believers (Qur'an, 9:128). God's clear order to the

Prophet Muhammad (peace be upon him) is to embrace forgiveness. The verse Adopt the way of forbearance and tolerance, and enjoin what is good and right, and withdraw from the ignorant ones (Qur'an, 7:199) indicates this.

By the blessing of God, the Prophet succeeded in establishing unity among people by acting with compassion and mercy. If he had treated the people around him severely and rudely, they would have left him and their unity would have collapsed (Qur'an, 3:159).

Since God and the Messenger of God are merciful and compassionate to believers, those who take the divinely prescribed ethics and the prophetic character as their example should obviously treat one another with mercy and compassion. Therefore, those who have received the Prophet Muhammad's (peace be upon him) message can never be severe, arrogant, antagonistic, or hostile.

Furthermore, God Almighty advises His Messenger to be forgiving and to consult people by asking for their ideas (Qur'an, 3:159; 42:38), since exchanging ideas increases feelings of unity and cooperation while reducing tension between people. As a result, a desire for change that transforms hatred into peace and serenity appears in society.

According to the Messenger of God, people are equal before God as the teeth of a comb are equal. Characteristics like language, ancestry, race, wealth, and poverty are not signs of superiority. In the thirteenth verse of the chapter Al-Hujurat, the creation of humankind from a female and a male, the division of humanity into ethnic groups or nations and tribes in order to know one another, and the importance of fearing God in order to become valued in God's view are pointed out.

The verse approves having an identity and being known by an identity; nonetheless, it rejects the abuse of affiliation (to different gender, social or ethnic groups) as a means of superiority. Thus, it assesses a person's honour and value in terms of universal values that he or she gains through his or her own will and effort, and not in terms of gender or ethnic ties, which are not obtained through free will.

In Islam, the individual is considered as a person that gains value within the society, as someone who is responsible to the community in a social context. According to Islam, the life of a human being is a trust from God, irrespective of his or her ancestry, colour, or language, and hence should be protected meticulously. The main idea in Islam is to praise God the Almighty (Qur'an, 1:1; 6:45), to show compassion to creation. Humankind is the best of all creations (Qur'an, 17:70) and is created of the best stature (Qur'an, 95:4). So, every human deserves respect by nature; approaching them with lenience, tolerance, and humility is certainly virtuous. Hence, staying away from hatred and having a tolerant attitude is essential for humanity.

God the Almighty asks from the Messenger of God (peace be upon him) in particular and from all Muslims in general to be forgiving (Qur'an, 42:37; 3:134). Thus, God loves good attitudes such as spending and serving for the sake of humankind at all times under all circumstances, forgiving people, and avoiding doing something wrong when we become angry.

Even if one has the right to retaliate in response to an evil action, forgiveness is more appropriate for those who are more pious. The Qur'an enlightens all humanity on this issue: The recompense of an evil deed can only be an evil equal to it; but whoever pardons and makes reconciliation, his reward is due from God. Surely He does not love the wrongdoers (Qur'an, 42:40; see also Qur'an, 42:43).

Besides, each of us lives on the path that God has ordained for him or her. For this reason, it is important to emphasize serving rather than fighting. God says in the Qur'an (5:48), Strive then together as if competing in good works, and also, say: Everyone acts according to his own character (made up of his creed, worldview and disposition), and your Lord knows best who is guided in his way (17:84). Therefore, individuals should not dispute and fight over their different ideas to satisfy their ambitions and self-interests. Rather, on the contrary, they should compete to show good character and to serve in the best way; they should support each other not in wrongdoing, but in doing well.

Trustworthiness

An important dimension of being a Muslim is trustworthiness. Every Prophet is introduced in the Qur'an with the attribute of trustworthiness. Qur'an, 7:68; 26:107, 125, 143, 178; 44:18. First and foremost, the Prophet Muhammad, the most trustworthy of the heavens and earth, and all the prophets preceding him, made efforts to promote trustworthiness in their societies.

In a place where trust does not exist, love, respect and solidarity are also absent. The lack of trust destroys family, as well as social, cultural, and economic life. For this reason, the Prophet Muhammad (peace be upon him) states that trustworthiness and treachery cannot exist together and asserts, "One, who betrays, harms, or deceives a Muslim, is not of us." He describes the ideal Muslim as thus: "A

Muslim is one from whose hand and tongue people are safe. A believer is one from whom people know that their wealth and lives are safe." In one hadith, the Messenger of God describes those who are good and those who are bad: "The good amongst you is the one from whom good things are expected and by whom people are sure that they will not be harmed. The bad amongst you is the one from whom good things are not expected and from whose evil people do not feel safe." From this, it can be understood that a believer is one who is trustworthy, and therefore, no one would fear any danger from him or her under any circumstances.

In Islam, good morals, love and respect for God and the Prophet Muhammad (peace be upon him) are expected from believers. Appropriate love, mercy and compassion are to be shown, not only to people but also to every creature in nature since, according to Islam's core understanding, every creation is a blessing from God and the protection of a blessing is the most fitting behaviour for a human being.

Social Peace

In Islam, the right to life is an absolute value. He who kills a soul unless it be (in legal punishment) for murder or for causing disorder and corruption on the earth will be as if he had killed all humankind; and he who saves a life will be as if he had saved the lives of all humankind (Qur'an 5:32).

When the Messenger of God (peace be upon him) explained Islam's potential to contribute to safety and peace in society, he specified one goal in his time as the following:

> "A rider will travel from Sana'a (a city in Yemen) to Hadhramaut (a region in the southwest of the Arabian peninsula) fearing none but God, or a wolf as regards his sheep."

If we consider the troubles due to the extreme violence Muslims were exposed to both in the Medinan and Meccan periods, we can understand how meaningful was this message expressed by the Prophet. It does not include any desire for revenge against any person or any group; instead, it only expresses an ardent desire for a violence-free world for all.

The Prophet commanded us to maintain social solidarity and cooperation, to open our hearts to our fellows, and to help one another at all times. He said, “Do not cut relations between each other! Do not turn your backs on each other! Do not grow hatred between each other! O God’s servants! Become brothers and sisters!”

Peace between Labour and Capital

The other great problem which is seriously undermining the peace of the world is the discontent prevailing in the working class against the capitalists. Islam claiming to bring about harmony and peace among warring interests has not failed to solve this baffling question also. On the one hand it recognises private ownership because there is no spirit of competition and incentive to progress left without the recognition of this fact, because if those who work harder than others or can bring a superior intellect or higher business capacity into the conduct of their affairs are to be deprived of the just rewards of their labour, all this competition and striving after better results would cease and the world would come to a standstill. On the other, Islam recognises in principle the right of the poor in the wealth of the rich. The Holy Qur’an says that in the wealth of the rich, those who can and who cannot ask have a right.

Islam suggests three remedies to remove the vast disparities of wealth and poverty. Firstly, it enjoins the distribution of inheritance. No man has the power to bequeath the whole of his property to one man, so as to promote its accumulation in a few hands. Under the Islamic Law of inheritance and succession, a man’s property must be distributed among his parents, all his children, his widows, brothers, sisters, and nobody can interfere with or divert this mode of distribution.

Secondly, Islam prohibits the giving and taking of interest. The possibility of being able to raise loans on interest enables people with established credit, to enhance it to any extent they please by borrowing. The huge trusts and syndicates which at present monopolise the sources of the national wealth would not be possible without interest, and wealth would be more evenly distributed among the people.

Thirdly, it is the institution of Zakat. Zakat is a charge of two and a half per cent levied by the Government on all capital, money, precious metals, and merchandise etc., which a person has been in possession of for one year or more. It is not a tax on income, but is a tax on capital. The proceeds of this tax may be provided to those who possess the necessary business capacity, but who are unable to make a start owing to want of funds. By this institution of Zakat, Islam provides for the discharge of all those rights that the poor have in the wealth of the rich, and thus brings about reconciliation between the haves and the have-nots.

International Peace

The third problem which is destroying the peace of the world is the unsatisfactory condition of the international relations. For the settlement of international disputes Islam lays down rules for Muslim states which contemplate a body like the present League of Nations [replaced later by the United Nations – Editor]. The Holy Qur'an says:

> *And if two parties of believers fight against each other, make peace between them; then if after that one of them transgresses against the other, fight the party that transgresses until it returns to the command of Allah. Then if it returns, make peace between them with equity, and act justly. Verily, Allah loves the just.* (Ch. 49: V. 10)

This verse lays down the following principle for the maintenance of international peace: as soon as there are indications of disagreement between two Muslim nations, the other Muslim nations, instead of taking sides with one or the other of them, should at once serve a notice upon them to submit their differences to the 'peace makers' for settlement. But, if one of them refuses to submit to the League, or having submitted refuses to accept the award of the 'peace makers', and prepares to make war, the other nations should all fight it. It is apparent, however, that one nation, however strong, cannot withstand the united forces of all other nations and is bound to make a speedy submission.

Peace between the Rulers and the Ruled

The strained relation of the rulers and the ruled is another factor disturbing the world's peace. Islam prefers a democratic government but does not preclude any form of government. The Holy Qur'an has used the word 'Amanat' (trust) in describing the Islamic concept of Government.

For a full appreciation, however, of the Islamic concept of the State, it is necessary to quote the verse, which in brief but comprehensive terms, describes the nature and duties of the rulers and the ruled. The Holy Qur'an says:

> *Verily, Allah commands you to make over the trusts to those entitled to them, and that, when you judge between men, you judge with justice. And surely excellent is that with which Allah admonishes you! Allah is All-Hearing, All-Seeing.* (Ch. 4: V. 59). According to this verse, government is a trust, and not in the nature of property, and the rulers are required to rule justly. And another verse of the Holy Qur'an states:
> *O ye who believe! Obey Allah, and obey His Messenger and those who are in authority among you...* (Ch. 4: V. 60) enjoins all men to obey those who are in authority over them and thus cuts at the root of all kinds of rebellion and anarchy.

Peace in the Family

By recognising the social status of woman and securing her rights in inheritance, in the guardianship of the children, in the management of the affairs of the family and in worship (in short, in Church and State), Islam has established peace in the family on a firm basis. If men have rights over women, women according to the Qur'an, likewise, have rights over men. According to Islam, women are the keystone of the arch of family life. Unity in the family is essential to a progressive state. Let it not be forgotten that of all religions, Islam alone has accorded woman status which after thirteen centuries of progressive development, working with the legacy of a prior civilisation, under the most favourable circumstances, the most civilised country in the world has not given her. By raising women from the condition of a mere chattel in which they were held before the advent of the Holy Prophet Muhammad, and giving women their rightful place in society, Islam settled those knotty family problems 1300 years ago which in the present progressive state of woman have wrecked many homes.

Peace among Individuals

Islam has laid down detailed injunctions which regulate the relations of individuals towards one another: *God commandeth you to do justice, beneficence and kindness to kith and kin* (Ch. 16: V. 91). In this verse of the Holy Qur'an God has set forth three injunctions. The first step is the step of justice. A Muslim is enjoined to discharge his duty and obligations quite faithfully and honestly and in the best way he can. No violation of the rights of others is permitted. When justice becomes to him a matter of course, he is required to do more than mere justice. He should be beneficent to others. When beneficence begins to appear to him not a very high stage of morals, he should be kind to his fellow people as a mother is kind to her son.

The first stage of morals is of doing good in proportion to the good received; the second stage is of doing more good than the good received; and the third and the highest stage of morals consists in doing good to others, not in return of a good received, nor in doing more good than the good received, but in doing good as prompted by natural impulse without the expectation of any reward or even any appreciation or acknowledgement.

Nothing seems more ironical than that the religion of which the very name signifies peace, which stands for freedom of conscience, which has enjoined upon its followers to respect the religious beliefs of other peoples and to protect their places of worship even at the risk of their own lives, a religion which has struck at the very root of religious acrimony by requiring its followers to believe in the missions of all the Prophets of God and in the Divine origin of their teachings, a religion which has laid down teachings that if fully acted upon would bring about an era of perpetual peace, should be looked upon as a religion breathing war and preaching hatred and a religion propagated at the point of the sword. But such really is the prevailing view about Islam. Let there remain no doubt about it that Islam positively forbids the use of force for the propagation of its teachings.

Peace, Reform, and Virtuous Deeds

The Arabic terms 'islah' (reform) and 'sulh' (peace) are from the same root. Islah means one's reach of peace and serenity while leaving conflicts and deviations; in other words, it refers to leaving confusion by settling a dispute between two people or two sides. Good deeds are actions that are beneficial for people and society, as well as actions that are taken to establish peace and serenity. This concept not only includes offering worship and spending in a good cause but also smiling, behaving warmly to others, establishing friendships, pleasing people by kind words, exchanging greetings, having warm conversation, and controlling bad feelings such as pride, arrogance, anger, envy, animosity, hypocrisy, rancour, and burning ambition. Thus, essentially, virtuous deeds are acts that purify humankind of aggression and bring them to peace.

In the Qur'an, it is recommended to cease disagreements by peace and not to commence further disputes, fights, confusion, and discord; in addition, people are asked to take a balanced approach and seek justice (Qur'an, 8:1; 49:9–10). It is forbidden to spoil peace and tranquillity by corruption; there are penalties for those who do. It is possible to apply the verse, Peace is better (Qur'an, 4:128) which was specifically revealed to eradicate disagreements between couples, to all kinds of human relations. Islam recommends a united and mutually helpful society, and this vision does not only refer to the level of nation, but includes international relations, too. In this sense, from an Islamic perspective, international law should take the establishment of peace as a foundation.

The Qur'an emphasizes peace and reconciliation as basic to all social and even international relations. As mentioned in the Qur'an, Paradise, which is the reward for the pious, is a place of serenity. One of the ninety-nine names of God is Salaam, which means peace. Throughout history, Muslims have made every effort to establish peace and serenity everywhere in all divergent fields, only taking military measures when their enemies tried to hinder these efforts for humankind. Over the course of history, the general approach of Muslims has been supportive of maintaining peace, spreading an environment of serenity and trust, and constructing a civilization of love, compassion, and mercy to share with other people in peace.

Islam Prohibits Violence and Promotes Peace and Justice

As mentioned earlier, the Qur'an—the holy words of none other than Allah Almighty—can best bear the witness for Islam's inclination towards peace, justice, and harmony amongst human beings while negating and discouraging violence, terrorism, and injustice. This becomes very evident if one vows to read the Qur'an and apply it on personal basis. Doing so in modern times is much more convenient as people can read the Qur'an online. Listed below are a few verses that support the claim that Islam is a true religion of peace and tranquillity.

- "O ye who believe! Stand out firmly for justice, as witnesses to Allah, even as against yourselves, or your parents, or your kin, and whether it be (against) rich or poor: for Allah can best protect both. Follow not the lusts (of your hearts), lest ye swerve, and if ye distort (justice) or decline to do justice, verily Allah is well-acquainted with all that ye do." (Surah 4, Verse 135).
- "God advocates justice, charity, and regarding the relatives. In addition, He forbids evil, vice, and transgression. He enlightens you, that you may take heed." (Surah 16, Verse 90).
- "And if ye do punish them, punish them no worse than they punished you: but if ye show patience, which is indeed the best (course) for those who are patient." (Surah 16, Verse 126).

These are just a few references from the Holy Qur'an. You may find many more of them that promote nothing else but peace and justice.

Historical Evidences Favouring the Peace-Loving Attitude of Muslims

The peace-loving attitude and behaviour of Muslims is not a myth. An absolute historical truth is very evident from their deeds when they were in command of different areas of the world where multiple religions were practiced:

- Muslims ruled Spain for about eight centuries. No significant evidence is found that suggests Muslims used force or unnecessary means to oppress non-Muslims living there.
- India is another place that was once ruled by Muslims for a period of over 1,000 years. Currently, about 80 per cent of the population is comprised non-Muslims. If Muslims had used force to convert people from other religions, the status would have been quite different.
- Arabia had been under Muslim influence for 1,400 years. Yet there are about 14 million Coptic Christians found in that region. Had Islam used the sword for its propagation, the situation would have been very different.

Conclusion

As mentioned earlier, the best way to find the truth about teachings of Islam with regard to its propagation can be seen easily from the content of the Qur'an. All you need to do is search the Qur'an online and see countless verses verifying this claim. The only sword Islam believes in, as far as propagation of the religion is concerned, is of logic and intellect:

- "Let there be no compulsion in religion: Truth stands out clear from error" [Al-Qur'an 2:256].
- "Invite (all) to the way of thy Lord with wisdom and beautiful preaching; and argue with them in ways that are best and most gracious." [Al-Qur'an 16:125].

The Qur'an emphasizes peace and reconciliation as basic to all social and even international relations. As mentioned in the Qur'an, Paradise, which is the reward for the pious, is a place of serenity. One of the ninety-nine names of God is Salaam, which means peace. Throughout history, Muslims have made every effort to establish peace and serenity everywhere in all divergent fields, only taking military measures when their enemies tried to hinder these efforts for humankind. Over the course of history, the general approach of Muslims has been supportive of maintaining peace, spreading an environment of serenity and trust, and constructing a civilization of love, compassion, and mercy to share with other people in peace. Islam is a religion of peace; it promotes peace and peaceful existence in all human relations. Islam is aware of the destructive impacts of aggressive use of language to human relations and therefore, strongly warns against this. Peacemaker are agents of good and those who breach it are elements of violence. It is observed that peace and peacemaking are seen in Islamic tradition as part and parcel of human development. Therefore, Islam encourages that one should be very selective when communicating with others because an aggressive word is destructive; it hinders both human relations and societal integration at large and consequently tends to produce destructive results. Islam promotes climate for caring and mutual understanding that respect the unique needs and characteristics of individuals. Every individual is required to practice etiquettes of communication in order to consolidate human relations in societies.

References

Abu, D., (n.d.) *Jihad*, 97.

Andersson, L.G. (1990) *Bad Language*, Oxford, Basil Blackwell, 1990, p. 194.

Arrazi, A. & Zakariyah, M. B. (1978) *Al-tiib al-Rawhaani*, Cairo: Maktabat al-Nahdah al-Misriyah, pp. 17-18.

Bukharî, Iman, 3, 5; Muslim, Iman, 64, 65; Nasaî, Iman, 8, 104, 105.

Bukharî, Manaqib, 25, Ikrah, 1.

Hanbal, A.B. (n.d.) Musnad, V, 110-111

Hasan, V. (2005) *The Study of the Qur`an by Non-Muslim Indian Scholars*, New Delhi, Adam Publishers & Distributors, p. 119.

Julne, D.(1996). *Status and Power in verbal interaction*, Amstardam, John Benjamin Publishing Co., p. 139.

Karamani Hayrettin, *et al.* (edited by). Kur'an Yolu, Türkçe Meal veTefsir, Ankara: Diyanet Isleri Baskanligi Yayinlari, 2006, V, 97–98.

Kidwa, A.R. (n.d.): *The Qur'an: Essential Teachings*, Markfield: Islamic *Foundation*, 2011, pp. 167-168.

Muslim, Birr, 23.

Muslim, Iman, 101,102.

Musnad, II, 349.

Qur'an 10:25

Qur'an 14:24-26.

Qur'an 4:148.

Qur'an 49:11.

Qur'an, 1·6-7; 11:112.

Qur'an, 7:68; 26:107, 125, 143, 178; 44:18.

Qur'an Al Baqarah, 2/27, 205; Al Ma'idah 5/32-33; Al A'raf, 7/56, 85; Ar-Ra'd 13/25; Ash-Shu'ara' 26/183.

Tirmidhi, Fitan, 62; Ahmad b. Hanbal, Musnad, II, 368.

Tirmidhi, Manaqib, 73; Abu Dawud, Adab, 111; Ahmad b. Hanbal, Musnad, V, 411.

Tirmidhi, Tafsir, 58.

2
Two Streams of Education in South Asia: A Brief Study

Muhammad Tariq Ghazi

It is time that South Asia – at least South Asia – revisits its academia. It is time to take account of the past and prepare for the future, especially if Muslims desire a future different from where the recent past has brought them down. For obvious reasons I am not talking about other parts of the world here, but they are free to take a leaf out of this brief study.

Renovation is an Islamic sociological principle of religious import. The centennial phenomenon is essentially of Faithic nature but the principle still guides society in general. It is involuntary in matters of Faith as one or more Renovators appear divinely at the turn of every century in different parts of the Muslim World which need them. However, this principle can be applied voluntarily to restructure adversely affected areas of life, especially where regeneration becomes a societal necessity. In the realm of Faith when Muslims stray from the original course, Deen rebounds and society re-evolves upon finding itself amidst creeping evil. Then the community's collective will rises out of decadence. Temporal life is not so fortunate, as it is devoid of Faithic insight. Education having several disciplines is one such area. To be restructured it needs more than the visionaries.

Relation of Knowledge to Islam

In Islamic epistemology, if we have something like that, knowledge is the kernel that is preserved in the divine storehouse to be used as and when society demands, by anyone who is qualified to use it. System of education, on the other hand, is the crust and coat that has to be devised and developed. Knowledge is constant by nature, academia is variable. Syllabus is a service. One can gain knowledge under a streetlamp, or squatting on the floor, or sitting on a cushioned chair in an air-conditioned lecture theatre, but the essence of wisdom remains the same everywhere in all conditions. Moreover, knowledge is what remains firmly rooted in divine scheme and not in its manifestations which modern people tend to accept as knowledge.

History of education in Islam shows that Dar Arqam in Makkah and the Masjid an-Nabawi in The Madinah were also schools. The Suffah served as hostel for resident students and as classroom where they would regularly revise the knowledge obtained thus far. The Rasool(s)-Allah and the Khulafaar-Rashidin[r] would often give lectures from the minbar, as is evident from the Hadith compendia and what are known as *Aathaar* – interpretative or original wisdom of the scholar Sahabah. In later generations renowned scholars would sit in different corners of city's Masjids imparting knowledge and permitting the qualifying disciples to pass on the torch to the next generations. As number of students and subjects grew, governments and philanthropist felt the need to expand academic facilities. They established colleges and universities adjacent to or separate from Masjid. Saljuqi grand vizier Nizamul Mulk Tusi (1018-1092) established a chain of universities – Madrasah Nizamiyah – in Baghdad, Nishapur, Amol, Balkh, Herat, Isfahan etc. These universities provided free education in Islamic and natural sciences and philosophical thought. Poor or foreign students were additionally provided free residential facilities with stipends for their daily needs. In Islam, knowledge is the birthright of man. And nothing was charged for it in the tradition of prophets who did not charge anything for their teachings. Edward Gibbon admitted that "both rich and poor students had equal opportunities of receiving the highest education in this institution. Education was free and the entire expenses of the poor students were met by the university. These universities "turned out to be the predecessors and models of modern universities that were later established in Europe," Gibbon added.

These schools had produced world's pioneers of science and technology, philosophy and arts – men who were primarily masters of Islamic sciences, who could derive natural sciences from these basic Faith sciences. They knew that The Qur'an was characteristically different from other Scriptures. They experimented with The Book and discovered what was unknown to man.

Similar institutions sprang up all over the countries under Muslim rule in cities of Rey, Bukhara, Eskişehir, Bursa, Edirne, Fustat, Kairouan, Timbuktu, Marrakesh, Cordova, Seville, Toledo and Granada. When Pathans and Turks brought Islam to South Asia in the tenth century, hundreds of centres of higher education were established in almost every city: Multan, Uch, Agra, Delhi, Lahore, Panipat, Jallandhar, Sialkot, Srinagar, Thanesar, Narnaul, Lucknow, Bilgiram, Barnawa, Saharanpur, Jaunpur, Anbehta, Murshidabad, Burhanpur, Ahmadabad, Ahmadnagar, Bijapur, Bidar, Bahawalpur, Malerkotla, Hyderabad, Golconda, Aurangabad, Arcot, Madras etc. to name but a few.

Academic Debacle After 1857

Most of these centres of learning were either destroyed or closed down under European onslaught. Mughal Delhi alone is said to have more than 5,000 such universities, colleges and schools before 1857, prominent ones being Madrasah Muizziyah founded by Sultan Qutbuddin Aybek, Madrasah Razia Sultanah, Madrasah Firuzia established by Firuzshah Tughlaq, Madrasah Nasiriyah by Sultan Nasiruddin Mahmud, Madrasah Shaykh Abdul Haq Muhaddith Dehlawi founded by Jahangir, Madrasah Fatehpuri Begumby one of the queens of Shahjahan, Madrasah Mir Jumlah, Madrasah Maulana Sama'uddin, Madrasah Bazar Daribah built by Nawab Roshan ad-Dowlah, Madrasah Iradatmund Khan also in Daribah, Madrasah Ghaziuddin Khan (now Zakir Husain College), Madrasah Rahimiyah established by Shah Waliullah's father, Madrasah of Shah Ghulam Ali, Madrasah Abul Baqa attached to the Jama Masjid, Delhi headed by Mufti Sadruddin Azurdah etc. (*India During Muslim Rule* – 'Educational Institutions in Muslim India'). This chapter of the English version of the original book in Arabic gives thumbnail sketches of hundreds of only the notable "institutes of higher learning" spread all over South Asia, setting at rest the widespread misconception that Indian Muslims were an illiterate mass before Syed Ahmad's Aligarh movement. Most of these universities were noted even by Syed Ahmad in *Asar as-Sanadid.* They are also discussed in *Tarikh Farishta, Maathir al-Umara, Tarikh i Kashmir, Basatin us-Salatin, Nuzhatul Khawatir.* Most of them were levelled to the ground by the vengeful British.

In the fateful post-Ghazali period, Muslims academia was fractured into two conflicting streams running in opposite directions. That was not the first time in Muslim history, but the total alienation of the two streams was so. Imam Ghazali (1058-1111) had also found himself in somewhat similar situation where, unlike the post-1850s India, the issue was of more emphasis or less on a particular side of education, not on negation of one or the other. The process of alienation and hostility began with the advent of European colonialism. Various individual forces worked in different countries in varying circumstances but all efforts were directed to achieve parallel goals in the Ottoman Empire, Egypt and Mughal South Asia. In the eighteenth century the Muslim World was still active academically, but suffered political decline and economic mismanagement when Europe was reinventing itself. The clash was economic; it imploded into political depression and resulted in Europe's academic victory that it is still enjoying for about seven decades after its defeat in political sphere and forced adjustment in economic zone.

That was the circumstance in which South Asia found itself standing indecisively in the 1800s. Agents of the East India Company, who would beg Mughal emperors in the 1600s for tax-exemption in Surat and Bengal, were already imposing taxes, and famines, on the local populace and deciding amounts of penury stipends to the descendant of earlier Mughal emperors. A section of scholars sensed the danger and began reform movements. They could not stem the rot, but showed people how to get out of the ditch.

A Look at Three Geniuses

The eighteenth century South Asia produced three Muslim geniuses: two of them are most talked about men, and one, who died youngest of the three, is the least noted of the three. Yet each of them influenced Muslim mind and action in his own distinct way. Two of them were directly connected with education and spread of knowledge; one had a temporary association with education as a profession rather than a movement. In chronological order these three were Syed Ahmad (1817-1898), Muhammad Qasim Nanautawi (1833-1880) and Muhammad Iqbal (1877-1938).

Muslims of South Asia have written so much about Syed Ahmad and Muhammad Iqbal that undue devotion to them has given rise to a general misconception that Muslims of South Asia are a barren societal group that is incapable of producing prominent people hence eulogising the duo that was surprisingly born in a sterile and unproductive community.

Maulana Nanautawi, on the other hand is the least remembered person. Little, if any, research is done on his writings, social and educational thought and academic philosophy. Ironically he is more ignored at the institution he established than outside it.

This trio was a product of the failed 1957 War of Independence or its sociological outcome. They might have left a different kind of impact on the society if British had not captured India, and if after gaining power the colonialists had not decided to politically control, economically plunder, socially change, and religiously disintegrate the subcontinent. So much new can still be learned by comparing contribution of this trio with pre-1857 Muslim geniuses like Shaykh Abdul Haq Muhaddith Dehlawi (1551-1642), Shaykh Ahmad Sarhindi Mujaddid Alf-Thani (1564-1624), Ustad Isa Muhammad Effendi (c.1600s), Ustad Ahmad Lahauri (c.1600s), Lutfullah Muhandis (c.1650s), Mulla Nizamuddin Sihalwi (1678-1748), ShahWaliullah Dehlawi (1703-1762), Qazi Sanaullah Panipati (1730-1810), Shah Ghulam Ali Dehlawi (1743-1824) and Shah Abdul Aziz Muhaddith Dehlawi (1745-1823).

Syed Ahmad's Life of Trials

Syed Ahmad was a Mughal title-holder who could visualize the imminent collapse of a degenerate political system. In 1838 after his father's death, according to his biographer Altaf Husain Hali, he changed sides partly because Raja Sohanlal – then secretary to Akbar-II's first crown prince Salim, who would sometimes look after the truncated empire's Finance Department – had stopped all stipends and had withdrawn freehold lands granted to his family (*Hayat i Jaweed* 60). Hali said Syed Ahmad did not complete education and had "forgotten all that he had learned" as a teenager. Later at the age of 29 he re-studied under a couple of teachers a few books of Dars i Nizami like *Quduri*, *Sharh Wiqayah* and *Usul Shashi* in Fiqh and principles of law, *Maqamat i Hariri* and some odes of *Sab'aMu'allaqat* in Arabic grammar and literature, some parts of *Mishkat*, *Muslim* and *Tirmizi* in Hadith (*Hayat i Jaweed* 64). Hali confirmed that he was not a diploma-holding scholar, unlike his other contemporaries. Syed Ahmad himself recognized that.

Raja Sohanlal's unexplained enmity to his family could be a major factor in Syed Ahmad's forming a particular viewpoint and later developing his rigid opinions about Indian Muslim society vis-à-vis British culture. Hali noted that on Hakim Ahsanullah Khan's recommendation Bahadur Shah Zafar awarded to him ancestral title of Jawwad-ud Dowlah with an additional title of Arif Jung (*Hayat i Jaweed* 63). Hakim Ahsanullah Khan was a British spy in the Mughal Court and perhaps he introduced Syed Ahmad to the Raj bureaucracy and in the employ of the East India Company. It was in that atmosphere and the company where Syed Ahmad worked out his academic plans for which he received support from British officials who had been studying Indian – Muslim and Hindu – society, culture and vernacular languages since the days of Fort William College (1800) and John Gilchrist (1759-1841).

Syed Ahmad was not the man of the world he lived in. He was born and raised in conventional Muslim culture of later Mughal era but in his writings in *Tehzibul Akhlaq* he criticised that life-style so much as not caring to complete his education in that traditional academic system; he marvelled at Europe's technological and scientific makeover through the Industrial Revolution and concluded that by simply emulating the British Indian Muslims could attain the same degree of greatness. He was not familiar with the socio-cultural undercurrents that had sparked the Industrial Revolution and effected the change in Europe. He was ready to pay any price in order to help Muslims match the British.

Conflicts of a Poet's Views

Muhammad Iqbal was a product of Victorian South Asia. He was groomed in European academics, with an early sprinkling of traditional tutoring. As a poet he was an admirer of Syed Ahmad, yet in a brief seven-verse poem "To the Students of Aligarh" – 'Talaba i Aligarh ke Naam' (*Kulliyat – Bang i Dara* 114) he advised them that since their "wine is not fermented yet and their yearning still short of attainment; let there be the church lid atop the wineglass." And he said that "Deobandi is the title of every rational religious person." (*Maslak i Ulama i Deoband* 80). Education and academia was his profession, not a means to achieve societal goals. He was unsuccessful as a lawyer and academic, and immensely successful as a poet. However, Iqbal is beyond the purview of this study since his contribution to academic revival is hardly noticeable.

Farmer's Son Cultivates Future

Maulana Muhammad Qasim Nanautawi hailed from an Ashraf family line of the indistinct town of Nanautah in Saharanpur, north of Delhi, but unlike the other two, his background was not remarkable. His father Shaykh Asad Ali was a literate pious farmer tilling a small tract of farmland in Nanautah, a few miles West of Deoband, for the living of a middle class family. Others in the extended family were, however, qualified Ulama of the time. His mother's sister was married to Maulana Mamluk Ali Nanautawi (1789-1851), known as Teacher of Scholars – *Ustaz al-Ulama*. Maulana Ansar Ali from nearby town of Ambehta was a student and son-in-law of Maulana Mamluk Ali and by extension a cousin-in-law of Maulana Nanautawi. At a young age he went to Delhi for education and studied under such scholars as Maulana Mamluk Ali and Shah Abdul Ghani Dehlawi, son of Shah Waliullah. It is believed that Syed Ahmad was also a student of Maulana Mamluk Ali, but Hali does not confirm that.

Ironically, the two lesson-mates before Maulana Mamluk Ali, Syed Ahmad and Maulana Nanautawi, parted ways in spite of coming to similar conclusions about the prevailing situation, which was perhaps one common lesson they had taken from their teacher. Overall decline had set in after the death of Aurangzeb in 1707. The country had lost leadership and direction. Disruptive forces, local and alien, were out to create chaos all around the county. Aurangzeb had sensed academic decline when he drew attention of court scholars to the study of natural sciences but ironically his call was taken for a revival of dry philosophy as became evident later in the formulation of a syllabus by Mulla Nizamuddin Sihalwi, whose father Mulla Qutbuddin of Sihali was an admirer of Mir Fat'hullah Shirazi (c.1582), but only for the study of philosophy and Ptolemaic astronomy. A polymath, Shiraz was an Islamic jurist, economist, mathematician, astronomer, philosopher, artist, physicist, mechanical engineer and inventor. His services were later secured by Ali Adil Shah I of Bijapur to head the Madrasah Aliyah. His influence faded after the era of Shahjahan. By the time of Syed Ahmad about 250 years later he was a forgotten Indian scholar.

The problem with academics in South Asia was that under the Mughals they could not discover a balance. Akbar's era was influenced more by free-thinker Abul Fazl and Faizi rather than an inventive scientist Shirazi. Few people know that Shirazi had originated the idea of machinegun, with multiple gun barrels, for use against the infantry.

Interestingly those cannons could be used in battles, and in peace time simultaneously for grinding corn and commuting passengers. His science was definitely more human-friendly. His inventive influence grew, especially in the sphere of engineering, under Shahjahan, a devout ruler who had sponsored science and technology wrought in the hard or delicate stones of the Red Fort and Taj Mahal and Jama Masjid. India's economy during his reign was so strong that a British visitor would give 50 British sterling pounds to get just one Mughal Tanka. By the time of Aurangzeb, greater focus was laid on Islamic sciences, while his single-minded mission to unite South Asia for the first time in history had demanded both armies of scientists and Islamic scholars. However, focus on religious sciences was obviously for the same reason that would later determine the post-1857 direction of Muslims: a degenerate society needed men like Mirza Mazhar Jan i Janaan (1699-1781) and Shah Ghulam Ali. Aurangzeb had sought to revive a combinitive approach as a device for political stability. He was failed by the academia and later rulers and bureaucrats. The result was a steady rise in the power of the British and overall Indian decline, with growing threat to Muslim belief system itself.

On the Opposite Sides of the Raj

That was the society inherited by Syed Ahmad and Maulana Nanautawi, although they stood on the opposite sides of the socio-political division, British had created. In 1857 a twenty-five years old Maulana Nanautawi was a fighter against the British, while a 40 years old Syed Ahmad was on the side of the British. Their philosophical difference of opinion on other issues is a long story for which one can refer to Hali's *Hayat i Jaweed*, Tayyab Bakhsh Badauni's *I'tiqadat i Sir Syed aur Sharar Badauni*, and Maulana Nanautawi's *Tasfiyatul Aqa'ed* in response to Syed Ahmad's 15 and then 13 questions of religious nature. Their differences on the issue of education were generally clouded by relative accent on system and syllabus, overlooking the need for a revision of academic philosophy. Both of them were in a hurry and did not have time for theoretical hair-splitting, leaving the matter to practical experiences of future generations.

Educational philosophies of Syed Ahmad and Maulana Nanautawi were focused on the well-being of Muslims of South Asia. Both of them were dissatisfied with the present and wanted a different future for their community. But they were looking at things from opposite vantage points. The divergence surfaced in the choice of syllabus. Syed Ahmad was not worried about what was to be taught at his college since the task was given to Europeans: like a 24-year old fresh Oxford graduate Henry George Impey Siddons and eight years later to Theodore Beck, another 24-year old, this time afresh Cambridge graduate of arts. They were obviously, backed by the Establishment.

Before going that far, Syed Ahmad was already convinced that most of the books written by early 'Asian' (Muslim) writers "are either proved wrong, or are incompatible with modern researches and discoveries, so much so that now learning them is useless." (*Sir Syed ka Maghribi Ta'limka Tasawwur* 12). Although this assessment was proved wrong in the next few decades, Syed Ahmad's journey towards the West was very slow. He took time to give up the idea of vernacular university, finally ridiculing the idea of gaining equality with the ruling Europeans through education in vernacular languages. "It is exactly like encouraging America's original natives to learn native sciences in native language to make progress and attain wealth, respect, pomp and governance among the ruling nation" (*Sir Syed ka Maghribi Ta'limka Tasawwur* 17 ref: *Tehzibul Akhlaq* 1886. 132-133). Time proved this theory also wrong in America itself. Educated in Europe as system, Native Americans could achieve nothing remarkable.

Nonetheless, Syed Ahmad was genuinely worried about the fallout of political collision of two major civilizations in the second half of the nineteenth century and resultant destruction, devastation, tension and tribulations. He thought that political collision had brought Muslims face to face with some critical truths. He was right to assess that "almost whole of North India especially Muslims were victims of widespread disorder, mindless and useless politics was the order of the day, industry, agriculture and economy was frozen which were strengthening the power of colonialists." (*Sir Syed ka Maghribi Ta'limka Tasawwur* 19-20). European power was global, and in Syed Ahmad's view, Muslims could not attain that power without learning their arts and sciences, philosophy and technology and by undergoing a major cultural and intellectual revolution.

Practical Problems for Syed Ahmad

Syed Ahmad had a burning desire to achieve parity with Europe, even though he knew that Europe was not just a different continent, but a different planet. From a practical side, however, a lot of debris of socio-political degeneration had accumulated over the past 150 years and to rebuild the social structure Muslims were first required to clear the mess and level the ground. Continual political aftershocks were adding more rubble and a decade after Syed Ahmad's death Muslim elite led by Viqarul Mulk and Nawab Salimullah huddled together in Dhaka to see how best to protect their interests. This political development was planned by the British, according to documents that have recently surfaced in Pakistan. The Congress, just like the Muslim League, was the brainchild of Raj bureaucrats. British hand was visible in every development. The only group that would not allow the colonialists to meddle in national affairs was that of the Ulama.

Maulana Nanautawi was in another proverbial boat. Away from the epicentre of political earthquake, he did not invest time in situation analysis, identification of micro problems, appeals to the government or to the Muslim elite. His prescription was consultation with some like-minded scholars and hit the rot at the root. His outlook was equally global, or more so if one revisits the international outreach of the Silken Letters Movement launched by Maulana Nanautawi's first disciple, Shaykhul Hind Maulana Mahmudul Hasan and Maulana Muhammad Miyan Mansoor Ansari. It was different in nature from the running about of Aligarh's Khairi Brothers, although both movements failed.

Policy of Slow But Sure Steps

Maulana Nanautawi was moving slowly and he was sure of every small step. He displayed stability of intellect. He had a bright inner eye to see things clearly. For him the problem was just two-folds: Muslim elite and Muslim masses – (a) collapse of Muslim political power was due to misdeeds of the elite; and (b) ignorance of Muslim masses about the very basics of religion and their involvement in all sorts of nonsense – innovations and superstitions (بدعات و خرافات) in the name of Deen, and a fresh threat posed by government-backed if not funded Christian missionaries who had spread all over the country. After the 1857 war there was no chance of regaining of independent political power immediately, so the issue had to be put on backburner until the time when qualified people were ready to oust the colonialists and reclaim the lost authority. The immediate task was to bring the masses back to original Islam. The remedy prescribed by Syed Ahmad generally attracted the Muslim elite – children of landed aristocracy whose economy was adversely affected by the revolt and who could retain and protect it only by keeping the colonialists in good humour. Maulana Nanautawi's strategy attracted middle and lower middle classes who had been surviving and could still survive on meagre means but would not agree to trade off their Faith.

That was why Maulana Nanautawi did not waste time on fine-tuning of the syllabus as long as it served the primary goal. He opted for a syllabus developed more than 100 years ago by Mulla Nizamuddin still known as DarsiNizami, but with certain modifications. He did not have time to thoroughly revise it or to prescribe a different syllabus. Nonetheless, he issued specific guidelines in the convocation (Dustar-bundi) address eight years after the establishment of the Darul Uloom, Deoband. That speech is preserved in the archives of the Darul Uloom Deoband and discussed at length in Sawaneh Qasmiby Maulana Nanautawi's biographer Maulana Manazir Ahsan Gilani. It was a revolutionary educational philosophy which, if introduced with the insight of Maulana Nanautawi, could have taken Muslims of South Asia to the days of Jabir Ibn Hayyan (c.721-c.815), Abu Bakr Muhammad Razi (865-925), Ibn al-Haytham (965-1040), Abu Rayhan Albiruni (973-1048), Ibn Sina (980-1037), Ibn Rushd (1126-1198), and Ibn Khaldun (1332-1406). What distinguished these men was that they were astronomers, biologists, botanists, celestial mechanics, chemists, chronologists, geographers, geologists, historians, linguists, logicians, mathematicians, musicologists, philosophers, physicians, physicists, poets, polyglots, psychologists, sociologists, surgeons, zoologists. And all of them were Maulawis first, if I am pardoned for using a current title for them: In varying degrees they were masters of Hadith, exegesis, Fiqh, Usul Fiqh, Usul ad-Deen, even Muftis and Qazis in some cases.

Different from existing or many of the destroyed past madrasahs, Darul Uloom Deoband was started with a purpose. Hakim ul Islam Maulana Qari Muhammad Tayyab (1897-1983), grandson of Maulana Nanautawi, said "the objective of establishing this Madrasah was not just education since basic necessities of such education were already available in the Dars i Nizami (madrasahs), and those associated with the Madrasah were already exponents of those sciences (philosophy and astronomy). The main purpose of the Madrasah was first to prepare freedom-loving Ulama, in addition to training human-friendly experts in Deen" (*Maslak i Ulama i Deoband* 3). He asserted that the Darul Uloom was not just a Madrasah, "It is a school of thought, a school of deeds, a school of proliferation" (*Maslak i Ulama i Deoband* 73).

According to him, Maulana Nanautawi oncc said that the Madrasah was actually "a citadel of Islam which I have dressed up with education."

Islamic Concept of Education

Islamic concept of education is spiritually different from materially-oriented Western system of education. In Islamic environment, even natural sciences acquire spiritual significance because there they are studies in relation with Attributes of Allah, the *Allaam* – Most Knowing, the Creator of *Alams* (worlds/multiverses عالمين), Original Source of *Ilm*. *Ilm* covers intellectual awareness of everything in the Creation. Arabic word *Ilm* has no synonym in any other language; knowledge does not convey the full meaning of the Arabic word, yet it is generally accepted as English synonym for *Ilm*. According to linguists and lexicographers, *Ilm* is congnition and certitude (معرفت و يقين), exertion to find the Truth, cognition of reality, faculty to attain certainty, talent to strengthen Faith. If 'knowledge' fails to attain any or all these objectives, it falls short of *Ilm*, though it could still be regarded as a kind of gainful information. Since this word and its derivatives are often used in the Qur'an, Imam Raghib Isfahani defined it as "cognition of reality of a thing in addition to awareness of the law concerning its assertion or negation." He further said *Ilm* is both visual (نظرى) and functional: visual (or pre-theoretical) knowledge of all that exists and functional which leads to actual worship of the Creator of what exists; hence education "is to counsel the self on concept of meaning, while learning is to advise a person on the concepts itself." (*Mufridat Al-Qur'an* 355-356). Hence, intellectual insight takes one closer to the intent of *Ilm*.

Hazrat Abdullah Ibn Amr[r] said "knowledge is limited to three things: Constant Signs, that is The Qur'an; eternally established Sunnah, that is authentic Hadith; and duties and deeds derived from The Qur'an and the Sunnah (that is Fiqh covering all aspects of human life). Anything else is in excess which one may or may not obtain." Hazrat Ali[r] said *Ilm* was something that should "take the seeker to the path to salvation"; therefore, if knowledge does not lead to salvation, it is not *Ilm*. Hazrat Abdullah Ibn Abbas[r] advised his disciples to "go to the Masjid, teach The Qur'an, Fiqh or Sunnah, since that is better than going to Jihad." He added: "If you can't do that, then learn these sciences, and if you can't do even that, then at least do not despise Ulama. Love and respect them." (*Hayat us-Sahabah* 1:172-179).

Divergent Views of Contemporary Society

These definitions of knowledge and purpose of its spread among the people was generally lost to South Asia of the nineteenth century, but the issue before the pioneers was its application or negation. That is where the paths of Maulana Nanautawi and Syed Ahmad separated. Their divergent views about contemporary society reflected in their conclusions and remedies they had prescribed. Syed Ahmad believed that material supremacy was what Muslims needed to stand up to shoulders of the Europeans; Maulana Nanautawi did not oppose material resurgence: in fact that was his objective as well, but only after ensuring that Muslims had rediscovered their roots in authentically transmitted Faith that was target of British ecclesial onslaught. For him progress without remaining Muslim was of no benefit. He did not want to copy the British. Probably he did not wish Muslims to always remain behind Europe – as is the case today that provoked Muslim Swiss-British Cambridge scholar Charles le Gai Eaton (Hassan Abdul Hakeem) (1921-2010) to warn that "Muslims would always remain behind the West as long as they emulate it." For those who would not be able to understand this statement, Charles le Gai Eaton asserts that only creative people lead the world.

Sir Syed himself arrived at similar conclusions in later years when he recognized that by simply copying the Europeans and by learning their language Muslims cannot overtake the British. It was realization that copycats cannot act as lions.

Here unmistakable emphasis is on being original and innovative where lay the secret of unmatched progress that Muslims had made during the ninth-fifteenth centuries. They were followers of none and originators of natural sciences which they had derived directly from The Qur'an and the Sunnah. For example, long before Ibn Khaldun put his pen to historiography and analyze it in the *Muqaddimah,* he obtained *ijazah* in The Qur'an, Hadith, Fiqh and Uloomash-Shar'iyah, in addition to mastering mathematics, logic and philosophy. He was a bureaucrat attaining the position of grand vizier. Apart from his chequered and eventful life, in writing history and *Muqaddimah* he was essentially guided by frequent advice in The Qur'an to its reciters to "see and analyze fate of people who lived before you, if you have the intellect." Ibn Sina once said that whenever he faced a problem or difficulty in understanding a technicality, he would make fresh ablution, offer two raka 'atsalat with the intention of seeking divine guidance, and everything would become clear by the time he finished the prayer. Farabi, known as the Second Teacher after Aristotle, admitted that the Qur'an – not Greece – was the very basis of his philosophy and a contented heart. For philosophical answer he would refer to The Qur'an before looking back into ancient Greek masters.

The greatest damage done to the post-1857 Muslim society was a clear disconnect, which became more pronounced on the side of those who were regarded as "bright minds" ("moderates" in current parlance). The bright minds (روشن خیال) would, however, accept anything coming from the West as ultimate truth on the issue concerned as against the views of compatriots or coreligionists who would have a different opinion on the same subject. Rashid Ahmad Siddiqi quoted at length a piece from (William Montgomery) W.M. Watt, asserting that "the Muslim intellectuals (more particularly, those of the religious institution) were not adequately prepared to meet the challenge which now come to them" (*Sir Syed ka Maghribi Ta'limka Tasawwur* 22 ref. Watt. *Islam and the Integration of Society* 236-237). This statement emerged from a specific perspective which may not necessarily be true when placed in the opposite perspective. Watt was a priest of the Scottish Episcopal Church. Ironically opinion of a Christian "Maulawi" about Muslims of South Asia, Iran and Egypt was treated with deference in comparison to what a local "Maulawi" would say about his people's condition. This debate is of least interest here, except to highlight general ignorance about the crosscurrents that were going to define and decide the future of Muslims in South Asia. Another such example was a statement of Muhammad Ahmad Khan (*Iqbalaur Mas'ala i Ta'lim* 237 cf *Sir Syed ka Maghribi Ta'limka Tasawwur* 22) that "Deoband was a stagnate (جامد) movement (stagnation and movement are opposite conditions) which had closed its eyes to the pace of time. It was unaware of the calamitous storm which in the form of secular education was breaching the four walls of Islamic Nationalism, therefore, it opposed modern sciences from the outset." (*Sir Syed ka Maghribi Ta'limka Tasawwur*, jeem). This is a self-contradictory statement: Deoband was the bulwark against "the calamitous storm in the form of secular education" that was breaching the social structure, not otherwise. Its objective was that secular education should not be allowed to demolish religious foundations of Muslim society. Khan did not refer to original sources about Deoband's viewpoint and depended on hearsay or what came from Christian priests like Wattet al. at Cambridge and Oxford.

Syed Ahmad's plan was to gain as much of the modern knowledge as possible, but that was not the intention of the British. Calcutta correspondent of *The Times* of London in a report on 22 January, 1877 admitted that the British faced a double problem in educating Hindustani people. Hindus of Bengal had boorishly accepted impact of how they wanted to train their minds. "They have learned our language, they have also got lessons in our history and got a little understanding of our science but their knowledge is no more than coating which has made them arrogant." As for Muslims, they were more rigid and hard to control because "they rival us with their history and way of life and seek to regain the lost power." (*Sir Syed ka Maghribi Ta'limka Tasawwur* 135-136 – retranslation from Urdu). This statement suggested that the British were ready to impart only such modern knowledge that would make Indians good subordinates–oblivious of their own languages, history, culture and glory.

Efforts to Merge Two Systems

Future was not a destination city on a map. It was to be built out of a void. Both Syed Ahmad and Maulana Nanautawi and their immediate successors had to undertake similar tasks. Deoband already was studying different options on how to harmonize the two systems. Others were also experimenting variously. A conference of Ulama – Nadwatul Ulama – held in Kanpur in 1894 decided to open a "modified version of Deoband" with a view to "counter the challenge of Western education." The meeting was attended by Maulana Muhammad Ali Mungeri and Maulana Shibli Nomani, together with five senior representatives from Deoband: Shaykhul-Hind Maulana Mahmud ul Hasan, Maulana Ashraf Ali Thanwi, Maulana Muhammad Khalil Ahmad Saharanpuri, Maulana Fakhrul of Hasan Gangohi and Maulana Abdullah Ansari, who was founder Nazim Deenyat in Aligarh. Later Nadwa as a school was moved to Lucknow. And there it lost sight of its goal as it tilted to one side when John Briscott Hewitt, Lieutenant Governor of India, was invited to lay its foundation stone on November 28, 1906.

Osmania University, Hyderabad established in 1918 merged the two systems in its Department of Deenyat while Aligarh made separate arrangement for theology (literally meaning mythology, or Hindi *deomala*–tales of gods) with option of a B.Th. degree. All these experiments were taken note of with dissatisfaction. (*Sawaneh Qasmi*

2:276). They did not produce the desired results. There is nothing to be ashamed of, though: important factor was that a society amidst a critical situation was struggling hard to find the right path. It is still in the middle of the journey. But the challenge is that it has no clear concept of a destination. Obtaining degrees and securing jobs hardly make a nation great and its members respectable.

Maulana Gilani discussed the issue at length in the second volume of *Sawaneh Qasmi*. He said the problem was how to patch up the two systems: should the Madrasah teach modern sciences and language together with Islamic traditional sciences of their syllabus, or make university syllabus more Islamically oriented. Both ideas were experimented in some institutes in South Asia. The first option was cumbersome. Maulana Nanautawi did not approve of it, at least in the early days of the Madrasah. The second plan was experimented in Nadwatul Ulama, Osmania and also in Aligarh. Gilani himself taught at Osmania for more than a quarter century and said from his personal experience that in Western-oriented academia even a semblance of involvement and association with Islamic sciences was clouded by Westernized approach among the students: they ultimately prefer to ape the West rather than emulate Islam. (*Sawaneh Qasmi* 2: 84). That preference in universities was a direct outcome of Syed Ahmad's opposition to traditional subjects of education. His objective was to westernise Muslims. No wonder if in Aligarh and other universities all over South Asia only orientalist interpretations of Islam are still valid.

Teaching of Islam was given charge to departments of Islamic Studies, a concept again borrowed from the West. It was destined to fail since in these departments and institutes Islam – religion, history and culture – is taught from books written and viewed with overt or covert disdain by the likes of Garcin de Tassy (1794-1878), Gustav Flügel (1802-1870), Victor Hugo (1802-1885), William Muir (1819-1905), Reinhart Dozy (1820-1883), Theodor Nöldeke (1836-1930), Ignaz Goldziher (1850-1921), David Samuel Margoliouth (1858–1940), Carl Brockelman (1868-1956), Leone Caetani (1869–1935), Arent Jan Wensinck (1882-1939), Philip Khuri Hitti (1886-1978), Alfred Guillaume (1902–1969), William Montgomery Watt (1909-2006), Wilfred Cantwell Smith (1916-2000), Bernard Lewis (1916-), Francis E. Peters (1927-), Wilfred Madelung (1930-) etc. Patch-up remains the problem. A patch-up does not necessarily match-up.

No-Bargain Attitude of Europe

Ironically, Europe which was supposed to be emulated was never a subject of academic study in any South Asian university. Asian academics also did not give a thought to what role Christianity – and later Judaism – played in preparing Europe to plunge into a revolution. While Oxford, Cambridge, Harvard, UCLA, Princeton, McGill, Carleton, Sorbonne, Leiden universities had departments and institutes to study Islam, of course, from a colonial-western angle, it was never a Muslim priority to make such studies of the West – Christianity and Judaism – from their Asian or Islamic standpoint. Madrasah could be excused because it was inward-looking. College overlooked an essential element of its *raison d'être*.

Yet another problem that was not in the estimation of Maulana Gilani in the 1970s when he was writing *Sawaheh Qasmi* and Syed Ahmad in the 1870s was underlined in 1992-93 by Dr. Mahmud Ahmad Ghazi (no relative of this writer). He stumbled on it during a weeklong symposium held in Germany on *Is Islam a Threat to the West and Europe?* In the midst of 13 Jewish and Christian Western scholars he was the only Muslim invited to address the issue. So much for academic fairness. In his presentation, Dr. Ghazi told his audience about a new trend gaining strength among Muslims that they should accept good things of the West like science, technology, amenities etc., and reject their philosophies, secularism and irreligiosity, and total man-woman freedom etc. "The symposium had men from France, Germany, Australia. All of them controverted me. They said the West would not allow *you* to benefit from *their* (emphasis is added) technology, *their* civilization and culture on *your* terms. Before that I had never thought whether the West was ready to let you benefit from its technology and tehzib on your terms." (*Maghribkafikri o tehzibichallanjaurulamakizimmedariayn*, Quarterly *Islam Aur •Asr Jadid*. JMI, New Delhi. January 2011, vol. 43 No 1, pp. 70-71). Several years before Dr. Ghazi could understand the modern Western mind, Charles le Gai Eaton said in a lecture in Lahore, Pakistan, that Muslims could not enjoy benefits of modern technology "without taking on board and principles, the suppositions and ideology which produced this technology." (*The Muslims in the west*, http://mysite.mweb.co.za/). That makes the issue more serious and complicated to handle. The West has made a 180-degree turn since Syed Ahmad saved the lives of the family of Bijnor's district collector, one Mr. Shakespeare. Muslims are still camped at the 1858 declaration of Queen Victoria.

Maulana Nanautawi's Viewpoint

A close look at the educational philosophy of Maulana Nanautawi suggests that he was aware of scientific distinction of early Muslims and wished to revive that legacy rather than merely imitating the modern West. That became evident in his convocation address to fresh graduates of the Darul Uloom on 19 ZiQa'dah 1290/9 January 1874. He said Muslim intelligentsia knew education of modern sciences was progressing rapidly because it was offered in liberally funded government schools. Traditional sciences did not make such progress under any sultan of the past. "However, traditional sciences (علوم نقليه) are in decline as never before anywhere in the world. That is why many people have found it of no benefit to open private schools on the lines of government schools." (*Sawaneh Qasmi* 2: 279).

Here Maulana Gilani offered an analogy that a man having only a shirt of coarse cloth, and no pair of trousers, logically needs a pair of trousers instead of another shirt of a finer cloth. Therefore, a reasonable course of action for the Ulama (of Deoband) was to leave government-sponsored modern education to government-funded schools, and focus on the areas neglected by the government and schools run by it since those were the sciences "without which people cannot even remain Muslim." Maulana Nanautawi could foresee that the trend of government's negation of Islamic traditional sciences "will further strengthen in future." (*Sawaneh Qasmi* 2: 280). He was not wrong.

Choice between Attitude and Education

Dars i Nizami was certainly not the panacea. Nonetheless, one of the two reasons Maulana Nanautawi accepted a slightly revised version of it was that he did not have time, nor peer support, even for a thorough revision of it, let alone develop a new syllabus. On the positive side, the syllabus had some emphasis on theoretical and practical sciences as logic, philosophy and astronomy and medicine which, according to Gilani, helped Darul Uloom students to gain enough proficiency for an appreciation of modern sciences, which they could increase individually if they wished. It is important to note that in his convocation address Maulana Nanautawi had advised interested

Deoband graduates to join government schools. Because of this allowance Maulana Anwar Shah Kashmiri, Sheikh al-Hadith at Deoband, had read some books on modern sciences and would teach them to selected students. (*Ulama i Hind ka Shandar Mazi* 5:222). Darul Uloom could not go for courses in modern sciences for many reasons.

There is a general misconception that the Ulama were against English language. Of course, there are some individual instances – like Maulana Khalil Ahmad Saharanpuri's – when a young man would quit a government school for the Madrasah and later his biographer describing that as his distaste for English language or modern sciences. Projected out of perspective, these narrations rely on misplaced emphasis. Do students of faculty of arts detest science and commerce, or students of law abhor medicine? Does an expert exegete discount a Faqih? It must be seen as an individual preference. Socially, popular dislike of the British was understandable, especially due to the post-1857 atrocities, oppression and genocide of more than 51,200 Ulama as noted by British official Edward Thompson. Others put this figure variously from 7,000 to 27,000 However, at the highest level of Islamic intelligentsia, while British officials and their policies were not seen favourably, everything about the West was never considered hateful. Maulana Nanautawi fought against the British on the Shamli warfront in Muzaffarnagar, yet he would accept many thing British. In his biography, Gilani said that during Haj journey European captain of the ship asked Maulana Nanautawi questions about Islam and he gave answers through an interpreter. The captain was impressed and promised to see him later in India. Maulana Nanautawi had then decided to learn English, but he died soon after the return (*Sawaneh Qasmi* 2:299-300). His inténtion, according to Hakim ul Islam, was to visit Europe and tell the Europeans in their language that "wisdom and science (حکمت) is not what you believe it is, but it emerges from the teachings of prophets and spreads into the bright hearts" (*Maslak Ulama i Deoband* 71).

Hakim ul Islam's Plans Impeded

Maulana Muhammad Tayyab who served as the most prominent Mohtamim of the Darul Uloom for more than 50 years, himself regretted that he could not learn English to have direct contacts with Europeans during his many journeys to the West. He was happy when his son Maulana Muhammad Aslam Qasmi learned English while still studying in the Darul Uloom, and did not object when his youngest son Dr. Muhammad Azam Qasmi decided to go to Aligarh. This was in line with Maulana Nanautawi's vision that Madrasah graduates' stint at modern education institutions "will further increase their expertise." (*Sawaneh Qasmi* 2: 281).

Few people know that at one time the Darul Uloom provided facility for teaching Sanskrit language in order to refer to original Hindu Scriptures when Arya Samaj leaders began debating Islam. (*Maslak Ulama i Deoband* 71). Later the facility was discontinued due to paucity of funds. I wish it could survive and expand. In the 1960s, Hakim ul Islam opened a department of English language despite stiff opposition from three Shura members: Maulana Abul Hasan Ali Nadwi, Maulana Muhammad Manzoor Nomani and Maulana Minnatullah Rahmani, who had refused to grant even Rs. 400 monthly salary of a single teacher from more than Rs. 2.7 million annual budgets in those days. The teacher's salary was paid by Hakim ul Islam from his resources. This was what he had told this writer in April 1963, then a fresh graduate from Aligarh. During that discussion, he agreed to the need for introducing modern Western philosophy replacing Socrates and Aristotle and general science and modern astronomy in place of Ptolemaic astro-myths. But he lamented that opposition in the Shura for any reform was strong. Like his grandfather, he too was a visionary, but his far-reaching plans were scuttled by myopic peers, administrators of "rival" institutions and narrow-minded men having politically ambitions. Muslims were the ultimate losers.

Issues Dividing the Academia

There were some practical problems as well. Education in Deoband was totally free, including all textbooks, three-meals and provision for other necessities, as compared to the price students would pay in Aligarh to purchase knowledge. The two styles produced mutually exclusive mindsets that would not fit into each other. This problem could have been overcome. But the greater problem in the two-way traffic was psychological adjustment of students in a dissimilar atmosphere. One aspect, as noted by Gilani, was disparity in the style of teaching and learning. In madrasah they are disciples, in college they are students. Teachers in the madrasah would instil in disciples full faith, devotion and respect for the teachers, elders and academic ancestors; while in universities, ostensibly encouraging inquiry, teaching was couched in doubt and debate, unpredictability, suspicion, misgivings, lack of confidence, and ego (*Sawaneh Qasmi* 2:283-284), which would be passed on to successive generations. In this conflict students would be the main sufferers. University graduates go for doubt as basis for research. That is a psychological makeup. In the process they tend to develop doubts about religion too, taking constants for variables. A short stay in a madrasah would be difficult to reshape thinking, unless a university graduate realized misconceptions much later in life, as was the case with Maulana Abdul Majid Daryabadi.

In addition, the stumbling block for Aligarh graduates remained their rigid social approach and the scare that Islamic sciences would stir in their hearts, as against flexibility of the Ulama and fearless determination of the few to tame the genie of modernity. In spite of the desire of Maulana Nanautawi, Aligarh has not opened its doors for the Ulama to learn modern sciences, although they are often accused of being "ignorant of modern knowledge." All they are allowed to learn there is "theology" (*sic*) or do masters or doctorate in Arabic or Urdu language. That negative frame of mind defeats the whole idea of revival as an objective of Syed Ahmad.

As for provision of full-time courses in modern sciences in Deoband, Maulana Nanautawi felt that multiplicity of compulsory subjects would overburden students and affect their ability to imbibe. In his view modern sciences should be open only for those interested in them. One major obstacle in not opening such departments in Deoband was total absence of Muslim teachers in those subjects. Even Syed Ahmad was forced to import novices like Siddons and Beck from England. Of course, a high class professor would not be available to an institution that would not augment their existing honour. Men like Siddons and Beck were misfit and of little benefit in the post-1857 Muslim South Asia. They did not, could not, would not produce another Ibn al-Haytham or Jabir Ibn Hayyan out of their students. This was the issue Aligarh had not addressed then, as now.

Fatwa Against Syed Ahmad

Syed Ahmad's non-conformist opinions about religious issues drew ire of many and he fought for his views in *Tehzibul Akhlaq*. He was unyielding and would not revise his views. His attitude enraged one person: Haji Ali Bakhsh Sharar Badauni who was a scholar of Barelwi persuasion. Sharar opposed Syed Ahmad's religious views and fallacy of justifying Islam by modern science through his own understanding of Nature. Maulana Sharar too was not opposed to modern education, yet he had taken many long steps against Syed Ahmad's beliefs as published in *Tehzibul Akhlaq* and what Syed Ahmad presented as his Tafsir. (*I'tiqadat* 9-10, 25). One among many reasons for his opposition was inclusion in Aligarh syllabus of a book on the Seerah written by former Scottish Governor of Bombay Mountstuart Elphinstone (1779-1859) – educated only up to high school – in which he had shamelessly attacked the Rasool^(s)-Allah (*I'tiqadat* 30). For such reasons Maulana Sharar had gone to Makkah to bring a Fatwa against Syed Ahmad. He was not alone. Jamaluddin Afghani (1838-1897) during his three-month sojourn in Hyderabad wrote an essay denouncing Syed Ahmad's views on Islamic beliefs and urged then reigning Nizam Mir Mahbub Ali Khan to open a university to counter "destructive Nature-bound influence" of Syed Ahmad. That was the reason for starting of the Osmania University, according to Muhammad Abduh (1849-1905). Jurji Zeidan had published Afghani's essay with Abduh's introduction in a special issue of Cairo monthly *Al-Hilal*.

On the contrary as a matter of policy, the Darul Uloom and its Ulama desist from calling any Muslim a Kafir, even though they have been condemned as such by votaries of mutually contradictive Muslim sects. Maulana Nanautawi considered Syed Ahmad's views about Islam a different subject that should be dealt with separately from his educational movement, as he did in *Tasfiyatul Aqa'ed*. Even there he did not call him an apostate, and in a language couched in humility, advised him sincerely to recant those beliefs. He and Maulana Muhammad Yaqub Nanautawi had declined membership of MAOC Court for reasons not related to modern education or Syed Ahmad's religious views. Their academic descendents understood these fine points of differences and were enthusiastic about opening a two-way street between Deoband and Aligarh. Thirty years after the death of Maulana Nanautawi, many modern educated Muslims were invited to the Darul Uloom's convocation of 1328/1910; prominent among them being Sahibzadah Aftab Ahmad Khan from MAO College. (*Sawaneh Qasmi* 295).

The issue of combining the two movements or at least bridging the gulf between the two systems was raised again and it was resolved that college graduates should be sent to the Darul Uloom and Deoband graduates should go to the College. Sending Darul Uloom graduates to Aligarh did not produce any notable result, at least in those early days.

The other part of the experiment proved disastrous. The first Aligarh graduate who came to Deoband was an agent of the British secret police CID who played a key role in the arrest and exile of Shaykhul-Hind Maulana Mahmudul Hasan (1851-1920) to Malta and collapse of the Silken Letters Movement for independence. The British spy was promoted as CID superintendent. Since then no Aligarhian came to Deoband, and Aligarh did not send any other graduate as it had lost the trust (*Ulama i Hind ka Shandar Mazi* 5:117).

Deoband's Contribution to Aligarh

Nonetheless, one neglected factor is that Deoband did not stay aloof from Aligarh, as is evident in Aligarh about Deoband. Exclusion, if not aversion, has always been greater in Aligarh than in Deoband. Initial failure to produce results from sending Deoband graduates to Aligarh did not deter them and many Darul Uloom graduates were still encouraged to follow the Nanautawi Doctrine. Maulana Hamidul Ansari Ghazi, a Deoband graduate and noted Urdu journalist of the freedom struggle era, had gained such proficiency in English language as to translate news and articles into Urdu. He would regularly read English newspapers, even though he did not attend any modern school. His knowledge of modern sciences was greater than a high-school graduate's. There were many other combinitive graduates, all of them originally from the Madrasah. Maulana Saeed Ahmad Akbarabadi, Prof. Qari Rizwanullah, Mualana Mufti Muhammad Taqi Usmani, Maulana Dr. Saud Alam Qasmi, Maulana Prof. Muhammad Wali Razi Usmani, Maulana Shahabuddin Nadwi, Maulana Dr. Mahmud Ahmad Ghazi, Maulana Dr. Muhammad Najeeb Qasmi Sanbhali, Maulana Burhanuddin Qasmi, Qari Abu Sufyan Islahi, and many others who have yet to make a name. On the contrary, in the last 138 years, Aligarh has yet to produce a double graduate from Deoband.

In 1983 Deoband missed a historic opportunity when it gave little attention to the advice of Maulana Hamidul Ansari Ghazi that at the head of a new century, the Darul Uloom needed a new set of aims and objectives in a changed national and global situation, that the centenary conclave should be tasked to define those objectives. Due to conflicting influences the Centenary Dustar-bundi was reduced to a political mela by political upstarts and their obscure and obvious sponsors. Today, it stands bifurcated with reduced influence, instead of being able to guide the nation and lead the Muslims.

Aligarh, on the other hand, is an institution run by the Government of India, and its Vice Chancellor acts like a CEO, not as the lead-bird. There also the internal situation is no better than what it is in Deoband. In fact Aligarh has little room for manoeuvre, while Deoband still being relatively free provides firmer ground to launch the Muslims into a new era with a new outlook. A new opportunity can be created to find common ground. A Deoband student committed to the educational philosophy of Maulana Muhammad Qasim Nanautawi can take the lead, of course in association with Aligarh. Otherwise Aligarh alumni serious about the future and not just about running personal economies, should offer a Sajda i Sahw, invite the Darul Uloom – institution and graduates – to visualize a point in time where they want the future Muslim generations to be in about one hundred years.

Notwithstanding a determined move, the process of reaching the point of confluence cannot be stopped now. It is not a spate, yet a trickle of Deoband graduates steadily flowing towards Aligarh is noticeable; mostly without sacrificing their religious appearance and legatic connection to it. Muhammad Qasim Zamanhas described the Ulama as the "custodians of change." The Ulama who are finding a place in the west-oriented academia have set a future role for themselves. Incidentally, the Madrasah is proving to be the trail-blazer. It is a one-way street, though. True that these double-qualified Ulama have not yet given society another Jabir Ibn Hayyan or Ibn Khaldun, *per se*. It will take time, probably another century. Moreover, it is not necessary that every graduate of Aligarh or Deoband should be equal to the past masters. The whole idea then as now is to keep both doors open for those who can attain that sublime stature of the paragons of Islamic Civilization. The progress made so far is not enough. To realize that dream, the Madrasah as well as the society have to make serious study of the philosophy of Maulana Muhammad Qasim Nanautawi.

Aligarh must resolve on frequent Sir Syed Days to do just that. It will still play a meaningful role in the civilizational resurgence. It is on the horizon, despite shadows of night getting darker by the minute. But that is the first sign of daybreak. Can anyone stop the Sun from rising?

References

Abdul Hai, Sayyid. *India During Muslim Rule* – 'Educational Institutions in Muslim India', http://www.imamreza.net. En tr of *Al-Hind fi al 'Ahd al-Islami*. Da□ irat al-Ma□ arif al-□ Uthmaniyah. Hyderabad. 1972.

Badauni, Tayyab Bakhsh. *I'tiqadat i Sir Syed aur Sharar Badauni*. Badaun. 1985.

Eaton, Charles (Hassan) le Gai. *The Muslims in the West*.http://mysite.mweb.co.za/residents/mfj1/eaton2.htm

Ghazi, Dr. Mahmud Ahmad, *Maghribkafikri o tehzibichaylanjaurulamakizi mmedariayn*, Quarterly *Islam Aur Asr Jadid*. (Editor Prof Akhtarul Wasey) Zakir Husain Institute of Islamic Studies Jamia Millia Islamia, New Delhi. January 2011. Vol. 43 No. 1.

Ghazi, Muhammad Tariq. *Darul Uloom Deoband Split*. Ottawa" Canada. 2011.

Ghazi, Muhammad Tariq. *Madrasah History and Its Problem*. *Radiance Views Weekly*, New Delhi. 6 June-2010.

Ghazi, Muhammad Tariq. *Madrasah – Past, Present and Future*. Ottawa, Canada. 2006.

Gilani, Maulana Manazir Ahsan. *Sawaneh Qasmi*. Daftar Darul Uloom, Deoband. 1973.

Hali, Maulana Altaf Husain. *Hayat i Jaweed*. Taraqqi e Urdu Bureau. New Delhi. 1990.

Iqbal, Muhammad. *Kulliyat Urdu – Bang i Dara* and *Zarb i Kalim*. Shaykh Ghulam Ali and Sons, Lahore. 1985.

Isfahani, Imam Raghib, *Mufridat Alfaz Al-Qur'an*. Dar al-Fikr, Beirut. 1972.

Kandhlawi, Maulana Muhammad Yusuf. *Hayat us-Sahabah*. Maktabah Al-Hasan, Lahore. 1965.

Miyan, Syed Muhammad. *Ulama i Hind ka Shandar Mazi*. Tayyab Publishers, Lahore.

Nanautawi, Maulana Muhammad Qasim. *Tasfiyatul Aqa'ed*. Kutubkhana Rahimiyah, Deoband.

Siddiqi, Rashid Ahmad. ed. MehrIlahi Nadeem and Latifuz-Zaman Khan. *Sir Syed ka Maghribi Ta'limka Tasawwuraurusska Nifaz Aligarh Mayn*. Maktaba Danyal, Karachi. 1993.

Tayyab, Hakim ul Islam Maulana Qari Muhammad. *Maslak i Ulama i Deoband*. Tayyab Publishers, Lahore. 1997.

Watt, William Montgomery. *Islam and the Integration of Society*, Routledge & Kegan Paul, London. 1961.

Zaman, Muhammad Qasim. *The Ulama in Contemporary Islam: Custodians of Change*. Princeton University Press, Princeton. 2007.

3

Impact of Religious Factors on Development of Education System

Ismail Thamarasseri

Introduction

A national system of education is often defined from the perspective of formal education system. This includes institutionalized formal education from early childhood education, primary education, secondary education, tertiary education and university education. The informal and non-formal education subsets are often assumed to be part of the formal education and if not ignored altogether, they are given little attention. However, it is important the national educational system should be wholly inclusive of all the subsets of the educational system, that is, formal, informal and non-formal education.

In light of this simple understanding of a national system of education, it is important to note that, behind every system of education, there are factors or features that determine or influence and hence shape each one of the system. However, the national character of a given system of education is never determined by one factor, but rather a combination and interweaving of several factors. Some factors are dominant in one particular system while in another system, they would be less dominant. Consequently national factors of a country are closely related with nationalism and national system of education. As such, in the study of comparative education we should study the factors which make the education of a country national. These factors include geographical, economic, social, cultural, historical, religious, political, language and technological. In this chapter we shall study some such factors.

The influence of religion is very powerful as it penetrates the emotional depth of human nature. The *Brahmanic* system of education, the Buddhist education and medieval Islamic education were dominated by religion. In Europe the Protestant countries were wedded to the education of the masses and the Catholic countries to the education of the classes.

Religious loyalties also dictate aims, content and even methods of instruction in education. Indeed, religion and beliefs have also been known to influence and shape aspects in education system.

In Africa, European Christian Missionaries did influence and continue to influence the education system. The initiative taken by the Christian churches to extend education and their power to control development often explains many of the common elements which can be discerned in education systems in countries that were colonized by the Europeans. For example, school days are from Monday to Friday and resting days are Saturday and Sunday. This is more so because some people have their worship days as Saturday and others on Sunday. Religious organizations have also been and are still involved in educational development through building of educational institutions. For example, the Catholic Jesuits succeeded in building up some of the greatest systems of secondary and higher education institution known in history. There is currently a Catholic university established in Kenya besides many Catholic sponsored primary and secondary schools. The Muslim faithful also have their own established institutions of learning as well as other religious groups such as the Hindus and Buddhists.

In Africa, the present systems of education have been influenced by the work which was initiated by European Christian missionaries who included Catholics, Protestant and Muslim. All these have influenced features in the education system in the areas, they occupied. Most current is that the primary and secondary curriculums have religious subjects being taught in schools of Kenya. Religion has played an important part in the development of education ever since the beginning, even before the creation of schools. The first schools, which were monasteries, started around the Dark Ages, approximately 450 A.D.; Back then, education's only purpose was to people of the religious persuasion, especially Christianity. Christianity is the religion that has most affected education, and so was the case back then, too. The pope commanded more respect and authority than the king, the church taxed the people, and the church dictated the laws of the land.

Religion occupies a very important place in an individual's life. History is testimony of the fact that thousands of persons have sacrificed their lives for the sake of religion. The history of Europe is full of such examples. In a religious country, the public is generally conservative and resents any change in its old traditions.Therefore, in the organisation of an educational system we have to be careful about the religious sentiments of the people. In an industrialised country, due to scientific developments, old traditions usually begin to break-down and the society is reconstructed according to the needs of the time. Education has to pay a special role in this reconstruction.

But opposite to this, in an agricultural country, the public is conservative and views any change with suspicion and it wants to preserve its religious traditions intact. Accordingly, the educational system has to be organised. Needless to remark that the religious sentiments of the people have to be honoured in any educational system. Therefore, the religious factor cannot be ignored in the study of comparative education. Indeed, a comparative discussion of how different religious loyalties have given birth to various educational systems in different countries of the world will be very interesting. Now we shall understand some such factors which may be regarded as results of scientific developments in the world. These factors are those of socialism, humanism, nationalism and democracy. The influence of these factors on education came to surface from the beginning of the modern age.

Religion and Education, two of humankind's most ancient endeavours, have long had a close relationship. Historians and social scientists have written about this relationship and about how the two may influence each other. Religion is certainly not the only reason for this variance; many other factors may play an equal or greater role, including economic, geographic, cultural factors and political conditions within a country or region.

Looking to the Past

Contemporary access to schooling – a solid pathway to educational attainment – depends on a country's educational infrastructure. In many instances, the foundations of that infrastructure are based on facilities originally built by religious leaders and organizations to promote learning and spread the faith.

In India, the most learned men and women of ancient times were residents of Buddhist and Hindu monasteries. In the Middle East and Europe, Christian monks built libraries and, in the days before printing presses, preserved important earlier writings produced in Latin, Greek and Arabic. In many cases, these religious monasteries evolved into universities.

Other universities, particularly in the United States and Europe, were built by Christian denominations to educate their clergy and lay followers. Most of these institutions have since become secular in orientation, but their presence may help explain why populations in the U.S. and Europe are highly educated. Apart from their roles in creating educational infrastructure, religious groups were foundational in fostering societal attitudes towards education.

Islam

There is considerable debate among scholars over the degree to which Islam has encouraged or discouraged secular education over the centuries. The first word of the Qur'an as it was revealed to Prophet Muhammad is "Iqra!" which means "Read!" or "Recite!." Muslims are urged to pursue knowledge in order to better understand God's revealed word. Early Muslims made innovative intellectual contributions in such fields as mathematics, astronomy, philosophy, medicine and poetry. They established schools, often at mosques, known as *Maktab* and *Madrasa*. Islamic rulers built libraries and educational complexes, such as Baghdad's House of Wisdom and Cairo's Al-Azhar University, to nurture advanced scholarship. Under Muslim rule, southern Spain was a centre of higher learning, producing such figures as the renowned Muslim philosopher Ibn Rushd *alias* Averroes.

But other scholars contend that these educational attainments, and the regard that Muslims had for intellectual inquiry in realms outside religion, were gradually attenuated by a complex mix of social and political events over several centuries. These events included foreign invasions, first by the Mongols, who destroyed the House of Wisdom in 1258, and then by Christians, who pushed Muslims out of Spain in 1492. Some scholars argue that the educational decline began earlier, in the 11th and 12th centuries, and was rooted in institutional changes. In particular, contends Harvard University Associate Professor of Economics Eric Chaney, the decline was caused by an increase in the political power of religious leaders who prioritized Islamic religious learning over scientific education. Their growing influence helped bring about a crucial shift in the Islamic approach to learning: It became dominated by the idea that divine revelation is superior to other types of knowledge, and that religious education should consist of learning only what Islamic scholars had said and written in the past.

In the view of some historians, this shift severely constricted intellectual inquiry in the Muslim world as the natural sciences, critical questioning and art were downplayed. Education became primarily the study of established, traditional religious and legal canons. This change also tightened religious scholars' control over the education of Muslims in Africa and the Middle East – a hold that was not broken until colonial governments and Christian missionaries introduced Western-style educational institutions.

Some scholars argue that the decline in secular learning and the narrowing of intellectual inquiry among Muslims have been exaggerated, or did not take place. Columbia University history professor George Saliba writes: "In particular, the decline of Islamic science, which was supposed to have been caused by the religious environment ... does not seem to have taken place in reality. On the contrary, if we only look at the surviving scientific documents, we can clearly delineate a very flourishing activity in almost every scientific discipline" after the twelfth century. Now-a-days, Islamic religious leaders and religious schools still have great influence on education in some Muslim-majority countries, but they compete with government and private schools offering secular topics.

Christianity

In the view of some scholars, the sixteenth-century Protestant Reformation was a driving force for public education in Europe. Protestant reformers promoted literacy because of their contention that everyone needed to read the Bible, which they viewed as the essential authority on doctrinal matters. Driven by this theological conviction, religious leaders urged the building of schools and the translation of the Bible into local languages – and Reformation leader Martin Luther set the example by translating the Bible into German.

Some scholars, however, argue that the "Second Reformation" of the German Pietist movement in the seventeenth and eighteenth centuries was even more influential in promoting literacy. Historians Richard L. Gawthrop of Franklin College and the late Gerald Strauss of Indiana University note that in addition to stressing the need for personal Bible reading, the Pietists persuaded German authorities to mandate Bible reading as "the chief instrument of religious instruction in primary schools, [which was] a powerful impetus to the spread of mass literacy."

In more recent times, religion was a prime motivator in establishing U.S. schools run by faith groups – including Quakers, Protestants and Catholics – that educated generations of immigrant families. Historically, however, Christianity and science often have come into conflict with each other, as illustrated by the seventeenth century clash between astronomer Galileo Galilei and the Roman Catholic Church, as well as the condemnation by prominent religious leaders of Charles Darwin's 1859 theory of human evolution. The Scopes Monkey trial in 1925 further highlighted the rift between science and some branches of Christianity over the theory of evolution, a contentious relationship that endures even today.

In sub-Saharan Africa, meanwhile, scholars describe how religious missionaries during colonial times were the prime movers in constructing educational facilities and influencing local attitudes towards education. These missionary activities, the scholars conclude, have had a long-lasting positive impact on access to schooling and educational attainment levels in the region. Research by Baylor University sociologist Robert D. Woodberry, for instance, suggests that Protestant missionaries in Africa "had a unique role in spreading mass education" because of the importance they placed on ordinary people's ability to read scripture. As a result, they established schools to promote literacy wherever they went and translated the Bible into indigenous languages.

Harvard University economics professor Nathan Nunn, who contends that education was "the main reward used by missionaries to lure Africans into the Christian sphere," says that in addition to establishing schools, "missionaries may have altered people's views about the importance of education." Woodberry and Nunn conclude, however, that Protestant and Catholic missionaries had differing results. Except where they were in direct competition with Protestant missionaries, Catholic missionaries concentrated on educating African elites rather than the masses, Woodberry observes. And Nunn notes that Protestant missionaries placed greater stress than Catholics on educating women. As a result, Protestants had more long-term impact on the education of sub-Saharan African women.

Buddhism

Scholars of Buddhism note that Siddhartha Gautama, the religion's founder, often is called "teacher" because of his emphasis on "the miracle of instruction." He considered learning essential for attaining the Buddhist goal of enlightenment." In many ways, Buddhism is particularly dedicated to education because unlike many other religions it contends that a human being can attain his or her own enlightenment (salvation) without divine intervention," writes Stephen T. Asma, a professor of philosophy at Columbia College, Chicago.

Buddhism is "also extremely empirical in its approach, suggesting that followers try the experiment of *dharma* (i.e. Buddha's Four Noble Truths) for themselves to see if it improves their inner freedom," Asma notes, adding: "Because the philosophy of Buddhism takes this pragmatic approach favouring education and experiment, Buddhism has little to no formal disagreement with science (as evidenced by the Dalai Lama's ongoing collaboration with neuro-scientists)." This theoretical openness to scientific knowledge, however, did not always play out at the practical level within Buddhist communities, Asma contends. "Powerful Buddhist monasteries, especially in China and Tibet, frequently resisted modernization (including science) for fear of foreign influence and threats to entrenched Buddhist power structures," he writes.

Despite this tension between theory and practice, Buddhism has been a major influence on the educational systems of many places, especially India, Sri Lanka, Thailand, Myanmar, Cambodia, Laos and Tibet. From around the fifth century onward, Buddhist monasteries emerged as centres of education, not just for monks but also for laymen. Several monasteries became so large and complex that they are considered prototypes of today's universities. In India, the most famous of these educational centres – Nalanda, in what is now Bihar state – is said to have had 10,000 students from many different countries, and offered courses in what then constituted philosophy, politics, economics, law, agriculture, astronomy, medicine and literature.

In Thailand, monastic schools located in Buddhist temples were the main source of education for male children for many centuries, though they offered primarily religious education. When the Thai government introduced Western-style, secular education around the beginning of the twentieth century, it used monastic schools as the vehicle for reaching the wider population. As of the 1970s, "almost 50 per cent of Thailand's primary schools [were] still situated in Buddhist monasteries." Similarly, in Japan the Buddhist monastic education tradition was so influential that one nineteenth-century scholar of Japan wrote that "Buddhism was the teacher under whose instruction the nation grew up."

Hinduism

For Hindus, education vanquishes a fundamental source of human suffering, which is ignorance, says Anantanand Rambachan, a professor of religion at St. Olaf College. As a result, education has been highly valued in Hinduism since the religion's inception in ancient times. Hindu scriptures urge adherents to seek knowledge through dialogue and questioning, and to respect their teachers. "Learning is the foundational stage in the Hindu scheme of what constitutes a good and a meaningful life," Rambachan says. Since ignorance is regarded as a source of human suffering, he adds, "the solution to the problem of ignorance is knowledge or learning."

The Hindu esteem for education is reflected in different ways. To start with, the most authoritative Hindu scriptures are the Vedas, a word that comes from the Sanskrit root word *vd*, which means knowledge, Rambachan says. University of Florida religion professor Vasudha Narayanan says Hindus regard two types of knowledge as necessary and worthwhile. The first, *vidya*, is everyday knowledge that equips one to earn a decent and dignified life. The second, *jnana*, is knowledge or wisdom that brings awareness of the divine. This is achieved by reading and meditating on Hindu scriptures.

Historically, the caste system in India was a huge barrier to the spread of mass literacy and education. Formal education was reserved for elite populations. But in the seventh and eighth centuries, the vernacular language of Tamil began to be used for religious devotion in southern India, which led to greater access to all kinds of knowledge for a wider group of people. "That is when you start having men and women of different castes composing poems of praise for God, poems that are still recited in temple liturgy today," Narayanan says.

Later, in the eighteenth and nineteenth centuries, both secular and religious education came to be seen by Hindus as a universal right, and it gradually began to be extended to all members of the faith. Still, today, the vast majority of Hindus (98%) live in developing countries – mainly India, Nepal and Bangladesh – that have struggled to raise educational standards in the face of widespread poverty and expanding populations, which helps explain why Hindus have relatively low educational attainment compared with other major religious groups.

Judaism

High levels of Jewish educational attainment may be rooted in ancient religious norms, according to some recent scholarship. The Torah encourages parents to educate their children. This prescription was not mandatory, however, until the first century. Sometimes around 65 C.E., Jewish high priest Joshua ben Gamla issued a religious decree that every Jewish father should send his young sons to primary school to learn to read in order to study the Torah. A few years later, in the year 70, the Roman army destroyed the Second Temple following a Jewish revolt. Temple rituals had been a pillar of Jewish religious life. To replace them, Jewish religious leaders emphasized the need for studying the Torah in synagogues. They also gave increased importance to the earlier religious decree on educating sons, making it a compulsory religious duty for all Jewish fathers. Over the next few centuries, a formal school system attached to synagogues was established.

These developments signalled "a profound transformation" of Judaism, according to economic historians Maristella Botticini of Bocconi University and Zvi Eckstein of the Interdisciplinary Centre, Herzliya. Judaism became, they write, "a religion whose main norm required every Jewish man to read and to study the Torah in Hebrew and to send his sons from the age of 6 or 7 to primary school or synagogue to learn to do so. ... Throughout the first millennium, no people other than the Jews had a norm requiring fathers to educate their sons."

This religious obligation meant that male Jews, to a greater degree than their contemporaries, were literate, which gave them an advantage in commerce and trade. Jewish scholarship was enhanced in the early Middle Ages, beginning in the late sixth century, by the emergence of Talmudic academies of Sura and Pumbedita in what is now Iraq. In the late Middle Ages, centres of Jewish learning, including the study of science and medicine, emerged in what is today northern Spain and southern France.

Until the early nineteenth century, however, most education of Jewish boys was primarily religious. That began to change with the Haskalah, the Jewish Enlightenment movement initiated by East and Central European Jews. This intellectual movement sought to blend secular humanism with the Jewish faith and to encourage openness to secular scholarship among Jews. It revived Hebrew as a language of poetry and literature, which reflected the reformers' appreciation of their Jewish religious heritage. At the same time, they were strong proponents of reforming Jewish education by including secular subjects, such as European literature and the natural sciences. This educational project often brought the reformists into conflict with more orthodox Jewish religious leaders.

Scholars also have explored how religions' cultural norms and doctrines may affect educational attainment by determining which subjects are taught in schools, how much emphasis is placed on religious knowledge *versus* secular education, and if there is gender parity in educational attainment. There has been considerable research on ways in which religious teachings on gender roles may be linked to women's educational attainment. Some scholars have noted that from the Reformation onward, Protestant groups encouraged educating women, with effects that still resonate today. "Martin Luther urged each town to have a girls' school so that girls would learn to read the Gospel, evoking a surge of building girls' schools in Protestant areas," write economics professors Sascha O. Becker, of the University of Warwick, and Ludger Woessmann, of the University of Munich. Looking at 1970 data for European countries, the two conclude that countries with higher shares of Protestants were "clearly associated" with greater parity between men and women in years of education.

Woodberry and Nunn, experts on missionary activity in sub-Saharan Africa, both highlight the Protestant missionaries' insistence that girls and women be educated. In the missionaries' view, "everyone needed access to 'God's word' – not just elites," writes Woodberry. "Therefore, everyone needed to read, including women and the poor."

By contrast, cultural and religious norms in Muslim societies often hinder women's education. Lake Forest College political scientist Fatima Z. Rahman examines how family laws in Muslim-majority countries can affect women's higher education. She finds that when a country's family laws closely conform to a strict version of *sharia*, or Islamic law, the share of women in higher education is smaller. This is not the case when family laws are based on more general Islamic precepts. The stricter laws "impose a limit on physical mobility which is typically required for pursuing higher education or a career," Rahman concludes. There are signs that this could be changing, however, as women make gains in higher education in some conservative Muslim countries in the Gulf Cooperation Council – including Saudi Arabia.

Some academic studies have probed ways a particular religion's attitude towards secular knowledge – whether it is seen as a necessity for spiritual growth or as a distraction from achieving personal salvation – can affect the pursuit of formal education. In this regard, sociologists Darren E. Sherkat, of Southern Illinois University Carbondale, and Alfred Darnell, a visiting lecturer at Washington University in St. Louis, find that "fundamentalist beliefs and conservative Protestant affiliation both have significant and substantial negative influences on educational attainment." Young followers of fundamentalist religious leaders, they add, "will likely limit their educational pursuits." They suggest that Christians who regard the Bible as inerrant – that is, as the error-free word of God – are less likely to enrol in college preparatory classes and "have significantly lower educational aspirations than other respondents."

While Darnell and Sherkat focus their research on Christians in the United States, their observations about how religious attitudes towards secular knowledge may affect attainment offer possible insights into attainment patterns seen in other religions and other parts of the world. Some scholars, however, hypothesize that higher levels of religious observance and engagement produce greater educational attainment. They posit that religious involvement enhances an individual's social capital in the form of family and peer networks, which promote educational success. University of Texas sociologists Chandra Muller and Christopher G. Ellison, in a study of U.S. teenagers, find that there is "a positive influence of religious involvement on several key academic outcomes," such as obtaining a high school diploma. Similarly, in her study of women raised as conservative Protestants, University of Illinois economics professor Evelyn L. Lehrer observes that those who frequently attended religious services during adolescence completed one more year of schooling than their less observant peers.

Strong social capital also is proposed by Paul Burstein, a sociologist at the University of Washington, as a topic needing further research to explain the high educational attainment of Jews. Research focused on the social capital approach, Burstein argues, provides "a framework for showing how Jewish religious beliefs and practices, and the organizations created to sustain them, help Jews acquire skills and resources useful in the pursuit of secular education and economic success."

Burstein argues that previous studies looking at "beliefs or behaviours that are specifically Jewish," or at Jewish "marginality" – either from traditional Judaism or Western society in general – have not offered complete explanations for Jewish educational success.

Religion in Education

Religion seems to be avoided in schools, educators are reluctant to raising the topic of religion in the classroom. Understandably they worry about offending students, or favouring a belief for that matter. Addressing religion in schools is essential to learning, and can adequately provide students with a diverse connection to the world. It is legal to discuss and teach students about religion in an unbiased and academically correct way. Therefore, it is the educator's choice whether to do so or not. Religion is an important factor in education for various reasons. Including religion in education will help decrease the amount of religiously motivated hate crimes. Along with making the student body more diverse, and enhancing the students education. Students have a First Amendment right to religious expression in school and should be able to exercise that right.

Religiously motivated hate crimes are on the rise, therefore to decrease this we should be teaching students about religion during school hours. Research shows that the percentage of hate crimes led by religion bias was about three times higher in 2012 than in 2004. Many of the violent hate crime leaders are school age. If educators encourage students to understand and respect people of different religious beliefs, it will immensely help lower the percentage of these hate crimes. Without teaching religion in schools some children feel that crime is acceptable, along with acting out because they aren't taught any better.

Today, our student bodies are much more diverse. Which means that students are going to come across students of different race, culture, and religions. Students need to learn how to be able to accept these differences, and not be judgemental. To ensure that students of less familiar cultures and religious backgrounds feel included and accepted in their learning environment, teachers need to begin providing different types of opportunities for all of the students to share unique features about themselves. As their classmates become more educated about these differences, the likelihood of exclusivity and bullying will largely decrease.

Religious literacy is key to a well-rounded education; this will enhance the student's education by teaching them more knowledge about different religions around the world. If students are going to function as global citizens, and be members of society; they will need to understand religion's impact on history, politics, society, and culture. Students should know basic religious facts and should be able to recognize the diversity that exists in each belief system that surrounds them. Students will also be encountering different types of people throughout their lives, and they are going to need to know how to deal with it and accept it.

Students have a First Amendment right to religious expression in school. With that being said, the U.S. Constitution contains two different types of clauses, known as the religion clauses. They are there to inform the relationship between religion and public schools. As government employees, public school teachers and administrators must follow these two clauses and are required to be neutral about religion while educating their students. Students have the right to believe in what they had like to believe, and say what they want to say. Students are allowed to express how they feel, and they do indeed have the right to religious expression.

Students who are taught about religion seem to have a better grasp on reality. Allowing them to have a better concept about what is going on in the world around us dealing with different religions, cultures, and values. Along with being more open minded about other peoples beliefs, instead of just focusing on their own and acknowledging others. Religious education is easily ignored when it comes to teaching it in schools. People feel that religion does not need to be discussed. That it is better to just keep to themselves, in fear that it could offend someone and their own beliefs. When religion is brought up in education we seem to ignore it, and not appreciate it the way that we should. Religion gets merged in with citizenship and social studies, instead of talking about it separately. Students should be taught about religion. It can teach them valuable ways of thinking, which can help them throughout life. Religion is a key concept and helps broaden people's knowledge about the world around us. There are so many different types of religions, which is why it is necessary for us to have an understanding and idea of the other religions that people are a part of and value.

References

Abiogu, G. (2014). "Philosophy of Education: A Tool for National Development?" *Open Journal of Philosophy*, 4, 372-377. doi: 10.4236/ojpp.2014.43040.

All Answers Ltd. (November 2017). Social And Political Factors That Shape Education Available Education Essay. Retrieved from https://www.ukessays.com/essays/education/social-and-political-factors-that-shape-education-available-education-essay.php?vref=1

Chakraborty, A.K. (2003). *Principle and Practice of Education*. Meerut: R. Lal Book Depot.

Factors influencing National Systems of Education. retrieved on 10-03-2018 from http://camponotes.blogspot.in/2013/01/factors-influencing-national-syastems.html

How religion may affect educational attainment: scholarly theories and historical background. (2016). retrieved on 10-03-2018 from http://www.pewforum.org/2016/12/13/how-religion-may-affect-educational-attainment-scholarly-theories-and-historical-background/

Manjari, A. *11 Important Factors Responsible For the Growth of Comparative Education*. retrieved on 10-03-2018 from http://www.share youressays.com/knowledge/11-importance-factors-responsible-for-the-growth-of-comparative-education/ 115574

McLaughlin, E. (March 25, 2015). *Religion in Education*. retrieved on 10-03-2018 from https://www.hastac.org/blogs/emmamclaughlin22/ 2015/03/25/religion-education

National Academy of Sciences, Washington (2001). *Contextual Forces that Influence the Education System* retrieved on 10-03-2018 from https://www.nap.edu/read/10023/chapter/9.

Taneja, V.P. (2003). *Educational Thought and Practice*. New Delhi: Sterling Publishers (P) Ltd.

Thamarasseri, I., and Bhat, M.S. (2014). *Comparative Education*. New Delhi: Kanishka Publishers.

Thamarassseri, I. (2008). *Education in the Emerging Indian Society*, New Delhi: Kanishka Publishers (P) Ltd.

The Effect of Religion on Education Essay. retrieved on 10-03-2018 from https://www.bartleby.com/essay/The-Effect-of-Religion-on-Education-FKSC HSZVC

Williams, J. (July 1, 2007). Cultural and social factors that affect development. retrieved *on 10-03-2018 from https://makewealthhistory. org*/2007/07/01/cultural-and-social-factors-that-affect-development/

4

The Need of Islamic Reform: An Analysis of Justification

Md. Tarique Anwer

Introduction

The founder of Aligarh Muslim University and the great social reformer as well as educationist Sir Syed Ahmad Khan (1817-1898) had lucidly argued in favour of re-reading the divine word to establish a harmony in the divine and the worldly, if there appears to be a contest between the two. According to him, "The Qur'an is the word of God, and everything that we see in the world is the work of God." He said it is impossible to imagine any contradiction between divine word and divine work: "If we perceive any contradiction, then it means that we have failed to understand the word of God. In such cases, we need to review our own understanding of the word of God and strive for a meaning that will establish total harmony between the two."

It can be justified from the following two events. The brutality of two recent events—the Peshawar school killings and the Paris attack—and the fact that perpetrators of both barbarities claimed to be the upholders of Islamic beliefs have led to questions being asked; at the top of the list are "Does Islam need reform, and can it be reformed?" The answer to both questions is "Yes".

So while the word of God would include guidelines on how to lead your life, their practicality and implementation is to be decided by the context and the needs of the time. Muslims constitute nearly 23 per cent population of the World and they rule themselves in 56 countries which are member-states of the Organization of Islamic Conference (OIC). Around one-third of them inhabit several major countries of the world as religious minorities but as full citizens.

The idea of reform and renewal is not actually new in Islamic history, as there have been a number of reformist and revivalist movements throughout many Muslim societies. Since the attacks of 9/11, there have been plenty of discussions about Islamic reform and a number of wide-ranging searches for reformers who are—or would be—leading such projects. There are those who say that Islam needs reform; those who say Islam does not need reform and those who say Islam cannot be reformed.

Among Muslims, there are those at one end of the spectrum that totally reject the idea of reform, whereas others in the middle desire a limited amount of reform and, on the other end of the spectrum, those who are calling for a total, open-ended, inside-and-out reform and reconstruction of Islamic theology and societies.

The idea of reform and renewal is not actually new in Islamic history, as there have been a number of reformist and revivalist movements throughout many Muslim societies. The important things for Muslims at this juncture in history is to figure out whether reform is necessary and, if so, what the reform's goals must be and what mechanisms to use to make it happen.

The History of Reform in Islam is Stated Below

There have been a number of revivalist and reformist movements, especially since the decline of the great Islamic empires, as permitted by the Islamic doctrine of *ijtihad*, or independent rethinking.

There are a number of reasons for the failure of these previous reformist movements.

First, the reform movements felt that adhering very closely to the literal meaning of texts kept them closest to the divine intent behind them. Instead of emphasizing the spiritual and ethical meanings, they focused on the letter of the texts.

Next, they overlooked the true nature of the sacred texts and presented their interpretations as foolproof and comprehensive. Also, the whole mental outlook and the ethos have been highly conservative and very suspicious of change and innovation.

Lastly, ignoring the continuous revelations to mankind provided from the arts, history and natural sciences resulted in stagnation and ossification and superficial interpretive changes, without transcending static interpretations.

The invention of the printing press and translation of the Bible into the vernacular languages made the Bible and its message more accessible to the masses and facilitated the reform of Christianity. In a parallel fashion, we now have the internet empowering Muslims worldwide to be better informed and ultimately take back their religion from the clutches of outdated dogmas.

On the other side, after every atrocious act of killing in the name of Islam, the average Muslim feels pressured—or voluntarily finds it important—to condemn the terrorists. They all point out that they do not belong to the same faith as the killers. But over time, with every passing attack, this response, albeit true, is becoming less and less convincing to the world that today sees Islam as a problem.

Man is an intellectual being. It is this faculty which makes man essentially different from other creatures, including animals. It simply signifies that human intellect is the focal point in life. Use of intellect sustains humanity and its non-use throws man into animal circle. Around forty nine times the term *ta'aqqul* in its various derivatives has occurred in the Qur'an.

The problem with Islam is that it has remained stuck in a time warp. While other religions had their reform movements and change-bearers early in the day, Islam has remained a seventeenth-century faith. Most other institutionalized religions struck their divine-worldly balance so that their followers do not see one versus the other, but as complementary. So that belief remains personal, not the prism through which to see the world. But Islam is yet to find that equilibrium where its followers do not have to choose or struggle to reconcile the two.

Do we blame an average Muslim for that? Or is there an inherent 'tribalism' in the religion itself which is at continuous friction with its surroundings? All religious texts are as good or as bad as their interpretations. And unfortunately, it is the most violent and abusive followers who are heard the most. On the other hand, the Islamic point of view subordinates human will to that of God, stressing the moral responsibility of human individuals and collectivity within the sphere of freedom afforded by God. Every success or failure of human societies must be attributed to the moral achievements or failings of human beings.

Coming back to the problem of reforms in Islam: the religion that started as a revolution and revolt against many prevalent "ills" of its time has to be dynamic to last in its true essence. What we have today in the name of the faith is based on a very twisted and orthodox reading of it. While the couple of initial centuries saw the Islamic world making great strides in scientific and modern innovations, thirteenth-century onwards, the intellectual environment got muddied and entrenched in orthodoxy. Education, scientific inquiry and innovation became bad words.

The condition of almost all the Muslim world today is a factual testimony to this assessment. Muslim countries, though some of the richest in the world, languish at the bottom of all human rights, gender justice, democratic, and innovations indices. When Muslim enterprise was derailed from its historical trajectory following the onslaught of colonial invasion, their response to the challenge of the new order was marked by an exaggerated awe of the colonial power and a cowardly acceptance of its rule. It seemed to them that the colonizer, being inherently invincible in their perception, has filled the whole space of their life world for good. Some people even accepted this phenomenon as part of their permanent fate and surrendered their will to resist.

The need is to rescue Islam, and in turn Muslims, from this Arab mindset. The need is to rescue the text and the religious philosophy from the orthodoxy and propagate ideas and interpretations that are in sync with modernity and scientific inquiry. While it may be true that Sunni Islam does not have a clergy as visible as, say, a Pope, the unholy nexus of the 'ulemas' (clerics) and state has ensured that the most patriarchal, undemocratic and medieval conclusions are drawn from the reading of the Qur'an. The 'ulemas' and the rulers sought justifications for the medieval acts in religion and more often than not twisted and moulded the divine word to suit their agendas.

The words of many Scholars about Islam from India and the World are under:

Islam and Islamic learning need to be democratised. As Maulana Azad said: "Our history is replete with the doings of ulemas who have brought humiliation and disgrace to Islam in every age."

Justice Amir Ameer Ali in his classic *'The Spirit of Islam'* quotes an Arab editor who says: "The Arabs might have been a nation of Galileos, Keplers and Newtons. By their denunciations of science and philosophy, by their exhortations that besides theology and law no other knowledge was worth acquiring, they did more to stop the progress of the Muslim world than most other Muslim scholists. And up to this day their example is held forth as a reason for ignorance and stagnation." Salman Rushdie says that there is a "deadly mutation in the heart of Islam." I would put it differently. There is obscurantist stagnation at the 'centre' of Islam (*read* Arab world) which has choked the flow of lifeblood to its heart.

The President of Egypt recently gave a call for "Islamic Reforms" at Al Azhar University in Cairo. He was widely hailed by some as the new Ataturk and even a Muslim Martin Luther. But I think the statist approach to reform is not the answer. The call for reform must come from below, from men and women who have a stake in an Islamic reawakening.

Gandhi's or Vivekananda's Gita is as different from Godse's or Bhagwat's as Maulana Azad or Maulana Wahiduddin Khan's Qur'an is from Baghdadi's or Bin Laden's. So while it is convenient to blame the text, it is not going to take either followers or opponents anywhere. The text was written in a time, in a context. When the context changes, our reading and interpretation of it must also change.

The five pillars of Islam are essential to the faith, so there is no serious effort by any credible groups or persons to reform them. These basic pillars are not a threat to anyone. However, beyond these five pillars, there are a whole host of issues that must be carefully examined. On the basis of these five pillars, the Sharia was formed to understand the Islamic Law.

We need to understand how Islamic law, or the *Sharia*, was formed and the role played by the interpretations of fallible people.

The limited comprehension of mortal human beings limits understandings of Islam and any interpretation of it. Historical Islam, as interpreted and understood by human beings, is not constant or infallible. It has evolved through every age and time based on the outlooks and mentalities of Muslims interpreting it.

Over a span of several hundred years after the passing away of the Prophet Mohammed, the Muslim scholars developed a set of principles known as the *Sharia* (The Way to Allah) and the *Fiqh/Ahkams* (understandings, commandments and laws).

The *Sharia/Fiqh*, as developed over the centuries, did not come directly from Allah, nor did it come from the unadulterated legacy of the Prophet Mohammed.

The Qur'an was progressively revealed to the Prophet Mohammed over almost 23 years and then compiled into its present form several decades after the passing away of the Prophet Mohammed.

In most cases, the Qur'an does not provide the background or context of the messages in sufficient detail. This was not a problem when the Prophet Mohammed was alive to explain it, but when he passed away without any contemporaneous notes left behind; the so-called "occasions of revelation (*asbab-ul-nuzul*)" were constructed over generations into the *Sunna* and *Hadith.*

The scholars worked for generations in writing commentaries and then commentaries on the commentaries, called the "*tafsir*". In order to reconcile contradictory passages, the theory of abrogation (*nasikh-wal-mansukh*)—the cancelling or superseding of one Qur'anic passage in favour of a newer passage—was invented, without prophetic or divine guidance.

Scholars in the first 300 years of Islam after the Prophet Mohammed's death determined which records of the his sayings and conduct (the *Sunnah*) would make it into the books of *Hadith*, giving different accounts varying degrees of authenticity and reliability. This science of *Hadith* authentication (*ilm-ar-rijal*) concentrated on the piety and personal character of the narrators, and not the historical accuracy or logical consistency of the narrators' reports.

No matter how meticulous and pious these scholars were, they were humans subjected to all the imperfections and limitations of being human beings. Plus, they worked in a highly charged political atmosphere, rife with sectarian conflicts between Muslims for power, wealth, glory and religious fanaticism.

This encouraged misinterpretation and altogether fabrication of *hadith*, both in terms of content and the chain of narrators. The *hadith* collection projects were neither done contemporaneously when the Prophet was alive, nor were sanctioned by the Prophet or his immediate successors, the so-called "Rightly Guided Caliphs". The collections were approved by later generations based on the perceived need (*darura*) and the consensus (*ijma*) of the scholars of the time.

The *sharia* is the codified consensus of these human scholars. Therefore, *sharia* is man-made and fallible. And because traditional Islam is based on this *sharia*, it has absorbed a lot of the values of the times in which the *sharia* was formed. As a result, traditional Islam has rough edges intermingled with a great deal of ethical goodness and serene spirituality.

In forming the *sharia*, the jurists' method was to follow the literal meaning of the clear-cut texts. Enormous effort has been spent in analyzing the lexical semantics and the linguistic morphology of the texts, at times employing casuistry and engaging in hair-splitting. This came at the expense of a historical-critical method marshalling a whole range of analytical methodologies to uncover deeper and fuller meanings.

These scholars categorized all human acts into one of five categories: obligatory, recommended, neutral, frowned upon and prohibited. It is important to note the ambitious goal of this *sharia* project: to categorize every human act—past, present and future—in order to be consistent with Allah's will.

However, the creation of God is so immense that no human project can encompass His will fully and completely. It is true that the message of the Qur'an is valid for all times and places, but it must not be interpreted literally by fallible human beings without having the full context available.

We have God-given reason (*aql*) so we can continuously work and use trial-and-error to get closer to the will of the creator. The accumulated experiences of human history must be incorporated into our understanding of the texts.

If God wanted us to follow blindly, then He would have given us an oracle or a search engine that would spell out all His detailed instructions for every question. Instead, He gave us ethical guidance in the form of the Qur'an and a brain.

There have been a number of revivalist and reformist movements, especially since the decline of the great Islamic empires, as permitted by the Islamic doctrine of *ijtihad*, or independent rethinking. There are **seven essential elements** for need of Islamic Reform. These recommendations for the renewal (*tajdid*) and reform (*islah*) are as follows:

(i) Acknowledge deep problems in classical Islamic thought: These problems are an inevitable product of God's message passing through imperfect human minds. We do not need to throw the baby out with the bathwater by rejecting traditional Islam wholesale, but we should continuously work to improve our understandings.

(ii) Educate about the Formation of Sharia: We must educate everyone about the sacred texts and how *sharia* was formed by humans interpreting them. We must make a solid case for avoiding literal interpretations and instead include all the relevant facts and analytical methodologies, textual and contextual and experiential.

(iii) Reform Traditional Sharia: The first step is separating the religion from the state. The core of Islam—the five pillars—are not about political governance. Traditional Islamic scholars can be experts on matters of ritual and worship and they are free to voice their opinions, but they must not be allowed to issue edicts for everyone to comply with.

(iv) Promote and Protect Freedoms: We must acknowledge that medieval misinterpretations are responsible for issues like slavery and concubines; blasphemy and apostate laws and unfair discrimination against women, minorities and non-Muslims. These are not consistent with universal human rights and freedoms or the fundamental Qur'anic principles of justice (fairness) and mercy.

(v) Accept the Equality of Humanity: Instead of demeaning and rejecting non-Muslims as *kafirs* or *infidels*, which are historically loaded terms, we must acknowledge the basic humanity and equality of everyone and accept that all of us, believers and non-believers, are all seekers of the Truth (*Haqq*) in our own way. This demeaning of non-Muslims must stop both in public and behind closed doors.

(vi) Hope and Patience: Be hopeful for a bright future for Islam, but do not expect quick changes. In fact, it might take generations. Therefore, assiduously cultivate the young but do not neglect the older believers.

(vii) Avoid False Reformists: There are many Muslim individuals and groups claiming they stand for reform and *ijtihad*, but if they do not embrace the above items, they are not for real reforms consistent with the universal values of justice and mercy.

Conclusion

From the above deliberations we are bound to conclude reforming traditional *sharia* is necessary and it is not apostasy. Doing so is in the best interest of Muslims and non-Muslims all over the world to avoid such terrorist attacks in the near future and it is also necessary to talk frankly and open minded so that the peace can be maintained the world.

The events of the so-called "Arab Spring" that began in 2010 and turned into the "Arab Winter" have amply demonstrated that the reform of religious ideas among Muslims is essential. This Islamic reform must take place before successful and meaningful political reforms can happen that lead to vibrant, prosperous, truly democratic and just Muslim societies.

The U.S. government has been turning a blind eye to the problematic nature of pro-*sharia* American groups and the importance of Islamic reform. It is unconcerned as long as these groups are not directly involved with violence, but these groups contribute to the radicalization of Muslims because the traditional *sharia* they support is inimical to the basic concepts of the U.S. Constitution. It is an Islamic Renaissance, guided by the masses, not the mullah, is long overdue.

References

Mohd Asim is Senior News Editor, NDTV (24x7).

Ahmed Vanya, "A Muslim's Case for Islamic Reform", *The Clarion Project*, 4th November, 2014, Ahmed Vanya is a Muslim-American activist and an electronics engineer in San Jose, California. He is a fellow with the American-Islamic Forum for Democracy.

5

Boko Haram Islamist Insurgency in Nigeria: Its Global Jihadist Connections

Zayon O. Nzegbulam

Introduction

Ordinarily, the Boko Haram jihadist movement was assumed to have been local Islamic rebellion against the Nigerian government that allowed corruption to thrive, thereby leading to the impoverishment and deprivation of its people, particularly those from the less educated northern part of the country. The religious and political dynamics and discourses that must have underpinned this Islamic jihads notwithstanding, most northern politicians/Muslims who even knew the background of the insurgency better, and their apologists in the U.S. and other Western analysts/observers viewed it as mere local response to and symptom of Nigerian socio-economic failures, which needed to be addressed by Nigerian authorities (Campbell, 2013).[1] However, a more critical and deeper look into the ideological framework, objectives and operational method of the Boko Haram jihadist reveals some kind of local agenda driven by a response to global Islamist jihadism initiated by Al-Qaida under the leadership of Osama bin Laden, from which today's ISIS emerged. Moreover, going back a bit to Nigeria's religious crises memory lane, two of the major religion motivated conflict in the country's history include the Maitatsine (the Al-Masifu sect) uprising of 1980 led by one Muhammad Marwa Maitatsine, and the Yobe Taliban (the Al Sunna Wal Jamm sect) of 2002. The uprisings by these two Islamist sects were based on the grounds that true Islamic worship and belief must be in accordance with the laws of "Prophet" Mohammed, and the Boko Haram terrorist insurgent group follows this same Islamic Fundamentalist narrative as mentioned above (George, A.T., 2013).[2] The Boko Haram radical ideology and violent operational tactics fit into other radical international Islamic movements such as the Taliban of Afghanistan/ Pakistan, the Al-Shabab of Somalia and the al-Qaeda terrorist group in the Islamic Maghreb across the Sahel region of Africa (George, A.T., 2013),[3] including those of the Islamic State of Iraq and Levant (ISIL), which evolved from the precipice and decrepitude of al-Qaeda, and to which the Boko Haram Islamist insurgents pledged allegiance in 2015 (Joscelyn, T., 2015),[4] (BBC News, March 13, 2015).[5]

Thus, although Boko Haram might have emerged as a local jihadist group to challenge what it perceived as corrupt government run by "infidels" in Nigeria, its ideological rhetorics and approaches expose its international link to other fundamental Islamist groups like Al-Qaeda and the Salafi jihadist movement. Ideologically, Boko Haram belongs to the Salafi Jihadist Islamist stock, which seeks to violently topple any government perceived as going against the Islamic way of life and impose Islamic regime based on the strict interpretation of the Qur'an. It is also on the same ideological basis that Boko Haram seeks to topple the Nigerian secular state. It was in pursuance of this objective that in February 2011, Boko Haram in a message sent to the media declared, "We are carrying out these attacks in order to propagate the name of Allah and to liberate ourselves and our religion from the hands of infidels and the Nigerian government" (Mshelizza, 2011).[6] As Freedom Onuoha aptly puts it, the sect's (Boko Haram's) ideology and operational tactics derive from the global Salafist Islamic ideology, which seeks the imposition of its own interpretation of Islamic Law and a safe haven for jihadists (Onuoha, 2014: 177).[7] According to other scholars like Denoeux & Carter (2009), "Salafi jihadi groups are motivated by a mix of religious and political objectives: they embrace a strict, literal interpretation of Islam, and combine it with an emphasis on jihad, understood here as holy war. They view jihad as the primary instrument through which their Salafi desire to 'return' to the original message of Islam will become reality. Unlike radical Islamists, they approach jihad as a global struggle that knows no borders, and that focuses on combating the West in general and the United States in particular. They form an amorphous, transnational movement, and disseminate an ideology that is fundamentally hostile to modernity, to the secular, democratic nation-state, to the logic of globalization, and to peaceful coexistence of different cultures and religions" (Denoeux & Carter 2009: 86).[8]

Furthermore, another evidential clue to the Boko Haram Salafi leaning came in the aftermath of the July 2009 revolt, which led to the death of its founder, Yusuf and other members. In March 2010, for instance, Boko Haram new leadership declared that it was "joining Al-Qaeda to avenge the murder of some of its members and leaders in a series of explosions across Nigeria" (The Jihadi Websites Monitoring Group, 2010: 14).[9] In an interview with Al Jazeera television on June 14, 2010, the Al Qaeda in Maghreb (AQIM) leader, Abdelmalek Droukdel (also called Abu Musab Abdel Wadoud) confirmed that his group had been talking to Boko Haram and intended to supply it with weapons to "defend Muslims in Nigeria and stop the advance of a minority of Crusaders." He further noted that Al-Qaeda had an interest in Sub-Saharan Africa for "its strategic depth that would give it a bigger scope for manoeuvres" (Stratford 2010).[10] Again, in a published manifesto in July 2010, Abubakar Shekau linked the jihad being fought by Boko Haram with jihadist efforts globally, especially that of "the soldiers of Allah in the Islamic State of Iraq" (Pham 2012: 4). Shekau expressed solidarity with Al-Qaeda and threatened the U.S. thus: "Do not think jihad is over; rather jihad has just begun" (Pham 2013: 4).[11] He also threatened attacks not only against the Nigerian state, but also against "outposts of Western culture", thus echoing the propaganda archetypical of Al-Qaeda's global Islamist rhetoric that Islam is under attack by "infidels" (Onuoha, 2014, *ibid.*).

It must also be appreciated that all splinter jihadist groups formed after al-Qaeda were responding to the archetypical propaganda according to their own local socio-political and economic circumstances and varied environments. Thus, even under their peculiar indigenous circumstances, they still seek and lend support to each other in various ways whenever the need arises. Any wonder then about the January 2012 report by the United Nations Security Council stating that Boko Haram members "from Nigeria and Chad had received training in [AQIM] camps in Mali during the summer of 2011." The report also confirmed that seven Boko Haram fighters "were arrested while transiting through the Niger to Mali, in possession of documentation on manufacturing of explosives, propaganda leaflets and names and contact details of members of AQIM they were allegedly planning to meet" (Joscelyn, February 2015).[12] It was also in that same month that an official from Niger confirmed that Boko Haram fighters had received training from both AQIM and Al Shabaab.

Besides, Boko Haram is known to have even a deeper history of involvement in Saudi Arabia. For instance, Muhammad Yusuf, the late sect's founder, was reportedly given refuge (in the guise of pilgrimage) in that country to escape the crackdown of Nigerian security forces in 2004 (Zenn, J., 2013).[13] Moreover, Boko Haram has reportedly received funding with the help of AQIM from organizations in the United Kingdom and Saudi Arabia; even as the sect's spokesman claimed that Boko Haram leaders met with al-Qaida in Saudi Arabia during the lesser hajj (umra) in August 2011 (Mark, M., 2012).[14]

However, even in the face of the glaring evidence of ideological and objective links between Boko Haram and some external jihadi forces, some analysts dismissed AQIM's intent to bond with Boko Haram as a mere wishful thinking or rhetoric. Some Western analysts particularly argued that "issuing statements claiming an alliance is easier than actually creating a meaningful accord and that several factors complicate AQIM's intent to move into Nigeria" (Stratford, 2010, *ibid.*). Even then, such dismissive arguments seem to have overlooked the fact that both Boko Haram and AQIM share the same Salafi Jihadist ideological philosophy and moreover that global Al-Qaeda had attempted to draw localised conflicts into an evolving but loose network of transnational jihadist and might be bent on replicating what it did in Iraq, Yemen, Afghanistan and other troubled and vulnerable places like Nigeria (Onuoha, 2014: 178, *ibid.*). Furthermore, as other scholars like Vidino, Puntuci and Kohlmann (2010) have rightly observed:

"Al-Qaeda, and more generally, the global jihadist movement, has repeatedly attempted to hijack conflicts that were largely nationalistic (local) in nature and turn them, both rhetorically and operationally, into battlefields of what they perceive to be a millenarian and global conflict between Islam and the world of infidelity. Local actors might maintain some of their parochial agendas, but by putting themselves under the banner of the global jihadist movement, they benefit from outside support in terms of funding, recruits, propaganda, and military expertise. The global jihadist movement also benefits, as it can expand its influence and add credibility to its narrative that Islam is under attack from non-Muslims" (Vidino, Puntucci and Kohlmann, 2010: 224).[15]

Following the onslaught of the Nigerian security forces during the July 2009 uprising, which saw the death of the Boko Haram founder/leader and its fighters, and subsequent crackdown thereafter,

Boko Haram ideologues and other Islamic demagogues within and even outside Nigeria seemed to have convinced themselves that not just the Boko Haram sect, but the place of Islam in Nigeria was largely threatened and impotent, and must do even the extraordinary to be able to liberate their religion from the hands of Nigerian "infidel" government. Thus, as Ayoob (2005) rightly stated: "When and where the sense of impotence becomes very acute, it provides extremist elements with the opportunity to exploit the prevailing climate of despair to undertake terrorist activities; extremist groups that arrogate to themselves the right to speak in the name of 'Islam' justify terrorism as the ... only strategy that can wrest the initiative from the hands of Western powers and those perceived to be their surrogates in the Muslim world" (Ayoob, 2005: 960).[16]

Viewed from the above understanding, therefore, one may argue that the sense of impotence could have driven Boko Haram ideologues and their local sponsors to establish links with like-minded Salafi Jihadist groups in Africa, particularly AQIM and Al-Shabaab, in furtherance of its ideological goal of Islamisation of northern Nigeria, and possibly extend same beyond their northern enclave. Consequently, many of their members fled to North Africa to train with Al-Qaeda in the Islamic Maghreb in the aftermath of the July 2009 revolt; and while there in the training camp, they chose Abubakar Adam Kambar as their leader" (Africa Confidential, 2013: 5).[17] Aside from this, Boko Haram militants also reportedly attended Al Shabaab-owned training camps in Somalia, where they were taught how to construct and detonate improvised explosive devices, as well as how to employ the use of suicide bombers, a practice, which until participating in the training camps, Boko Haram fighters did not engage in (Connell, 2012: 89).[18]

Meanwhile, just as the Nigerian security operatives and some analysts were still speculating on the possibility of foreign links of Boko Haram, on June 15, 2011, a statement released by Boko Haram had the sect boasting of its ties to the Somalia-based terror group, Al-Shabaab thus: "We want to make it known that our Jihadists (warriors) have arrived Nigeria from Somalia where they got serious training on warfare from our brethren (Al-Shabaab) who made the country of Somalia ungovernable; we want to assure all security agencies that we would frustrate their efforts; by the grace of God, despite the armoured carriers that they are boasting of, they cannot match the training we acquired in Somalia" (Safeafricagroup.com, 2011).[19]

As Connell (2012) observed, alignment and solidarity with AQIM and Al-Shabaab became evident as a true shift of radical ideological expansion; having acquired the tactical and ideological tools, the sect began to attack targets it considered as infidels and Western secular surrogates, which include Christians, moderate Muslims and secular institutions (both local and international) in Nigeria (Connell, 2012).[20] For instance, suicide attack on Nigeria's police headquarters in Abuja on June 16, 2011 was a practical show-off of the training Boko Haram earlier boasted of having acquired from established transnational jihadist movements in Africa. Sequel to this was the August 26, 2011 suicide-bombing of the United Nations' building in Abuja, showing glaring evidence that the group was seriously determined to internationalise its terror activities, in alliance with global jihadist agenda. In the aftermath of the UN bombing, a self-identified spokesman for Boko Haram had these to say, "All over the world, the UN is a global partner in the oppression of believers; we are at war against infidels; in Nigeria, the federal government tries to perpetuate the agenda of the United Nations" (Bashir, 2011).[21]

The UN bombing brought to the world's attention the growing danger Boko Haram posed(s) to regional and international security; it also exposed the unpreparedness of the Nigerian armed forces to the extent of the looming danger posed by the festering Islamic jihadists in the country. Prior to the UN bombing, and indeed, the abduction of over 276 school girls from Chibok community of Borno state in April 2014, there was very little awareness of, or attention paid to the ideology driving the Boko Haram Islamist sect and the extent they were ready to go in achieving their averred "caliphate." However, unlike previous years before the above incidents when the debate was centred on whether Boko Haram had links to other Salafi Jihadist movements, concern shifted to the extent of established ties and their consequences on the Nigerian national and regional security trends in Africa.

Unheeded Early Warning Signals

About 2011/2012 when the Boko Haram jihadi sect started intensifying their atrocities around the north-east of Nigeria, the intelligence community had confirmed that Africa's top three Salafi Jihadist movements, which include Al-Shabaab, AQIM and Boko Haram, were sharing funds, training, and explosive materials, which could possibly lead to the emergence of an 'extremist triangle' in Africa

(Shaughnessy, 2012).[22] The then United States AFRICOM Commander, Gen. Carter Ham, made mention of the possible threat in the following apprehensive expression: "What really concerns me are the indications that the three organizations are seeking to coordinate and synchronize their efforts, in other words, to establish a cooperative effort amongst the three most violent organizations; I think that's a problem for America and for African security in general (US Africa Command 2012).[23] Moreover, given that Al-Shabaab, AQIM, and Boko Haram subscribe to Salafi Jihadist ideology, it was possible for them to collaborate on certain areas of mutual interest such as training and weapons smuggling, while maintaining their distinctive local specificity and character shaped by the domestic environments in which they were then operating. The developments in Mali, which made that country slip into instability after a coup led by Captain Amadou Sanogo overthrew President Amadou Toumani Touré on 22 March 2012, seemed to confirm such connections. The coup created a power vacuum that enabled Tuareg rebels in the North, backed by a patch-work of Islamist forces of Ansar Dine, AQIM and the Movement for Unity and Jihad in West Africa (MUJWA) to take control of nearly two-thirds of the country; these groups, particularly AQIM and Ansar Dine, belong to the Salafi Jihadist stock (Onuoha, 2014: 181, *ibid.*).

In order to stem the insecurity situation posed by the Islamist groups who were poised on invading Bamako, and to restore stability to her former colony, beginning from January 11, 2013, France deployed her forces in a military intervention code named "Operation Serval." Nigerian troops, in addition to other African forces, joined French forces to roll back the Islamist occupation of northern Mali (Onuoha & Thurston, 2013).[24] The then Nigerian authorities justified sending forces to help in the France-led operation on the grounds that Boko Haram received training in Mali, making it imperative for Nigerian troops to join the international campaign to free northern Mali from Islamist militants. In a seeming corroboration of this, the Nigerian military convoy to Mali was ambushed by Boko Haram militants (*Premium Times*, January 21, 2013)[25]; (*The Nigerian Voice*, January 19, 2013).[26]

Some analysts observed that the above situation portended serious dangers to security not only to Nigeria as a nation, but to the entire gulf of Guinea and the Sahara-Sahel regions, given possible fusion of terrorist groups that have strongholds or footprints in the region who share in the Salafi Jihadist ideology. The analysts cite instances like

Niger which is Nigerian northern neighbour, whose southern part is dominated by the Hausa-speaking Izala-Salafi group and its northern region bordering Algeria and Libya, which is dominated by the Tabligh Tuaregs; while also in Chad, another northern neighbour of Nigeria, where Ansar al Sunna is another influential Salafi group which was or still receives huge funding from donors in Sudan and Saudi Arabia (Rasheed, 2012).[27]

In view of the above, the Sahara-Sahel region seems to offer both a potential safe haven and training grounds for Salafi Jihadists, including large unmanned spaces for them to generate funds for their terrorist activities through complex shades of criminal cross-border activities such as kidnapping, drug and human trafficking and arms smuggling. The security situation has also been compounded and worsened by the existence of porous borders and ineffective border control, which help to ease and facilitate movement of jihadists across borders and the exchange of ideas, resources and training centres. Nigeria being surrounded by intrusive Salafi movements and ideological influences, Boko Haram gained support from some Al-Qaeda-linked Salafist groups in the form of training, weapons, and ideological radicalisation of impressionable youth in northern Nigeria (Onuoha, 2014, *ibid.*).[28] The abduction of over 276 school-girls from government school in Chibok community of Boronu state in April 2014 without any trace until ransom was paid by the government and some detained Boko Haram commanders were swapped before some of the girls were released, and the recent scandalous mass abduction of another set of school girls in Dapchi of Yobe state and in fact, their dramatic release, really speak volume in this regard. This is despite government continued boast and claims that the Boko Haram Islamists have been "technically defeated/degraded and weakened" to fight and pose threat to the security of the country and the north-east in particular.

In addition, mention must also be made of some sharia-minded politicians in the north who gave the Boko Haram insurgents some political and moral backing for their own political opportunity and self-aggrandisement. For instance, the incumbent president, Mohammadu Buhari, who was the chieftain of a political party called "Congress for Progressive Change (CPC)," was quoted to have publicly condemned the state of emergency declared by his predecessor in the northeast to combat the Boko Haram insurgents in May 2013. At the first instance, while speaking as "Guest of the Week" on Liberty Radio Programme in June 2013, Buhari accused his predecessor's led federal government of "killing and destroying houses belonging to Boko Haram members, while the Niger Delta militants got special treatment"; he added that Jonathan (his predecessor) should "stop the clampdown on Boko Haram insurgents, claiming that the Niger Delta militants were never killed, nor their properties destroyed" (*Point Blank* News, June 2, 2013).[29] In another occasion also, the now incumbent president was quoted thus: "Military Offensive against Boko Haram, anti-north" (*The Nation*, June 2, 2013),[30] (*This Day*, 2013),[31] (NewsRescue.com, Aug., 2015).[32]

Although some persons had claimed that Buhari might have been quoted out of context, particularly in the second instance, (NewsRescue.com, 2015, *ibid.*), the fact remains that some politicians from the northern part of Nigeria, particularly those that shared some of the sentiments of the Boko Haram group (with or without their bloodletting tactics) condemned the emergency declaration in the three most affected north-eastern states; and also made some efforts to make political capital of the tragic security situation. The situation became even worrisome when some of these politicians used their position and influence to draw the attention of the international human rights organisations and the United Nations to the "atrocities" they claimed were being perpetrated by the Nigerian military against the north-east, while at the same time downplaying the extent of the Boko Haram security menace. It should not be forgotten in a hurry that this outright propaganda tilted the opinion of the international community against the then Nigerian government, leading to embargo on the sales of arms the government in power at the time (*Jerusalem Post,* January 26, 2015),[33] (Nigeria communicationsweek.com.ng, January 27, 2015).[34] Following the above development within Nigeria and the seeming lack of confidence it generated in international community among the major powers in particular, then government was constrained to resorting to start sourcing arms through black market (*The Globe and Mail,* January 30, 2015)[35] and the use of South African mercenary fighters against Boko Haram (*The Guardian,* April 15, 2015).[36]

Further Incontrovertible Evidence of Obvious Boko Haram Foreign Link

It must be recalled that following the weakening of Al-Qaeda and the onslaught of the Nigerian security forces against Boko Haram in a joint military operation with the neighbouring countries of Cameroon, Chad and Niger in 2015, which led to the jihadist group losing the chunk of territories it had earlier controlled within Nigeria, the leadership of Boko Haram declared allegiance to the Syrian-Iraqi based Islamic State in July 2015, calling itself the "Islamic State in West Africa", in a seeming desperation to find a stronger international godfather/ally (Joscelyn, T., March 2015),[37] (BBC, March 7, 2015).[38]

Since then, the extent of the relationship between the Islamic State and Boko Haram has remained a source of controversy. For instance, in May 2016, the former U.S. Deputy Secretary of State was quoted as saying: "We've seen that Boko Haram's ability to communicate has become more effective; they seem to have benefited from assistance from Daesh," (ISIS) and there were also reports of material and logistical aid; "so these are all elements that suggest that there are more contacts and more cooperation, and this is again something that we are looking at very carefully because we want to cut it off" (Reuters, May 14, 2016),[39] (*The Guardian,* May 14, 2016).[40] However, on June 9, 2016, a media report quoted a U.S. official statement, which claimed that more than a year after the group's (Boko Haram) pledge of allegiance it has no link with IS. The same source went further to state that "Boko Haram's loyalty pledge had so far mostly been a branding exercise designed to boost its international jihadi credentials, attract recruits and appeal to IS leadership for assistance; and that securities were closely watching for any increased threat to Americans from Boko Haram and any confirmation of media reports of deepening ties with IS (*Premium Times,* June 9, 2016).[41] It went further to state that "the U.S. has closely tracked ISIL's leadership, finances and other activities, including its cooperation with other groups such as its branch in Libya, to which Islamic State has sent fighters, commanders and other support. Multiple reports, according to the source, indicated no evidence that Islamic State leaders, based in Syria and Iraq, have transferred significant amounts of cash or weapons or sent high-level representatives to Nigeria (*Premium Times,* June 9, 2016, *ibid.*). At the same time, some sources described the Boko Haram-ISIS connections as mere propaganda stunt (*The Guardian,* March 8, 2015).[42]

Even in the face of the above double speak by the US officials whose government undeniably is in the forefront of fighting ISIS, albeit "terrorism" worldwide, there is no need denying the fact that Boko Haram-ISIS connection has come to stay and would probably remain. As the ISIS and its major allies and affiliates continue to lose grounds and battles both in the middle east and north Africa, they obviously must look elsewhere much attention had not been paid in the past in order to keep the hope of their members alive and continue to retain the loyalty of their followers and boost/uphold the morale of their fighters. One of such major elsewhere (s) still remain places like Nigeria and its weaker neighbours, with connecting porous borders through to the Sahel region, where there are vulnerable Islamic faithfuls who could easily be indoctrinated due to poor or outright failure of governance with its socio-economic consequences. Further evidences have emerged since the pledge of allegiance in 2015 that the two world most deadly terrorist groups have been cooperating at higher level with each other (*Independent,* April 21, 2016).[43] As a chief security analyst for the sub-Saharan region, Ryan Cummings aptly put it, "What we do know is that Boko Haram has become the largest ISIS affiliate anywhere and has increased its jihadist credentials within an area of sub-Saharan Africa where the prevailing social, political and economic climate is seen as conducive to radicalization" (Cummings, 2016).[44] This analyst went further to state the obvious thus: "the inconvenient truth is that Nigeria has not defeated Boko Haram but simply reversed the gains that the terror group has scored against it; while territory has been recaptured from rebel hands, innocent lives have, and continue to be taken by it" (Cummings, 2016, *ibid.*). In an apparent corroboration of this fact, despite several boasts and claims of Boko Haram defeat, and denials of ISIS-Boko Haram cooperation in the past, Buhari (the Nigerian president) in an interview expressed his worry over "ISIS support for Boko Haram" (Daily-post, October 19, 2017).[45]

Furthermore, the latest abduction and dramatic release of most of the Dapchi school girls by Boko Haram in northeast Nigeria speak volume of the ease with which the Boko Haram Jihadist can move in and out of the territories "controlled" by the Nigerian military and other security operatives. This shows further collaborations of Boko Haram with other terrorist groups beyond the watch-list of the Nigerian authorities. No doubt, despite all assurances by the Nigerian authorities, the abducted Dapchi school-girls have indeed been released, but not rescued. Even then, their release could not have been without a financial or a political give-and-take deal, which the government would not want to disclose (*Sahara Reporters,* March 21, 2018);[46] (This Day, March 22, 2018)[47].

Conclusion

The fundamental objective of this paper is to bring to fore the fact that the Boko Haram Islamic movement in Nigeria, which snowballed from the declaration of sharia by predominantly Muslim states in the northern part of the country in the early years of the current democratic experiment has actually slipped away from a mere local agitation for sharia against corrupt government, into a full-fledged Islamist jihadist project against the Nigerian state for the establishment of an Islamic enclave in line with ISIS agenda globally. Therefore, to continue to view the Boko Haram Islamist terrorist activities in Nigeria, albeit within its neighbouring states as local socio-security challenges and continue to engage this established global Islamist terror affiliate/franchise group as such would amount to regional security naivety or international security hypocrisy. By the latter I mean stance of some major powers which seem to portray attitudes which suggest that "your national security threats are your local challenges so long as they do not affect our own national values or strategic interests; an attitude which has remained the bane of finding lasting international peace and security since the end of the two great wars and since after the cold war era. Therefore, for Nigeria, and indeed, her entire West African neighbours not to slip away into the control of ISIS as was in the case of Syria and Iraq, the Boko Haram security threat in the region should stop being treated as a mere local security challenge.

Recommendations

From the light of the above discussions, it is obvious that Boko Haram, though started as Muslim youth's agitation in Nigeria for establishment of sharia system of government in predominantly northern Muslim states, some socio-economic dynamics and the initial local support it received among grassroots Muslims and some politicians in the north gave it the morale boost to establish link with other foreign jihadist terror groups like al Qaeda and later ISIS. Today, the ambition of the Boko Haram group for global attention has transformed its ideology, strategy and operational approaches to a trans-national terrorist organization as it continues to export its insurgency across the Lake Chad borders, drawing synergy from other global terror groups.

With the above understanding in view, the following recommendations have been put forward to help combat the Boko

Haram security menace.

- The Nigerian authorities need to do more than the present reactionary approach being adopted in the fight against the Boko Haram jihadi extremists. More should be done in terms of detailed security assessment and threat perception and take more proactive measures in order to deny the terrorists the initiative of choosing where and when to strike with ease.
- The government of Nigeria and the need to consider erecting fences along their porous border areas. Such fences or barriers have to be equipped with some monitoring gadgets that could trigger off and transmit alarm at designated security station whenever there is any attempt of entry. This option needs to be considered seriously by the Nigerian authorities around their northern borders with Niger and Chad in particular, through which the terrorists use as their major accessed route to Libya and even up to the Sahel region.
- As it is obvious that the security threat posed by Boko Haram has assumed a trans-national dimension around the Lake Chad region, the countries that share common borders with Nigeria, particularly Cameroun, Chad and Niger should articulate their security needs and present same along with Nigeria to the relevant international bodies for assistance. They should also co-ordinate their security efforts better for proper synergy among their military and other security operatives engaged in the fight against the jihadi terrorists.
- Nigeria and her affected neighbouring states need to engage in a more serious, vigorous campaign against the ideology underpinning and has been sustaining the Boko Haram insurgency. This could be achieved by using well known Islamic scholars and models to re-direct the attention and minds of vulnerable Muslim youth from the ideology of dying for their religion to that of living for it and making it the envy of other religions by the way they live rather than the way they die. Moreover, the al-majiri education system needs to be improved upon to instill the feeling of self-eliance and patriotic mind-set to live and serve in the name of "Allah" instead of dying in the name of whatever religion in the vulnerable children who may have no other option than going through the system.

- Nigerian government need to reconsider her option of paying ransom to and swapping unrepentant terrorists to free hostages from Boko Haram. This does not only embolden the group and encourage it in its child/human trafficking activities to sustain its terrorist insurgency, it also makes their alliance with other terrorist groups stronger. Moreover, it does not only make Nigeria seem to be treating the group as a "recognised sovereign terror organization" the government is always ready to do deal with; besides, it makes the claim of victory over Boko Haram a mere hoax or hocus-pocus intended to deceive.
- Finally, rather than claiming victory against Boko Haram by mere media propaganda and suppression of information concerning the actual security threat posed by the group, Nigerian government particularly should devote more serious and practical efforts and resources in tackling poverty, hunger, socio-economic injustice and ignorance, all of which have been made much worse by the Boko Haram terrorist activities, and even more so since the present regime took over power in 2015. As the International Monetary Fund (IMF) recently stated, "Nigerians have become increasing poor since 2016 (*Daily Post,* March 1, 2018)[48], (*Premium Times,* March 1, 2018)[49].

Notes

1. Campbell, John (2013) *Nigeria: Dancing on the Brink*; New York: Rowman & Littlefield; also visit: http://www.cfr.org/nigeria/nigeria-dancing-brink/p22833?co=C011803 (Accessed 12/03/018).
2. George, A. Temilola (2013: 316) *America's Intervention in Boko Haram,* Society for Peace Studies and Practice, Abuja: John Archers Publishers ltd.
3. George, A. Temilola (2013) *Ibid.*
4. Joscelyn, Thomas (March 2015) *Boko Haram Leader Pledges Allegiance to the Islamic State*, Foundation for Defence of Democracies (FDD) Long War Journal; also visit: ttp://www.longwarjournal.org/rchives/2015/03/boko-haram-leader-pledges-allegiance-to-the-islamic-state.php (Accessed 12/03/018).
5. BBC (March 15, 2015) *Islamic State Accepts Boko Haram's Allegiance Pledge*; also visit: http://www.bbc.com/news/world-africa-31862992 (Accessed 13/03/018).
6. Mshelizza, M. (2011) "Nigerian Islamist sect posters threaten uprising",

Reuters, February 2; @ http://af.reuters.com/article/topNews/idAFJOE7110GN20110202 (Accessed 04/08/016).

7. Onuoha, F.C. (2014: 177), *ibid.*
8. Denoeux, G. and Carter, L. (2009), *Guide to the Drivers of Extremism*, U. S. A.: United States Agency for International Development (p. 86).
9. The Jihadi Websites Monitoring Group (2010: 14), *Periodical Review*, March (2).
10. Stratford, R. (2010), *Nigeria: AQIM attempts to expand*, June 15 (2010); @http://www.stratfor.com/analysis/20100615_nigeria_aqim_attempts_expand (Accessed 04/08/016).
11. Pham, J.P. (2013: 4) "Boko Haram evolving threat", *Africa Security* Brief No. 20, April (2013: accessed 04/08/016).
12. Joscelyn, Thomas (2015) Jihadist Divisions Grow in Nigeria, FDD's War Journal; also visit: http://www.longwarjournal.org/archives/2015/02/jihadist-divisions-grow-in-nigeria (Accessed 113/03/018).
13. Zenn, Jacob (2013) *Boko Haram's International Connections, Combating Terrorism Centre*, February 14 (2013); also visit: https://www. ctc.usma.edu/posts/boko-harams-international-connections (Accessed 13/03/018).
14. Mark, Monica (2012) *Boko Haram Vows to Fight Until Nigeria Establishes Sharia Law*, Guardian, January 27 (2012).
15. Vindino, L., *Pantucci R. & Kohlmann, E. (2010: 224), Bringing global jihad to the Horn of Africa: Al Shabaab, Western fighters, and the sacralisation of the Somali conflict, African Security* 3(4): 216-238.
16. Ayoob, M. (2005: 960) *The future of political Islam: the importance of external variables*; *International Affairs* 81(5): 951-961.
17. Africa Confidential (2013: 5) *Nigeria: Taking the hostage road*, Africa Confidential 54(6), 15 March 2013.
18. Connell, S. (2012:89) *To be or not to be: Is Boko Haram a foreign terrorist organisation, Global Security Studies* 3(3): 87-93
19. Safricagroup.com (2011), *Boko Haram calls off proposed talks, promises wider attacks using Somali-trained hit men*, 16 June. http://saferafricagroup.com/2011/06/16/boko-haramcalls-off-proposed-talks-promises-wider-attacks-using-somali-trained-hit-men/ (Accessed 10/08 016).
20. Connell, S. (2012) *To be or not to be: Is Boko Haram a foreign terrorist organisation, Global Security Studies* 3(3): 87-93.
21. Bashir, M. (2011) *UN building: Boko Haram names bomber, Abul Barra, Daily Trust,* September 2 (2011).
22. Shaughnessy, L. (2012) *Extremist triangle, a growing threat to Africa and America;* June 25 (2012) http://security.blogs.cnn.com/2012/06/25/extremist-triangle-a-growing-threat-toafrica-and-america/ (Accessed 08/08/016).
23. U.S. African Command (2012) *Transcript: Ham discusses African security issues at ACSS senior leaders seminar*; June 27 (2012). http://www.africom.mil/getArticle.asp?art=8039&lang=0 (Accessed 13/03/018).

24. Onuoha, F.C. and Thurston, A. (2013) *Franco-African military intervention in the Mali Crisis and evolving security concerns*; Al Jazeera Centre for African Studies Report, February 19 (Accessed 08/08/016).
25. Premium Times (2013) *Three-man 'Boko Haram' gang killed Nigerian soldiers going to Mali* @ http://www.premiumtimesng.com/news/116273-three-man-boko-haram-gang-killed-nigerian-soldiers-going-to-mali.html (Accessed 13/03/018).
26. The Nigerian Voice (Jan. 19, 2013) *Boko Haram Attacks Mali-Bound Soldiers in Kogi* (Nigeria) @ http://www.thenigerianvoice.com/news/105951/boko-haram-attacks-mali-bound-soldiers-in-kogi.html (Accessed 13/03/018).
27. Rasheed, O. (2012) *Hidden roots of Boko Haram ... Why security agencies are worried about South West, Nigerian Tribune,* February 17 (Accessed 10/08/016).
28. Onuoha, F.C. (2014), *Ibid.,*
29. Point Blank News (2013) *Stop Killing Boko Haram Members – Buhari tells FG* @ http://pointblank.com/pbn/exclusive/stop-killing-boko-haram-members-Buhari-tells-fg/ (Accessed 14/03/018).
30. The Nation (June 2, 2013) Buhari*Faults Clampdown on Boko Haram Members*; also visit: http://thenationonlineng.net/buhari-faults-clampdown-on-boko-haram-members/ (Accessed 14/03/018).
31. This day News (2014) *Buhari: Military Offensive Against Boko Haram, Anti-North.*
32. NewsRescue.com (2015) REVEALED: BUHARI Said "A State of Emergency is Anti-North, NOT A War Against Boko Haram" @ http://newsrescue.com/revealed-buhari-said-a-state-of-emergency-is-anti-north-not-a-war-against-boko-haram/#ixzz4jlexvw4p (Accessed 14/03/018).
33. Jerusalem Post (January 2015) *US Vetoed Israeli Sale of Attack Helicopters to Nigeria 388985*; also visit:http://www.jpost.com/Israel-News/Report (Accessed 14/03/018).
34. Nigeria Communications Week (January 27, 2015) *Revealed: How US Blocks Arms Deal with Nigeria*; also visit: https://nigeriacommunications week.com.ng/revealed-how-us-blocks-arms-deal-with-nigeria/
35. The Globe and Mail (2015*) Nigeria buys Black-market Weapons to Fight Boko Haram;* also visit:https://www.theglobeandmail.com/news/world/nigeria-buys-black-market-weapons-to-fight-boko-haram (Accessed 14/03/018).
36. The Guardian (April 15, 2015) *South Africa's Ageing White Mercenaries Who Helped Turn Tide on Boko Haram*; also visit: https://www.the guardian.com/world/2015/apr/14/south-africas-ageing-white-mercenaries-who-helped-turn-tide-on-boko-haram (Accessed 15/03/018)
37. Joscelyn, Thomas (March, 2015) *Boko Haram leader Pledges Allegiance to the Islamic State*, Foundation for Defence of Democracies (FDD) *Long War Journal.*

38. BBC (March 7, 2015) *Nigeria's Boko Haram Pledges Allegiance to Islamic State*; also visit: http://www.bbc.com/news/world-africa-31784538 (Accessed 14/03/018).
39. Reuters (May 14,2016) *Boko Haram may be sending fighters to ISIS in Libya: U.S. Officials.*
40. The Guardian (May 14, 2016) *Boko Haram may be sending fighters to ISIS in Libya: U.S. Officials* @ https://www.theguardian.com/world/2016/may/14/boko-haram-may-be-sending-fighters-to-isis-in-libya-us-officials (Accessed 15/03/018).
41. Premium Times (June. 9, 2016) U.S. says no major link between ISIS, Boko Haram (Accessed 13/08/016).
42. The Guardian (March 8, 2015) Boko Haram-ISIS Alliance is nothing but Superficial Propaganda; also visit: https://www.theguardian.com/world/2015/mar/08/ (Accessed 15/03/018).
43. Independent (April 21, 2016) ISIS Increasing co-operation with Boko Haram the World's Most Horrific Terrorist Group-a6; also visit: http://www.independent.co.uk/news/world/africa/isis-increasing-co-operation-with-boko-haram-the-worlds-most-horrific-terrorist-group-a69 (Accessed 15/03/018).
44. Cummings, R. (2016) Buhari's Deadline, Inconvenient Truth about Boko Haram's Defeat, @ naija.ng.; also visit: https://www.naija.ng/684751-buharis-deadline-inconvenient-truth-boko-harams-defeat.html#684751 (Accessed 19/03/018).
45. Daily Post (October 19, 2017) *Buhari Expresses Worry over ISIS Support for Boko Haram*; also visit: http://dailypost.ng/2017/10/19/buhari-expresses-worry-isis-support-boko-haram/ (Accessed 19/03/018).
46. Sahara Reporters (March 21, 2018) *Nigeria Government Lied, Boko Haram Fighters, Money swapped for Dapchi Girls*; also visit: http://saharareporters.com/2018/03/21/nigerian-govt-lied-boko-haram-fighters-money-swapped-dapchi-girls-0 (Accessed 23/03/018).
47. This Day (March 22, 2018) *Boko Haram Returns 104 Dapchi Schoolgirls, Raising Concerns over Ransom Payment;* also visit: https://www.thisdaylive.com/index.php/2018/03/22/boko-haram-returns-104-dapchi-schoolgirls-raising-concerns-over-ransom-payment/ (Accessed 23/03/018).
48. Daily Post (March 1, 2018) *More Nigerians getting poorer under Buhari government – IMF*; also visit: http://dailypost.ng/2018/03/01/nigerians-getting-poorer-buhari-govt-imf/ (Accessed 20/03/018).
49. Premium Times (March 1, 2018) *Nigerians Getting Poorer, Says IMF*; also visit:https://www.premiumtimesng.com/news/headlines/260334-nigerians-getting-poorer-says-imf.html (Accessed 20/03/018).

References

Africa Confidential (2013: 5) *Nigeria: Taking the hostage road*, Africa Confidential 54(6), 15 March 2013.

Ayoob, M. (2005: 960) *The future of political Islam: the importance of external variables*; International Affairs 81(5): 951-961.

Bashir, M. (2011) *UN building: Boko Haram names bomber, Abul Barra*, Daily Trust, September 2 (2011).

BBC (March 15, 2015) *Islamic State Accepts Boko Haram's Allegiance Pledge*; also visit: http://www.bbc.com/news/world-africa-31862992 (Accessed 13/03/018).

BBC (March 7, 2015) *Nigeria's Boko Haram Pledges Allegiance to Islamic State*; also visit: http://www.bbc.com/news/world-africa-31784538 (Accessed 14/03/018).

Campbell, John (2013) *Nigeria: Dancing on the Brink*; New York: Rowman& Littlefield; also visit: http://www.cfr.org/nigeria/nigeria-dancing-brink/p22833?co=C011803 (Accessed 12/03/018).

Connell, S. (2012:89) *To be or not to be: Is Boko Haram a foreign terrorist organisation*, Global Security Studies 3(3): 87-93

Connell, S. (2012) *To be or not to be: Is Boko Haram a foreign terrorist organisation*, Global Security Studies 3(3): 87-93.

Cummings, R. (2016) Buhari's Deadline, Inconvenient Truth about Boko Haram's Defeat, @ naija.ng.; also visit: https://www.naija.ng/684751-buharis-deadline-inconvenient-truth-boko-harams-defeat.html#684751 (Accessed 19/03/018).

Daily Post (October 19, 2017) Buhari Expresses Worry over ISIS Support for Boko Haram; also visit: http://dailypost.ng/2017/10/19/buhari-expresses-worry-isis-support-boko-haram/ (Accessed 19/03/018).

Daily Post (March 1, 2018) *More Nigerians getting poorer under Buhari government – IMF*; also visit: http://dailypost.ng/2018/03/01/nigerians-getting-poorer-buhari-govt-imf/ (Accessed 20/03/018).

Denoeux, G. and Carter, L. (2009), *Guide to the Drivers of Extremism*, U.S.A.: United States Agency for International Development (p. 86).

George, A. Temilola (2013: 316) *America's Intervention in Boko Haram*, Society for Peace Studies and Practice, Abuja: John Archers Publishers ltd.

George, A. Temilola (2013) *Ibid.*,

Independent (April 21, 2016) ISIS Increasing co-operation with Boko Haram the World's Most Horrific Terrorist Group-a6; also visit: http://www.independent.co.uk/news/world/africa/isis-increasing-co-operation-with-boko-haram-the-worlds-most-horrific-terrorist-group-a69 (Accessed 15/03/018).

Jerusalem Post (January 2015) *US Vetoed Israeli Sale of Attack Helicopters to Nigeria 388985*; also visit: http://www.jpost.com/Israel-News/Report (Accessed 14/03/018).

Joscelyn, Thomas (March, 2015) *Boko Haram leader Pledges Allegiance to the Islamic State*, Foundation for Defence of Democracies (FDD) *Long War Journal*.

Joscelyn, Thomas (March 2015) *Boko Haram leader Pledges Allegiance to the Islamic State*, Foundation for Defence of Democracies (FDD) *Long War Journal*; also visit: http://www.longwarjournal.org/archives/2015/03/boko-haram-leader-pledges-allegiance-to-the-islamic-state.php (Accessed 12/03/018).

Joscelyn, Thomas (2015) Jihadist Divisions Grow in Nigeria, *FDD's War Journal*; also visit: http://www.longwarjournal.org/archives/2015/02/jihadist-divisions-grow-in-nigeria (Accessed 13/03/018).

Mark, Monica (2012) *Boko Haram Vows to Fight Until Nigeria Establishes Sharia Law*, *Guardian*, January 27 (2012).

Mshelizza, M. (2011) Nigerian Islamist sect posters threaten uprising", *Reuters*, February 2; @ http://af.reuters.com/article/topNews/idAFJOE7110GN2011 0202 (Accessed 04/08/016).

NewsRescue.com (2015) REVEALED: BUHARI Said "A State of Emergency is Anti-North, NOT A War Against Boko Haram" @ http://newsrescue.com/revealed-buhari-said-a-state-of-emergency-is-anti-north-not-a-war-against-boko-haram/#ixzz4jlexvw4p (Accessed 14/03/018).

Nigeria Communications Week (January 27, 2015) *Revealed: How US Blocks Arms Deal with Nigeria*; also visit: https://nigeriacommunicationsweek.com.ng/revealed-how-us-blocks-arms-deal-with-nigeria/

Onuoha, F.C. and Thurston, A. (2013) *Franco-African military intervention in the Mali Crisis and evolving security concerns*; Al Jazeera Centre for African Studies Report, February 19 (Accessed 08/08/016).

Onuoha, F.C. (2014) *Boko Haram and the evolving Salafi Jihadist threat;* in De Montclos, Marc-Antoine P., 2014:166); African Studies Centre (ASC) Institute Français de Recherche en Afrique (IFRA) West African Politics and Society Series, Vol. 2.

Onuoha, F.C. (2014: 177), *Ibid.*,

Pham, J.P. (2013: 4) "Boko Haram evolving threat", Africa Security Brief No. 20, April (2013: accessed 04/08/016).

Point Blank News (2013) *Stop Killing Boko Haram Members – Buhari tells FG;* also visit:http://pointblank.com/pbn/exclusive/stop-killing-boko-haram-members-Buhari-tells-fg/ (Accessed 14/03/018).

Premium Times (June 9, 2016) U.S. says no major link between ISIS, Boko Haram (Accessed 13/03/018).

Premium Times (2013) *Three-man 'Boko Haram' gang killed Nigerian soldiers going to Mali* @ http://www.premiumtimesng.com/news/116273-three-man-boko-haram-gang-killed-nigerian-soldiers-going-to-mali.html (Accessed 13/03/018).

Premium Times (March 1, 2018) *Nigerians Getting Poorer, Says IMF*; also visit: https://www.premiumtimesng.com/news/headlines/260334-nigerians-getting-poorer-says-imf.html (Accessed 20/03/018).

Rasheed, O. (2012) *Hidden roots of Boko Haram ... Why security agencies are worried about South West*, Nigerian Tribune, February 17 (Accessed 10/08/016).

Reuters (May 14, 2016) *Boko Haram may be sending fighters to ISIS in Libya:- U.S. Officials.*

Safricagroup.com (2011), *Boko Haram calls off proposed talks, promises wider attacks using Somali-trained hit men*, 16 June. http://saferafricagroup.com/2011/06/16/boko-haramcalls-off-proposed-talks-promises-wider-attacks-using-somali-trained-hit-men/ (Accessed 10/08/016).

Sahara Reporters (March 21, 2018) *Nigeria Government Lied, Boko Haram Fighters, Money swapped for Dapchi Girls*; also visit: http://saharareporters.com/2018/03/21/nigerian-govt-lied-boko-haram-fighters-money-swapped-dapchi-girls-0 (Accessed 23/03/018).

Shaughnessy, L. (2012) *Extremist triangle, a growing threat to Africa and America;* June 25 (2012) http://security.blogs.cnn.com/2012/06/25/ extremist-triangle-a-growing-threat-toafrica-and-america/ (Accessed 08/08/ 016).

Stratford, R. (2010), *Nigeria: AQIM attempts to expand*, June 15 (2010); @ http://www.stratfor.com/analysis/20100615_nigeria_aqim_attempts_expand (Accessed 12/03/018).

The Globe and Mail (2015*)~,Nigeria buys Black-market Weapons to Fight Boko Haram;* also visit: https://www.theglobeandmail.com/news/world/ nigeria-buys-black-market-weapons-to-fight-boko-haram (Accessed 14/03/ 018).

The Guardian (April 15, 2015) *South Africa's Ageing White Mercenaries Who Helped Turn Tide on Boko Haram*; also visit: https://www.theguardian.com/world/2015/apr/14/south-africas-ageing-white-mercenaries-who-helped-turn-tide-on-boko-haram (Accessed 15/03/018).

The Guardian (May 14, 2016) *Boko Haram may be sending fighters to ISIS in Libya: U.S. Officials* @ https://www.theguardian.com/world/2016/may/14/boko-haram-may-be-sending-fighters-to-isis-in-libya-us-officials (Accessed 15/03/018).

The Guardian (March 8, 2015) Boko Haram-ISIS Alliance is nothing but Superficial Propaganda; also visit: https://www.theguardian.com/world/2015/mar/08/ (Accessed 15/03/018).

The Jihadi Websites Monitoring Group (2010: 14), Periodical review, March (2).

The Nation (June 2, 2013) Buhari *Faults Clampdown on Boko Haram Members*; also visit: http://thenationonlineng.net/buhari-faults-clampdown-on-boko-haram-members/ (Accessed 14/03/018).

The Nigerian Voice (January 19, 2013) *Boko Haram Attacks Mali-Bound Soldiers in Kogi* (Nigeria) @ http://www.thenigerianvoice.com/news/ 105951/boko-haram-attacks-mali-bound-soldiers-in-kogi.html (Accessed 13/03/018).

This Day News (2014) *Buhari: Military Offensive Against Boko Haram, Anti-North.*

U.S. African Command (2012) *Transcript: Ham discusses African security issues at ACSS senior leaders seminar*; June 27 (2012). http://www.africom.mil/getArticle.asp?art=8039&lang=0 (Accessed 13/03/018).

Vindino, L., Pantucci R. & Kohlmann, E. (2010: 224), *Bringing global jihad to the Horn of Africa: Al Shabaab, Western fighters, and the sacralisation of the Somali conflict*, African Security 3(4): 216-238.

Zenn, Jacob (2013) *Boko Haram's International Connections, Combating Terrorism Centre*, February 14 (2013); also visit: https://www.ctc.usma.edu/posts/boko-harams-international-connections (Accessed 13/03/018).

6

Islamic Education and Politics: Readings in the History of Madrasah System in India

Khan Gulnaz Begum Md. Ishaque and *Hussein Ahmed Abdo Rajhy*

Introduction

Madrasa (or spelt as madrasah), which is an Arabic word which simply means a place of learning, is referred to as a traditional religious educational institution of Muslims. "Literally it means a place where Dars (lesson) is given to the students. The history of Madrasa system of education began from the Masjid, in Masjid al Nabavi (Prophet's Masjid) wherein there was a platform called al-Suffa which was reserved for the learning people, known as Ashab al-Suffa. So al-Suffa is the first Madrasa of Islamic Tradition." Mohammed Basheer, K. (2013:96).

"The word *Madrasah* is derived from the tri-consonantal Semitic Arabic root "*D-R-S*" which means "to learn, study." Therefore, *Madrasah* literally means "a place where learning and studying are done." In the Arabic language, the word *Madrasah* simply means the same as *school* does in the English language, whether that is private, public, or parochial school as well as for any primary or secondary school whether Muslim, non-Muslim, or secular. However, in English, the term *Madrasah* usually refers to the specifically Islamic institutions." Wani, H.A. (2016:236).

The word Madrasa includes four types of Islamic educational institutions prevailing all over the globe: (i) Maktab, (ii) Madrasa, (iii) Darul Uloom, and (iv) Darul Qur'an. Maktab is a primary centre which functions in a Masjid or a small modest building and provides instruction in religious as well as some secular subjects. Madrasa is an institution that provides education generally up to senior secondary level. Darul Ulooms are institutions of higher learning providing instruction up to post graduation and specialization levels. Darul Qur'an are sort of madrasa specialized in Hifz and Thajwid (memorizing the Glorious Qur'an and learning the art of reciting) [Mohammed Basheer, K. (2013)].

"Although no regular census of madrasa has ever been taken, government sources estimate that there are approximately 1,05,000 such institutions in India. Every Madrasa follows its own pattern in educational structure and curricula. There is no uniformity with regard to subjects, books, specializations, or duration of various degrees. Its nature, structure, management, curriculum and degrees are varied from state to state. So we have to understand the system of madrasa education in a wider sense" [Mohammed Basheer, K. (2013:97)].

Role of Madrasa in Society

Madrasa has played a vital role in different fields of society. First of all madrasas helped Muslims to preserve their identity as Muslims. Through Madrasas, Muslims not only managed to protect their Islamic identity but also they influenced the Indian culture and made a good synthesis of Indo-Islamic Culture. The great contribution that madrasas made during the freedom struggle is non-negligible. From 1857 to 1947 they never compromised with the British rule and always held the torch of freedom. Madrasas are the greatest NGOs that promote education among the people. Monarchs as well as masses were educated in the Madrasas in the yesteryears. And even today Madrasa education in India plays a vital role in educating lakhs of Muslim children. The importance of Madrasas lies in its potential to make education available to the poorer section of the society. Madrasas provided free education, free board and free books while the Government of India yet could not manage to provide children with free and compulsory education even after the landmark legislation of RTE—2009. The contribution in the field of literary and academic works also should be taken into account. Hence, the contribution of Madrasa system of education cannot be neglected [Mohammed Basheer, K. (2013)].

"There would be no exaggeration in mentioning this truth that if Islam and Muslim civilization is alive across the globe, it's because of these *Madrasahs* and its products. These *Madrasahs* are the main tools which transmit and transfer the Prophet's teaching to the present generations and posterity. These institutions are the main channels of

Da'wah (preaching in Islam). Another main aim is to lay the foundation stone of that society where nobody's rule is acceptable, except the sovereignty of the Allah" [Wani, H.A. (2016:241)]. *Madrasahs* have for centuries served as centres of Islamic education. They have played a key role in the development of Islamic thought and in the formation and progress of Muslim communities.

After assessment of the *Madrasah* education setup, it can be said blatantly that these Muslim institutions play a commendable role in preaching Islam towards whole humanity. It is noteworthy to mention here that if Islam is alive its credit goes to these *Madrasahs*. The products of the *Madrasahs* are the symbol of great discipline and conduct. They are truthful and honest in their activities [Wani, H.A. (2016)].

The Indian Muslim minority is quite backward in science education and its representation and participation in the scientific activity of the country is woefully low. This situation, if allowed to persist for long, would certainly hinder the growth/health of the progress of the country. In these days of fast expanding frontiers of scientific knowledge and its multiplying technological spin-offs, no nation can afford to have a sizable chunk of its population illiterate in science, and no community can hope for a respectable place in the national stream without equipping itself with science education.

"One important factor of the educational backwardness of Muslims in India is the system of *Madrasah* education, which has its own advantages and disadvantages. Most of the students socially, economically, and educationally backward sections of the Muslim community begin their education from these *Madrasahs* and *Maktabs*, where education is relatively cheap and in some cases free. The students and teachers of these *Madrasahs* also get an euphoric feeling that they are performing their religious duties by learning Qur'an by heart, no matter whether they understand it or not" [Wani, H.A. (2016:247)].

The Concepts of Promoted Islamic Education

Islamic education tries to promote a set of concepts in the individuals. These concepts constitute the sole teachings of Islam and Islamic philosophy along with the working politics of Islam which are nothing other than a way of life style and Islamic conventions. Dar Al-Ifta Al-Missriyyah, has mentioned the following concepts that Islamic education tries to promote and they include:

1. *Education is a duty and right for every human being:* Islam promoted knowledge and education, which helped give rise to the scientific movements and the rise of new fields of knowledge that varied to include secular studies and fine arts.
2. *Caring for childhood;* The Islamic child education stems from the Arabs' keenness on ties of blood and lineage and their purity. Arabs used to view the child as a means of extending families and a source of pride.
3. *Raising knowledge and scholars to an elevated stature of a divine mission* after purifying the souls from evils and imbibing within one self's virtues and fine morals. Prophet, wherein he says: "Whoever treads a path seeking knowledge, Allah will make easy for him the path to Jannah (Paradise)." In another Hadith, the Prophet, peace be upon him, says: "He who goes out in search of knowledge is in God's path till he returns."
4. Mind sets thought free where Islam asserted human freedom of the mind from enslavement of specific notions that entails clinging to the footsteps of previous generations, blindly following the suit of people of authority and demeaning fear of their might and power. The Prophet, peace be upon him, used to hold the human mind in high esteem and regarded it as the core of religion and its foundation, for there is no religion for he who got no mind and perception. The Prophet has also commanded people to communicate and interact using their intellect and resorting to it as a safe haven.
5. Equality and equal right to education.
6. *Inclusivity, Integration and Balance:* to shape the human personality in an all-inclusive physical and spiritual frame in way that best serves the well-being of humanity and achieves its happiness.
7. Education is not restricted to time or place. (Dar Al-Ifta Al-Missriyyah).

Objectives of Madrasah Education

Islamic education comprises a set of concepts and tenets pertaining to human nature, creed, intellect, and attitude, along with spiritual and physical values, all entwined in unified perceptual framework and relying, entirely, in its fundamentals and morals on the Holy Qur'an and the Prophet's Sunnah. "Through Islamic education, individuals are educated and cultured following an all-encompassing method that involves all aspects mentioned, without compromising any, or giving primacy of one over the other." That was in brief identifying the Meaning of 'Islamic Education' as stated by Dar Al-Ifta Al-Missriyyah.

The objective of the *Madrasah* system is "to teach Islamic subjects, for instance the education of the Holy Qur'an, *Hadith*, Islamic Jurisprudence, Arabic Literature, and Islamic History. *Madrasah* created thousands of the Muslim youth who were having strong knowledge about the gospels of Islam. The one of the main aim of the *Madrasah* was to produce such youth who after garnering the education of Qur'an and *Hadith* thereby to preach this among the people. Indeed, it is accepted notion that these *Madrasah* products played a very vital role in our society." [Wani, H.A. (2016:241)]. Islamic educational setup wants to create a society based on justice, peace, tolerance, world brotherhood, equality, and egalitarianism.

"Islamic education have played a vital role in building and shaping the fate of Muslims from the very inception of the Islam. Islamic education not only fulfil the religious needs of Muslims, but also providing a great contribution to the field of knowledge and art and try to make them complete human beings from every side. Islamic educations are imparted through Moktabs, different types of Madrasas, Khankas, Jamias, Religious Assembles, Tablik Jamat etc." [Khatun, J. (2016:80)].

Islam is the universal religion and its principles have a universal applicability. If one understands Islam only by confining himself to religious education, this is his misnomer and its nothing but illusion of irrationality. Islam has a broad paradigm and its emphasis is upon the universality principle not to be confined in home. Islam allows Muslim to have the plenty of information about the modern education so that they could adjust themselves at any fore. They will be not beggars but contributors to other sections of society [Wani, H.A. (2016:248)].

For centuries, *Madrasahs* were the centre of thought and intellectualism in Muslim communities, and influenced all sections of the society. *Madrasahs* produced religious scholars and guides as well as leaders in various "secular" or "worldly" fields, including traders, administrators, judges, and so on [Wani, H.A. (2016)].

The Concept and Meaning of Islamic Edu :ation

Dar Al-Ifta Al-Missriyyah stated that "Islamic education has a set of concepts which were described by Muslim educationists in various ways which include:

1. Cultivating all intellectual, emotional, physical and social aspects of the personality; based on Islamic teachings and values, with the aim of achieving the optimum goals of leading a dignified life entangled with a religious flavour.
2. Providing Muslim individuals with an all-encompassing preparation process that involves all aspects of his/her personality which continues throughout his growing phases to be able to handle this worldly life and the other, in light of the teachings and values of Islam, and in accordance with an educational methodology defined by educational specialists.
3. Individual and social activity that seeks to cultivate individuals intellectually, doctrinally, spiritually, socially, physically, ascetically, and ethically, thereby empowering them with the knowledge, approaches, ethics and proficiencies needed for sound growth that can best serve both their practical and spiritual life.
4. Purposeful process that is guided by Islamic Shariah and seeks to cultivate all aspects of human personality in a way that achieves total submission and worship to Almighty Allah."

Madrasah Educational Institution

Mosques in Islam served as the first educational institution. Since the Nabawai Mosque in Madina was built, it used for teaching purposes, especially for the teaching of law and theology. Gradually, as the Muslim society developed, study circles were held not only in the mosques but also in the palaces, in the streets and even in the market places. Nevertheless, the mosque remained pre-eminent for the teaching of theology and jurisprudence, where students sat in a circle at the teacher's feet.

In 750 and then after to the middle of the thirteenth century, during the Abbasid period, religious education became a branch of learning in its own right, with some teachers specializing in the Qur'an, theology and jurisprudence, and other teachers teach Arabic language, literature and history. Then the study circles also grew in number and quality during this period, forming the nuclei of what were to become the madrasas, or can be called colleges, intended for adults who had already received their primary education in mosques or Kuttabs.

The institution of madrasah emerged as an independent institution distinct from the mosque in the 10th century. However, Asimov, M.S. and Bosworth, C.E. (2000:37-8) wrote: "madrasahs in the early days were set up either for a single jurist or to teach the tenets of a particular legal school. Thus was born a new kind of educational institution, destined in future to become a centre of religious and secular learning in the Islamic world and a place where the representatives of the official class were educated in the spirit of Muslim orthodoxy."

Developing steadily, "Madrasah came to dominate learning in the Islamic Middle East as much as universities do in the contemporary West" (Mottahedeh, 1985: 89). Madrasah was something different in the arena of Muslim education: an independent institution which receives various kinds of endowments for funding the education and research following an established curriculum. The madrasah had set a model with education under the supervision of paid teachers (The founders of madrasahs, often viziers, sultans, wealthy people who financed expenditures of madrasahs) using a fairly a uniform curriculum for instruction. Hence madrasahs became an important part of every Muslim city, just like a mosque or bazaar [Asimov, M.S. & Bosworth, C.E. (2000)].

Progress of development in the madrasah educational system reached a higher level during the fifteenth and sixteenth centuries. "There were moves towards integration and specialization, and individual madrasas in Samarkand and Herat, under the influence of the scientific circles that had formed there, now acquired a more clearly defined and well-developed structure as centres of scientific education, with inquiries into such sciences as mathematics, astronomy, medicine, philosophy, theology, languages, literature and music." [Asimov, M.S. & Bosworth, C.E. (2000:39)].

In the second stage of schooling, as Madrasah was considered the second stage of Islamic education, coming after the stage of Kuttab which is considered the primary education, Ibn Sina called madrasah the period of specialization where pupils should, in his view, begin to acquire manual skills, irrespective of their social status. Ibn Sina's own preference was for the teaching of crafts, rather than the more risky trade and commerce, since 'the master of a craft, no matter what the circumstances, will always find a use for his skills." "The teaching of such crafts should begin immediately after completion of the study of the Qur'an and basic Arabic grammar. He advised parents not to be over-protective of their children and not to smother them with attention while they were being trained in a craft; rather, they should be given encouragement, and an interest should be taken in the final result of their efforts" [Asimov, M.S. & Bosworth, C.E. (2000:35)].

For selecting specialization in madrasah schooling system, Ibn Sina advised that children after the age of 14 should be allowed to choose and specialize in subjects they have an interest in, whether it was reading, manual skills, literature, preaching, medicine, geometry, trade and commerce, craftsmanship, or any other subject or profession they would be interested in pursuing for a future career. He wrote that this was a transitional stage and that there needs to be flexibility regarding the age in which pupils graduate, as the student's emotional development and chosen subjects need to be taken into account [Asimov, M.S. & Bosworth, C.E. (2000)].

During the Mongol invasion of the Muslim world, there was a temporary blow to learning, severing links between creative intellectuals and for a time disrupting the continuity of culture, but after the successful monetary reform introduced by the first Mongols, Mongke Khan and his minister Mascud Beg, economic life soon revived in the cities of Iran. Under Mascud Beg twin madrasas were built in Bukhara, where 1,000 students each could study [Asimov, M.S. & Bosworth, C.E. (2000)].

Promoting the research and scholarship, "under the leadership of al-Tusi, over 100 scientists worked and wrote there, and astronomical observations were carried out there for a period of over 15 years. Attached to the observatory was a madrasa, and lectures there were closely connected to the activities of the observatory. Its teaching covered philosophy, medicine, theology and handasa (technology)" [Asimov, M.S. & Bosworth, C.E. (2000:39)].

Regarding the infrastructure of madrasahs, "under the Mongols, and later under the Timurids, there was a growing tendency to build at major urban sites architectural ensembles that often included a mosque, a madrasa, a mausoleum and public garmabs (baths), and we have valuable accounts of the construction of madrasas undertaken by Mongol rulers and members of their families in Shiraz, Isfahan, Tabriz, Kirman, Gurganj and other cities in Iran and Central Asia." [Asimov, M.S. & Bosworth, C.E. (2000:40)]. Giving an examples of developed madrasahs building of the late fourteenth century, the madrasah in Samarkand was the Khanum madrasa opposite the famous great mosque of Timur.

The Madrasah Educational System

Education in the early centuries of Islam was being carried out in 'madaris' which were connected with a major mosque. The students were accommodated with boarding and lodging facilities in mosques. They were not restricted to finish their studies within a particular period of time as modern universities do. [Abdul Waheedu K. (2003)]. The expenses of the madrasas were met from the revenue earned from large estate given as endowments. Certain madrasas had libraries and hospitals attached to it [Abdul Waheedu K. (2003)]. The facilities for students' staying in the educational institutions were made which was later adopted by the system of modern education.

History of Islam has proved that Islamic Educational Institutions had their own curriculum and the philosophy of curriculum centred round the Islamic epistemology and axiology which were based on Qur'an and Hadith. It is stated that the mosque was the central institution in the system of Islamic education and Madrasas were attached to it.

"Based on these historical facts one can come to the conclusion that there was adequate shelter facilities in madris and a healthy teacher-pupil interaction which resulted in the increase in knowledge of the students and their character formation. Besides, the new system of arrangements made for the studies, and stay of the students make it clear that there was a system of management which was often supported by the rulers of the region as well as the community as a whole. The system of educational management was carried out in the interest of the society based on the principles of Islam" [Abdul Waheedu K. (2003:173)].

Curriculum in Madrasah

As the curriculum of any society will reflect its concepts of issues, the ideology and culture it inherits, the goals which it intends to achieve etc., the Islamic curriculum familiarizes the individual with his relation to his fellow beings and other creatures, his responsibilities in life, duties and role in the society, his social relation and his relationship with the universe as a whole.

Islamic Education distinguishes clearly between two types of curricula:

(i) Obligatory knowledge which must be studied by everyone. It includes the religious sciences and related disciplines such as linguistics and literature;
(ii) Optional knowledge, which are to be learned according to the interest and capacities of the pupil. They are in turn divided into: (a) revealed sciences and (b) non-revealed sciences [Abdul Waheedu K. (2003)].

Though the curricula of madrasahs vary not only according to the stipulations of the founders but also according to the preferences of the teachers and the wishes of the directors of madrasahs, the bases of Islamic curriculum are mainly Qur'an and Sunnah. So, it is the prime duty of the curriculum setters not to include any element which may adversely affect the Qur'anic principles. However, a man of integrated personality is expected to come out as a product on completion of the Islamic curriculum.

The madrasah has always been regarded as the institution for Islamic sciences. Thus, it is expected to provide the basic education in fiqh (religious law, Islamic jurisprudence). Students are expected to be acquainted with the arguments using Qur'ān, ḥadīth (sunnah) and sīrah. Over the course of time, other subjects – some foreign sciences – were introduced to the madrasah curricula. The Islamic curriculum is ideologically oriented; hence the nature and contents of it and the syllabi will be of the same nature. Islamic education is a life-long process. So, possibility of continuity should be ensured in all stages of education. Qur'anic concept of man is that he is, dignified honourable human being, the vicegerent of God on earth. Accordingly, the curriculum should be framed including the relevant and appropriate topics for preparing the man to undergo a stream of education that will prepare him to perform effectively the duties entrusted upon him [Abdul Waheedu K. (2003)].

The institution of madrasah, during its formative period, was referred to as a higher education institution whose curriculum initially included only the "religious sciences", whilst philosophy and the secular sciences were often excluded. The curriculum slowly began to diversify, with many later madaris teaching both the religious and the "secular sciences", such as logic, mathematics and philosophy. Some madaris further extended their curriculum to history, politics, ethics, music, metaphysics, medicine, astronomy and chemistry.

Curriculum Addressing the Needs of Globalized Era

The Madrasa have been changing over time, although the pace and scope of these changes may not be as spectacular as some of us would wish. The syllabus of schools and universities keep upgrading/ modifying at the interval of every 5-7 years. The dars-i-nizami, syllabus of the madrasas has not been changed for last 3-4 centuries. There is a need to modify Dars-i-Nizami madrasa syllabus, without altering its core subjects. "Madrasahs have continued to differ in their versions of this curriculum, and the latter has scarcely been impervious to change. The single most important of such changes concerns the relative prominence that the study of Hadith has come to have in the Dars-i Nizami from the late nineteenth century onwards. The primary emphasis of the Dars-i Nizami is on the "rational sciences" (ma'qulat), as distinguished from the "transmitted sciences" (manqulat)" [Zaman, M.Q. (1999:303)]

When we talk about reforming the madrasas we must keep in mind their basic goals and purpose. They are meant to train religious specialists and so reforms must be such that can help the madrasas better fulfil their purpose. Rather than the 'hard' sciences, we should be thinking in terms of incorporating the social sciences into the curriculum, along with basic Mathematics and English. Teaching social sciences in the madrasas is important in order that the students can go on to interpret Islam in a socially and contextually relevant manner [Mohammed Basheer, K. (2013:99)]

The modern madrasa system originated in Eastern Iran in the tenth century and spread to major urban centres throughout the Middle East by the late eleventh century. The architect of the madrasa as a state-sponsored institution of higher education was Nizam al-Mulk (died 1092 C.E.), the prime minister of the Seljuk empire. These residential colleges were designed by the ruling elite both as a training ground for state bureaucrats and as a Sunni Islam response to the propaganda of Ismaili Shi ism w at al-Azhar, the theological learning centre founded by the Fatimid dynasty in Cairo in 969 C.E. As part of a Sunni Muslim religiopolitical agenda, the madrasa spread throughout the Islamic world. The madrasa system augmented already extant mosque-centred training sites for the study of religion and law. Unlike these centres, the madrasa forged links between the ulama, the religious scholars who directed Islamic education, and the ruling government authorities whose financial support made their control of the madrasa possible [Mohammed Basheer. K (2013)].

Development of Islamic Education

The Islamic Education system has undergone significant developments along the line of the history of Islamic regime. "Dar Al-Ifta Al-Missriyyah" wrote an article on the "The Theory of Islamic Education" and observed three phases in the development of Islamic education. These phases are:

Phase I—The Advent of Islam

This phase started with the rise of Islam in the Arabian Peninsula in the seventh century AD, and it laid the foundation for the political, religious, social, educational and ethical life of people, which impacted the Islamic life for long centuries that followed, and till date. Islamic education in this era asserted the importance of seeking learning and gaining knowledge along with urging individuals to work their minds to analyze present realities, enhance human life, and contemplate the surrounding creation and natural phenomenon. During early age of Islam, the primary aim was to establish the primary political and social foundation for the state is credited to this phase of Arab history, in which scattered and warring tribes were brought together for the first time, under the guardianship of one leader who paved the way for unity and solidarity by adopting a unified set of fundamentals and calling for the worship of one god, after tribes used to worship several gods. With the expansion of Muslim conquests, Caliph Umar ibn al-Khattab sent convoys of teachers and judges to teach and educate new Muslim converts, as well as Muslim children, as a means of spreading knowledge and education all over Muslim lands. He also sent Qur'an teachers and preachers to all lands that were new to Islam. Such religious missions sent by the Caliph had a significant impact on the spread of knowledge and teachings of the Qur'an, as well as Jurisprudence, among other Islamic sciences. The ultimate aim of these educational missions was to develop a sound Muslim personality, sound society, a prosperous civilization and a well-organized Muslim state.

Phase II—Islamic Conquests and the Development of the Muslim State

This stage covers the period stretching between the end of the rule of the Rightly Guided Caliphs till the end of the Umayyad State, during which the Arab Muslim Empire grew significantly, with its boundaries extending from India Eastward, to the Atlantic Westward, and from the Caspian Sea Northward, till Sudan Southward. Besides being influenced by their political and social systems of the newly controlled famous civilizations, such as the Persian, Greek and Coptic civilizations. During this phase, Arabs were exposed to historic civilizations. The positive impact of such cultural mingling manifests in the kind of education. This phase of Islamic history witnessed significant development in the field of education, a kind of development that sought to:

1. Preserve the Arab identity of the state, and thus scholars set the teaching curriculums, giving special care for history of other nations.
2. Assert the Islamic identity of the state and teaching Qur'an and Hadith sciences.
3. Adapting to the overall development and rising needs of the nation, thus organizing the state administrative and economic institutions. Thus administrations were Arabized and the influence of Romans and Persians was eradicated.

Phase III—Creativity

This phase stretches from the second century AH/ eighth century AD till mid-fifth century AH/11th century AD, and reflects the special care which rulers gave to the affairs of their nations following a fluctuation in Islamic conquests. Hence the intellectual and scientific integration of different nations and civilizations eventually led to genuine intellectual prosperity. Having the Arabic language as the main language for cultural representation, science, and communication, was another helping factor, besides religion, that led to cultural integration and unity. The great advancement in the cultural movement and translations of foreign books, especially Greek, Persian and Indian, into Arabic gave rise to a set of new disciplines such as philosophy, Logic, Geometry, Astrology, Music, Medicine, Chemistry and Geography and had its impacts on the educational system and curriculum in Islamic educational institutions, Dar Al-Ifta Al-Missriyyah.

The Evolution in the Educational System of Madrasah

The Madrasah initially was a very simple institution teaching reading and writing. It has been under a palm tree, in a tent or in a private house; yet it was a Madrasa. The courtyard of mosques and the open halls running along the walls of the mosques were also used for the purpose of education as a Madrasah. However, there is a significant differences between the present day Islamic system education which got influenced by the Western education system and the old Islamic system of education. "Madrasas as seen in India today are the outcome of beliefs and practices that took root in the country several centuries ago. Over time, they have been shaped in significant ways by the nature of the state, as well as the changing relationships between the state and the ulema and religious leaders" [Nair Padmaja (2009:6)].

Islamic education has undergone several changes from the day of its beginning. At the beginning only Qur'an and Hadis and Fiqh was taught. Gradually other branches of knowledge were added to it. All the branches of secular and religious knowledge were taught. Frequent changes were introduced to meet the challenges of the time. But after the introduction of Dars-e-Nizami by Mullah Nizamuddin the madrasas could not keep pace with the changing times. They clung to the outdated syllabus of the Dars-e-Nizami in its degenerated form. That is why most of the madrasas graduates are unable to take part in the process of national development [Afzal Ahmed (2017)].

From the earliest years of their history, Muslims witnessed juxtaposition of their faith and worldly power. Within a hundred years after the death of the Prophet Muhammad, Muslims were ruling over a vast empire. The Qur'anic assurance that "they were the best community" (The Qur'an, 3:110) was nourished and confirmed by this situation, which continued for another thousand years or so [Panjwani Farid (2004)]. With the territorial expansion of Islam under the pious caliphate new political centres emerged such as Kufa, Basra, Palestine and Damascus. This necessitated the appointment of permanent teachers to these far-flung areas and opening of maktabs. The companions of the Prophet Muhammed were held in great esteem and their lectures and sermons were heard with great eagerness and devotion. The expansion of Islamic empire brought manifold problems because different races of men were brought within the fold of Islam who hitherto held different faiths and followed different polity. Accordingly to meet the requirements Islamic jurisprudence or Fiqh was developed [Afzal Ahmed (2017:26)].

Now-a-days a madrasah or a school constitutes a great building, a group of specialist professionals, a series of lectures for certain limited hours. The universities or college in the present time can be established only in cities, but old personified Madrasahs of that time could be established in every village, town or hut. In the old terminology, a Madrasah was in the name of a particular person where a great number of people flock towards him and surround him and whatever he would speak day and night, it would be his educational lectures; his manners, postures, gestures, his dress etc. all would be his silent educational lectures.

Reformation of Madrasah

The educational system of madrasah has encountered significant reforms especially during the colonial period. "From being the main education system during the Mughal period, producing administrators as well as religious scholars and teachers, madrasas' response to the establishment of a schooling system on the British model to produce local staff for the colonial administration was to retreat from their close relationship with the state to the provision of religious education" [Nair, Padmaja (2009:1)]. The format of education imparted to the students of *Madrasahs* ought to be modified keeping in view the shifting demands of the employers – a concern which can no longer be under-played. And this is perfectly possible without an erosion of the cultural and religious identity. *Madrasahs* need to recognize that the world has undergone a transformation. Employers have specialized needs which the current education is unable to meet. Global and private competition, not to mention financial constraints, is not likely to disappear in the foreseeable future [Wani, H.A. (2016:243)].

Education involves transference to others, of knowledge and values accumulated by mankind. Even though schools and teachers have been part of the process of education for hundreds or even thousands of years, it is the spirit of enquiry that has enriched mankind with knowledge. We learn through reading, experience, by watching others, and by observing the world in general. Inculcating a spirit of scientific enquiry in students will perhaps be the best manner of propelling them on the path of learning [Wani, H.A. (2016:244)].

"Reformation of Madrasah education is the process or a method which Muslim learned people can go for if they want to stabilize themselves and positions of the Muslim masses. No education system in the world is complete; every education system needs reformation time to time so that loopholes and problems could be removed by overhauling the system by inclusion of new subjects and new courses" [Wani, H.A. (2016:249)]. So, *Madrasah* needs this reformation for the betterment of their Muslim community which is the second largest community in the democratic India. A positive change is always beneficial for any society. Inclusion of Science, Mathematics, and Computer educations could pave a way towards bright future for Muslim youth [Wani, H.A. (2016)].

"*Madrasahs* have to change their age old curriculum such as logic, philosophy, and minimize the quantity of subjects just give the first priority to the education of the Holy Qur'an, *Hadith*, Islamic jurisprudence, and Arabic literature. But in the meanwhile, they have to include some arts subjects like Science, Mathematics, Urdu, English, Political Science, Sociology, Economics, and basic computer knowledge. By doing this reform work, *Madrasahs* will be to produce those talents which will be perfect in both Islamic education and modern education" [Wani, H.A. (2016:251)]. The reform proposed for the Madrasah system is a "reform in the sense of actively integrating modern with classical knowledge is suspect to many, however; for it is perceived as undermining the unity and integrity of madrasa education and as devaluing the credential so f those trained in it" [Zaman, M.Q. (1999:303)].

There were two groups, namely traditionalist and modernist, emerged in Muslim community as a result of calls for reformation of Madrasah system. Both distrusted each other and often referred each other in derogatory terms. The modernist led by Sir Syed Ahmad Khan, Badruddin Tayyab Ji and Sayyed Amir strongly believed that traditional education imparted in madrasas and maktabs would not deliver the good. The traditionalist on the other hand opposed them. They believed that education which was imparted in madrasas and maktabs was necessary and that the modern education was contrary to their faith [Afzal Ahmed (2017)].

Madrasah in India: An Outline of History and Curriculum

The history of *madrasa* education in the Indian subcontinent is spread over more than a thousand years. Initially *madrasa* education system came with the Arab settlers who came to the Western coast of *Kerala*. With the spread of Islam in India, the Muslims brought here the Islamic system of education. In which mosques have occupied the central position for imparting knowledge since the time of the Prophet Muhammed. With the expansion of Islam, mosques were built all over the conquered countries. "Madrasas came into existence in India with the advent of Muslim rulers in the sub-continent. They were established by the rulers and nobles of the Muslim states or were the result of collective community endeavours" [Nair, Padmaja (2009:10)].

"*Madrasa* education system was catering to the needs of religious education of Arab settlers and converted locals. The establishment of *Delhi Sultanate* in 1106 A.D. *madrasa* education was popularized and patronaged by the establishment and the rulers were taking very keen interest for establishing *madrasas*. A number of famous *madrasas* came into being at the point of time. During the reign of *Tughlaq* dynasty, hundreds of *madrasas* were established in Delhi alone. *Madrasa* education reached to its culmination during Mughal Empire when it became a formal educational institution where all the students, irrespective of caste, colour, creed and place of birth, used to study together under the same roof to get education" [Ansari, M.A. (2016:101)] .

The Mughals have been known for their magnificence in all spheres of life. They also were the great patrons of learning. They established some important madrasas and provided their fullest support to the development of public education. The institution of the madrasa was well known in the Indian subcontinent, where the first madrasa appeared as early as the thirteenth century. For instance, when Juzjani arrived in Sind in 1227, the local ruler Nasir al-Din Qabacha put him in charge of the Firuziyya madrasa there, and when he went to Delhi in 1236 he was appointed a judge and head of the Nasiriyya madrasa [Asimov, M.S. & Bosworth, C.E. (2000:42)]. Nair Padmaja (2009:10) has written about the establishment of madrasas in India "from the latter half of the 12th to almost the end of the 16th centuries, the number of madrasas grew rapidly under the patronage of the early Muslim and Mughal rulers. The first Mughal conqueror, Babar, is credited with establishing a separate department for the promotion and administration of madrasas between 1526 and 1530. Emperors Jahangir (1605-1658) and Aurangzeb (1658-1707) made financial provisions for the upkeep and maintenance of madrasas and for scholarships for poor students. They are also believed to have granted large amounts of land (*jagir*) to the madrasas. Even during the last days of the Mughal Empire in the early eighteenth century, under Bahadur Shah Zafar, madrasas continued to be established in Delhi with state patronage."

In India, during the Muslim ruling period a particular kind of education system was prevalent all over the country. Primary education was imparted in the 'Maktabs', and for secondary and higher education there were 'Madrasas'. In Islamic history, Madrasas have played a vital role in building and shaping the faith of Muslim Ummah (society) from the very inception of the Islam. "These Madrasas have a great contribution to religious education which helps Muslims to know deeply about Islam. Madrasas not only fulfil religious needs of Muslims, but also providing a great contribution to the field of knowledge and art, but also try to make them complete human beings from every angle. These institutions have also played an important role in the survival of Islamic practices, publication and dissemination of Islamic literature, protection of Islamic faith and development of culture and civilization besides contributing to the development of the country" [Khatun, J. (2016:82)].

Anzar, Uzma (2003:4) wrote "as Islam spread to further east, the *Sufi* orders of the Muslim faith were establishing Madrassas in the Indian Sub-Continent and Central Asia. In these *Sufi* Madrassas grammar, poetry, literature, logic, math and other disciplines of Islam and general knowledge were taught. As most of the knowledge about Islam was either recorded in Arabic and Persian, the Madrassas in Indian Sub-Continent became places for learning Arabic and Persian. Every student aspiring to reach the highest level of the Madrassa education had to learn these two languages whatever the mother tongue of the student. The most renowned poets of India at that time were, borrowing from the Sufi traditions of Persia and Central Asia, composing their poems in Persian."

According to Afzal Ahmed (2017: 25) "the first Madrasa of India was built by Naseruddin Qabacha for Maulana Qutbuddin Karhani in Multan (now in Pakistan) in which Sheikh Bahauddin Zakaria Multani received his education. But according to Maulana Abul Hasnat Nadvi the tradition of opening madrasas and Maktabs side by side of mosques came to India in the period of Mahmud Ghazani and his governors which got general acceptance slowly."

In India all the Muslim rulers were patrons of learning and did tremendous service for the promotion and universalization of education. Great scholars thronged their court due to their patronage by these kings. The rulers established new madrasas, rebuilt old moribund madrasas and gave large estates as endowments for their maintenance. The contribution of provincial rulers is no less praiseworthy. Apart from the rulers wealthy individual also established madrasas because it was the most easy way to get social recognition and it was considered an act of religious service. Delhi, Agra and Jaunpur emerged as the great centres of learning at different period of the history [Afzal Ahmed (2017:205)].

In India, during the Muslim period, educational institutions were not divided into religious and secular. There was only one type of school called the madrasa where both the religious and secular sciences were taught. Its graduates fulfilled both the religious and secular needs of the society and the country. But in British period the non-madrasa type of schools soon spread throughout the country. The Government established and patronized the moden schools and colleges for secular education and showed no inclination to support the then existing madrasa education. Gradually the doors of jobs were closed for its graduates. But the Muslims instead of introducing the changes to its syllabus to meet the challenges of the time, stuck to the old system of Dars-e-Nizami. The situation is no better even now [Afzal Ahmed (2017:202)].

The course of instruction at a madrasa included the Qur'an, tradition, Arabic language, theology, arithmetic, geometry, astronomy and, often, medicine; however, the study of Islamic law (Sharia) provided the core of the madrasa's rigorous curriculum. Initially, madrasas were founded to provide specialized instruction in one of the four Sunni legal schools. In time, legal instruction in one or more of the Sunni legal schools might be offered in a single madrasa. The method of instruction relied heavily on memorization – of the Qur'an and as many traditions as possible [Mohammed Basheer. K (2013)].

The syllabi of the madrasas need a radical overhaul. "Most of the madrasas use some form or the other of the Dars-e-Nizami—a syllabus developed in the eighteenth century by Mullah Nizamuddin. In Mullah Nizamuddin's time, madrasas functioned as schools for training clerk and officials for the Mughal state and the books they taught were meant for that purpose. However, most madrasas still continue to use many or at least some of those books!" [Afzal Ahmed (2017:202)].

The texts studied at present in most madrasas of India and Pakistan comprise what is known as the "Dare-e-Nizami," a corpus whose introduction in madrasas is attributed to the influence of Mulla Nizam al-din Muhammad (d. 1748). Many of these texts were being taught in Indian madrasas long before Nizam al-din's time, however; and several others were added considerably after his death. The texts themselves were, in most cases, composed between the ninth and the eighteenth centuries by scholars of Iranian, Central Asian, and Indian origin. [Zaman, M.Q. (1999)].

The Dars-e-Nizami, today, has become irrelevant to our needs. We can gain a great deal from the experiments in moden Islamic education being conducted in other countries. For instance, Al-Azhar, the greatest seat of Islamic learning, now teaches Islamic as well as moden subjects in thousands of the schools it runs in the Egypt. There is no reason why Indian madrasas should not do so [Afzal Ahmed (2017:202)].

Wani, H.A. (2016) commented on the subjects taught in the Madrasahs saying that "the subjects which are there in *Madrasah*, in fact, these all subjects are Islamic or religious oriented subjects. It's good that *Madrasahs* should have these subjects but at the same time, they have to provide modern or scientific education to the Muslim youth; this is way by which their conditions could be bolstered and enhanced. Islam is the identity and recognition of Muslim *Ummah*, nobody have a right to criticize that element. But one should see the other dimensions of the pathetic situations of Muslims in India, their condition become worst than *Dalits* of India. Millions of Muslims are illiterates; due to illiteracy, they are jobless; if thousands have read but due to lack of modern education, they are not in position to stabilize themselves in the modern scenario because of the complexity and the competitions of the modern world [Wani, H.A. (2016:247-8)].

Religious subjects should be given the top priority but teaching modern education cannot be ignored. Muslim civil society has to think regarding this very pertinent issue that is immediate reformation of *Madrasahs* curriculum. Muslims could understand the world by having the glances over the modern subjects. They can garner bunch of information of Science and Humanities thereby understanding the present challenges would be easier process [Wani, H.A. (2016:250)].

Sultan Masud, his son and successor followed in the tradition set by his father. But it was all in Ghazani and its surroundings except that he established some educational institution in Punjab. Hiring his reign Arabic and Persian acquired a rich store of knowledge through interaction with both Sanskrit and Greek literature. Mathematics, astronomy, philosophy, medicine, astrology, and pharmacology which had reached high level of standard in India, were the favourite subjects with Muslim scholars. Translation of Indian works including a large portion of narrative literature into Arabic and Persian provided an added incentive to their eagerness. The later Ghaznavids were, however, not noted for their literary zeal [Afzal Ahmed (2017:30)].

The pattern of education which reached its zenith during the Seljuk and Ghaznavid rule was adopted by the Ghori rulers. Mohammad Ghori was the first Muslim ruler who paid special attention for the promotion of education in India. He established some Madrasas at Ajmer. The exact date of these Madrasas is not known, yet probably there was no Madrasa before him. Hence, they can be called the oldest Madrasas of India [Afzal Ahmed (2017:30-1)]. Mohammad Ghori had developed a special programme for the education of his slaves. He supervised their education himself. The curriculum included all the branches considered necessary for the education of princes.

Madrasa Education in Colonial India

Historians and researchers on the development of madrasa educational system in the Indian subcontinent generally agree that "the advent of colonial rule and the downfall of the Mughal Empire was a critical turning point for the madrasas. The British introduced new systems of administration and, although initially averse to changing the system of education *per se*, eventually greatly influenced its profile. Their view of education was governed by their understanding of religion not only as being subordinate to the state but also as an aspect of life to be relegated to the 'private' sphere" [Nair, Padmaja (2009:11)].

Islamic education encountered modernity through colonialism. The British colonialists not only confiscated properties owned by indigenous religious institutions, but also established a parallel education system. In British India, the English education policies reflected a system of power and forcible Westernization. As Thomas Macaulay envisioned, the goal was "to form a class who may be interpreters between us [colonizers] and the millions whom we govern; a class of persons, Indian in blood and colour, but English in taste, in opinions, in morals, and in intellect." Consequently, English education became a necessary qualification for getting jobs (note how this legacy continues today). Although Muslims began to resist this (secular) education in the beginning, considering its utilitarian values, they eventually accepted it [Anwaruddin Sardar M. (2012)].

There was a conflictual relationship between Islamic and Western education in British India. Teachers and students in madaris (plural of madrasa) focused more on defending their faith against colonial infiltration. Instead of training people for government jobs, the foremost goal of the madaris was to defend religion and protect traditional values. The confrontational relation between Islamic and colonial education was a major obstacle for the madaris to modernize their curricula and focus on branches of knowledge that are necessary for the modern world [Anwaruddin Sardar M. (2012)]

There two significant changes took place with the advent of the British and were consolidated in the years after Independence:

Firstly, the madrasas, which initially offered secular as well as religious education, became more religion-oriented after the British policies, directly or indirectly, threatened their very existence. It was also during this period that a feeling of mutual suspicion and tensions between the state and the madrasas also began to grow.

Secondly, the social composition of the madrasas also began to change at this time, with more of the students coming from lower class families. The opportunities for upward social mobility, the attraction of free board and lodging, education and the prospect of a livelihood as an *imam, maulvi* or madrasa teacher encouraged many poor families to send their sons to madrasas [Nair Padmaja (2009)].

According to Anzar, Uzma (2003:5), "one particular region in which Madrassa went through a radical shift in ideology was the Indian Subcontinent. When this region came under the British rule and a new educational system was introduced, which was perceived to be a threat to the Islamic identity of the Muslims, the Madrassa system in India took upon itself the task of opposing the cultural and educational hegemony of the British. It is important to point out, however, that the Madrassa system in the Indian Subcontinent was the only one that underwent drastic changes in terms of Islamic education curriculum and teaching styles and quality and abandoning of the earthly science studies. The Madrassas in the Arab world also changed a little in terms of the orientation of the Islamic curriculum but they carried essentially the same system of education that was established in the early development of the Madrassa in Baghdad, and to this day accommodate the teaching of the secular subjects. This is especially true for Egypt where, under the Al-Azhar education system, the secular subjects compliment the Islamic education."

There emerged two major events behind the exclusion of many branches of knowledge during the formation of *madrasa* and a hostile relationship with Western education during the colonial era. These two events have hindered Islamic education from embracing modern knowledge. These two events are:

(1) The need to restore early medieval Islamic traditions of knowledge, which can be very helpful to re-conceptualize the Islamic curriculum and pedagogy.
(2) The need to re-consider whether inclusion of disciplines of modern knowledge will impoverish Islamic education and diminish its uniqueness [Anwaruddin S.M. (2012)].

"With the advent of *East India Company* as a colonial regime, not only the *madrasa* education system but also, in a larger term, the entire indigenous education system found it very difficult to survive because it was devoid of political patronage and the Western system of education posed a grave danger to the very existence of indigenous education system. Initially the *East India Company* did not interfere with the local education system but with the passage of *Charter Acts-1813* and *1833* by the British Parliament, the company got involved into the educational affairs of the company-ruled territory." [Ansari, M.A. (2016:101-2)]. Thus the Company, directly, became the in-charge of the education affairs of company-ruled territory. In 1837, Persian language was abolished as a court language and replaced by English language. Then, in 1844 it was declared that for all kinds of posts, a preference would be given to those who could read and write English language. Thus, the English language became a symbol of vertical progress and material well-being.

Tracing the Islamic education in India, we need to observe and categorize the impacts of policies applied by British Company on the Indian Muslim society during British India. In relation to its educational policies the Company's activities can be divided into four periods:

1. The First Period (1600-1700)

In this period the Company remained unconcerned with education. It focused all its energies on business activities. It constructed forts and buildings and employed force and gave jobs to thousands of people. But, it did not pay any attention to educational and religious necessities of the public. So much so that even the priests were not allowed to perform their missionary activities [Afzal Ahmed (2017:70)].

2. Second Period (1700-1813)

In 1868 at the time of renewal of the permit, the British Parliament, on being drawn its attention towards its lack of interest for education, made the Company liable to keep the priests for religious education of its population and open schools for the education of its children. But it was all restricted to its European employees. The Company's negligence continued as far as its Indian employees were concerned. After 1757, the Company became an important political power. After 1765 the Company became responsible for civil administration of Bihar, Bengal and Orissa. By the new permit of 1773, the company started its structure for administrative, civil and judicial system. But in education it did nothing of importance except that with individual efforts of the Missionaries educational activities were started. When the Company implemented its judicial and administrative system, the Britain's Common Law was introduced at first. But due to the public outcry against it an amendment bill was passed in 1781 in which Indian tradition of personal code and law of property were accepted. Courts were made liable to follow Hindu and Muslim Personal law. This necessitated the preparation of master of Hindu and Muslim law. As a result Madrasa Aliya, Calcutta Madrasa and Hindu Sanskrit College, Banaras were established. Fort William College was established to teach Persian language to its English employees [Afzal Ahmed (2017)].

3. Third Period (1813-1835)

This period marks the beginning of educational policy and its implementation. In the Charter of 1813 the Parliament for the first time made the company liable to take the responsibility of promoting Indian and classical sciences. One lakh rupees were earmarked for this purpose. The education of science was made compulsory. Missionaries also got the freedom to start their educational institution anywhere in India [Afzal Ahmed (2017)].

4. Fourth Period (1835-1947)

Lord Munto's educational policies were pursued up till now. But when Lord William Bentick came to India as Governor General, he passed the Resumption Act just after taking charge. As a result all the Auqafs, Mafi and La Khiraj (tax free) lands were taken over by the

Government. During the Muslim rule, the ruler, the Umara and viziers and wealthy persons used to give land and properties to Ulama, Fuqaha, Mashaikhs and Darwesh as Waqf, so that they may dedicate their life in teaching and learning without bothering for bread and butter. Muslim rulers never established Department of Education. It was only the above mentioned automatic system of teaching and learning which was in practice. The change of rulers did not have any impact on education. It was free from the interference of kings and its changes. As a result, thousands of Ulama and Fuzala used to get permanent employment without any botheration of bread and butter. It was the backbone of madrasa system, which received a deathblow in the form of Resumption Act of 1818. Lord William Bentick made a more severe law of Resumption Act in 1828. According to William Hunter the Act was enforceable with retrospective effect from 1765 (sixty years in the past). It was enforced in the most severe manner [Afzal Ahmed (2017)].

A large number of Muslim population was salaried class. The Company did certain things which went against them. First Governor General, Warren Hastings ended the court of Mall (revenue) of Mughal period. Cornwallis ended the department of country police (*chaukidars*). In 1844 Lord Harding shut all the doors of job for non-English knowing people. In 1860 the Sadr Adalat was changed into High Court and the proceedings were carried out in English instead of Urdu. In 1864 the Qazi Act was passed which ended the necessity of Muslim Qazi for judging the Muslim personal matters and Muslim advocates became jobless. In 1835 English was made state language in place of Persian which changed the direction of education from ancient sciences and tradition to Western sciences. Before that Western sciences were taught in Missionary schools and colleges [Afzal Ahmed (2017)].

Oriental sciences and languages also had a place. Now it all stopped. And after 1857 it became impossible for madrasa graduate to get any job. During this period, it was observed that there was scarcely a Government office in which a Muslim can hope for any post above the rank of porter, messenger, filler of inkpots etc. The Muslim lost the position, which they had enjoyed in the times of Lord Cornwallis when they held 75 per cent of Government jobs because of their knowledge of Persian language. The abolition of Muslim law with the introduction of Penal Code deprived the Muslims of all respectable appointments and also greatly restricted vernacular education [Afzal Ahmed (2017)].

Nonetheless, Madrasa system continued to enjoy some importance up to the middle of the nineteenth century and its graduates were considered to be qualified for certain government services. But after 1857 it became impossible for a madrasa graduate to get any Government job because Muslims in general and Ulama in particular were considered responsible for that revolution. We have already quoted Hunter in this regard.

"The radical changes introduced in the administrative and educational policies of the country demanded knowledge of the language of the ruler, but no order was made to make English education as compulsory. The orders of the Government, permitting candidates for the office of Munsif and pleader to take their examination either in English or Urdu, remained in force until 1864. But a year or two later the previous order was revoked and was declared that in future the examination for higher grade posts of Munsif and pleader would be conducted only in English. The step placed Muslims under further disadvantage" [Afzal Ahmed (2017:71)].

As a result two movements started. One headed by Ulama who realized that they could not depend on the Government for their religious education. They would have to run their own schools if they wanted their youth to know something about their religion. As a result of the calls to modernize the madrasa system, "one of the new madrasas established in response to the call for exclusively religious institutions was the Darul Uloom Deoband, which was set up in 1866 in Uttar Pradesh and quickly grew to become the most respected and traditional school of thought in the subcontinent [Nair, Padmaja (2009:11)]. Then after Madrassatul Uloom or Mohammedan Anglo-Oriental College in Aligarh (now called the Aligarh Muslim University) in 1875 and Nadwat-ul-Ulema in Lucknow in 1892, were emerged as a response to the calls to develop the Islamic madrasa system and thus to moderate the rigid and exclusive *dini* philosophy and strike a balance between the 'modern' and 'orthodox' schools of thought. "These institutions are said to have propounded a relatively moderate path and tried to introduce English, social and natural science into the madrasa curriculum, arguing that Islam is an 'eternal' religion "open to new developments in the realm of the aqli ulum (rational sciences)", according to Nair Padmaja (2009:11).

The Government established twelve maktabs and in appropriate localities had inspecting Maulvis, so that these institutions might improve and its education might become popular. All these measures were helpful in spreading English education among the Muslims. But they did not go far enough, yet the situation became a little more satisfactory.

All India Educational Conference in 1907 called for comprehensive scheme leading to high standard in Islamic education as its integral part. Urged by such demands for changes in madrasa education, the Government of Bengal appointed a committee under Archdale Earl who held a series of conference in 1907-08. The two questions discussed were:

1. An institution of degree for madrasa students in literature, law and theology similar to Sanskrit; and
2. The revision of existing course of studies to enable madrasa students to acquire such knowledge of English as would make them fit for Government services and other profitable employments.

Some changes in the syllabus of madrasa education particularly in regard to the introduction of Hadis, Tafsir, History, geography and Urdu was advocated. A suitable examination system on the pattern of 'Title' examination of Sanskrit in Arabic literature, Hadis, Tafsir, Theology, logic and philosophy, Muslim law and jurisprudence was recommended. However, it was recommended that English should be taught as an optional subject in the three top classes of junior section and in all five classes of senior section. Moreover, a two years' special course in English was also recommended for those who had passed fifth year of senior section with English as an optional subject as well as for those who had taken the Title course. It was also recommended that after successful completion of two years English course a madrasa student should be considered as equivalent to one who had taken a university degree for the purpose of Government service. Almost all the proposals were approved by the Government of Bengal except the most vital part of the recommendation—two years special course for English—thereby failing to open up greater opportunities for madrasa students. But the number of inspecting Maulvis and of Model Maktabs were increased during the period of Earl of Archdale as Director of Public Instruction. Ten *pathshalas* were also converted into maktabs. The classification of maktabs as into three categories by Sir Alfred Croft were reduced to two, namely 'recognized and unrecognized' depending on whether they adopted the courses prescribed by the education department or not [Afzal Ahmed (2017)].

In 1913, the All India Muslim Education Conference formed committees in every district for the promotion and reform of maktabs and also for looking after them. Maktabs were established in some places through the efforts of All India Muslim Educational Conference. It also opened some special maktabs for teaching Urdu and Qur'an and to impart some religious knowledge to the Muslims in rural areas. The Conference also passed resolutions for the establishment of schools for training Imams, where students coming from Arabic colleges can be trained for reforming the Muslims in rural areas. The Conference made strong recommendation to run the maktabs on modern educational principles. Some of these maktabs since then have been closed down, but others have been promoted to the higher secondary or even higher stages with the modified syllabus [Afzal Ahmed (2017)].

Thus, with a revised Nisab the maktabs or primary schools on an Islamic basis were brought in line with ordinary primary schools. Similarly, the high madrasas and junior madrasas were brought in line with Middle English schools and high schools and were made a part of general scheme of secondary education. Likewise, the general intermediate madrasas were brought on par with the general intermediate education. The objective was to bring madrasa system into the mainstream of modern life and incorporate it with university education, without sacrificing the truly Islamic founding. The scheme was introduced in 1915 from class third and was adopted by all the existing madrasas except Calcutta madrasa.

In 1921-22 a Superintendent of Islamic Studies was appointed to improve the madrasa system and a board of examination was established.

In 1938, the Government of Bengal constituted Muslim Advisory Committee under the chairmanship of Khan Abdul Momin. The Momin Committee submitted its report in 1934. But out of all the recommendations only one-namely the Department of Title, Fiqh and Usui should be made permanent was accepted by the Government.

Maula Bakhsh Committee prepared a questionnaire of madrasa education on September 26,1938 and circulated it among all those interested. Out of 168 completed questionnaires received 78 persons supported the retention of old scheme madrasa and demanded the closure of the reformed scheme madrasas; 15 were in favour of reformed scheme madrasas and closure of old madrasas; 70 were in favour of keeping both the types with suitable changes in syllabi and four or five were of the opinion that both types of madrasas should be closed down and new ones be opened on new patterns. In its last meeting on October 10, 1940 the Maula Bakhsh Committee adopted 68 resolutions. Some of the important ones were:

1. The object of retaining old scheme madrasas is to produce Islamic scholars; hence their continuance was essential.
2. Reformed scheme madrasas (high madrasas) have been functioning with purpose of providing secular education along with Islamic knowledge, to enable the student enter the various services and hence should also continue, with emphasis in religious books in their curriculum.
3. Up to class 4 in both types madrasas the standard of syllabi and course should be of the same standard while maintaining the distinctive features of each.
4. The old scheme of junior madrasas should also come under Government control and be given recognition.
5. At the end of junior madrasa education there should be public examination.

"In 1939, the Chief Minister of Bengal asserted that he not only wanted to promote madrasa education but was also in favour of establishing an Arabic University in Bengal. With this perspective Rs. 30000 were set apart to be spent on senior madrasas which were growing from year to year both in size and number. But due to the start of World War II the proposal could not be implemented [Afzal Ahmed (2017:78)].

Post-Independence Status of Madrasa Education in India

After India got Independence, for almost four decades there was little interaction between the state and madrasas. "Subsequently the state's engagement with the madrasas has become more formal, structured and project-based, with the objective of bringing about changes in the curriculum to align it with mainstream education, rather than making overall reforms. Support based on the recognized minority status of Muslims is reviewed in Section 4.1, the modernization programme in Section 4.2 and the response of madrasas to government reform attempts in Section 4.3" [Nair, Padmaja (2009:21)].

There has been continuous growth in the number of madrasas after Independence. Majority of the madrasas are maintained by the charity of the Muslims, though some of them are affiliated to the madrasa board and receive financial aid from the Government. The trend of not making any change in its curriculum, which started in British period when the doors of Government employment were shut for madrasa graduates, still continues. "Some of the madrasas have got their degrees recognized by Aligarh Muslim University, Jamia Millia Islamia, Lucknow University and Maulana Azad Unversity where its graduates can aspire to seek modern higher education in the Faculties of Arts and Social Sciences thereby providing its graduates limited opportunities for mainstreaming. In order to get recognition, they have introduced certain necessary changes in their curriculum" [Afzal Ahmed (2017:78-9)].

The State-Madrasa Relationships in India after Independence

"The madrasaa is a social institution relied heavily on the state and elites for political and financial support. Its function was to disseminate specific discourses for cultural reproduction and preservation. Muslim societies during the tenth and eleventh centuries were marked by enormous political, linguistic, cultural, and sectarian differences, and the madaris became an important instrument of social and ideological containment" [Talbani, A. (1996:71)]. The relationship between madaris and the state was generally cordial as madaris provided the knowledge, skills, and values that enabled its graduates to perform judicial, civil, and economic functions within the state bureaucracy.

Nair Padmaja (2009:1-2) has written "the State-Madrasa relationships are shaped by constitutional, political and educational factors:

1. Muslims in India have official minority status: their right to practise their religion and establish institutions (including educational institutions) is safeguarded in the constitution, enabling them to resist excessive state interference.
2. The nature and extent of state engagement with madrasas is influenced by the political ideology and electoral interests of national and regional political parties. When madrasas feel threatened, they may seek to protect themselves by organizing and seeking political backing.
3. Data on the numbers of madrasas and maktabs (part-time schools for religious education linked to local mosques) and

student enrolment are poor, although it is asserted that numbers have increased in some parts of the country in recent years.

4. In addition to their primary purpose of providing religious education, many madrasas have long included a few other academic and vocational subjects in their curriculum, although the coverage and quality was generally very limited.
5. At present 'modernization' of the content and quality of madrasa education is the stated objective of state interventions in the affairs of madrasas, but several critics expressed a belief that the government may be intending to make more extensive 'reforms' in the near future.
6. Although participation in the 'modernization' process is voluntary, in some States, such as West Bengal, extensive secularization of the curriculum of state-supported madrasas offering primary and secondary education, control over the recruitment of teachers and increased government monitoring in some states confirm critics' fear that the state intends to increase its control over madrasas.
7. Madrasas as a whole are not organized to negotiate with the state for support on their own terms. Therefore, while the better-resourced madrasas choose to stay out of state-funded programmes, a significant proportion of the poorly funded are happy to engage and to comply with the conditions imposed in return for the financial and other support provided.
8. A variety of support programmes are on offer (often centrally funded but delivered by State governments), but a variety of implementation problems were identified, especially in Uttar Pradesh." [Nair, Padmaja (2009:1-2)].

The Area Intensive and Madrasa Modernization Programme

"An Area Intensive and Madrasa Modernization Programme" sponsored by the Ministry of Human Resource Development was the first major planned intervention by the Central Government. It continues, in a modified version, to be the only significant programme of structured and formal engagement with the madrasas. In 1993-94, the revised Plan of Action (1992) of the National Educational Policy (1986) suggested short, medium and long term measures for the education of minorities. "The objective of the programme is to encourage traditional institutions like maktabs and madrasas to introduce the teaching of science, mathematics, social studies, Hindi and English, in order to provide opportunities for students to acquire education comparable to that available in the national system.

While in the first phase of the programme (under the Eighth Five Year Plan, 1992-97) primary classes were covered, in the second phase (since the Ninth Five Year Plan period, 1997-2002), the coverage has been extended to institutions providing education equivalent to the secondary stage. During the first phase, 100 per cent assistance for appointment of qualified teachers was given to madrasas, together with assistance for the establishment of a book bank and to strengthen their libraries. Provision of science and maths kits and essential equipment were also included. The scheme was then reviewed and continues in the current (Tenth) Plan, which proposes to cover 5,000 madrasas (less than 15 per cent of the total in the eight states where relatively large numbers of madrasas are found), with textbooks being provided by the National Council for the Promotion of Urdu Language, an autonomous Council set up by the central government" [Nair, Padmaja (2009:25)].

Summary

Historical evidence indicates that a kuttab-like institution emerged in the first century of the Islamic era, not long after scholars working at the instruction of the Caliphs 'Umar (634–44) and 'Uthman (644–56) completed their recensions of the Qur'an (Bulliet, 1994: 28). The madrasa developed only three centuries later. The first is thought to have originated in the tenth century, not in the Arab heartland, but in the province of Khurasan in eastern Iran. From there it spread widely, reaching Baghdad in 1063, Damascus in the 1090s, Cairo in the 1170s, and Spain and northern India in the first decades of the thirteenth century [Hefner, R. W. & Zaman, M.Q. (2007)].

"Prior to the historical emergence of madrasas, advanced study in the religious sciences was already taking place, but it does not appear to have been systematized and standardized to the degree that it would be after the rise of the madrasa. The setting in which advanced study had earlier taken place was the informal study circle or *halqa*. Study circles were organized in homes, mosques, or shops under the auspices of a master scholar (*shaykh*)" [Hefner, R.W. & Zaman, M.Q. (2007:6)].

In these changed circumstances, mosques specializing in advanced study built hostels for resident students. The tenth-century madrasa took this innovation one step further, providing classrooms, dormitories, and washrooms for students, all of whom in this early period were male.

Eventually, the typical madrasa came to include instructional rooms; residences for the founder, teachers, and students; and a mosque, which was used for study as well as worship. Many complexes also had mausoleums, where the school's founder and his relatives were entombed. [Hefner, R.W. & Zaman, M.Q. (2007)].

Madrasa Education is the largest non formal education network all over India. Even though it has its own strength and weakness, it should be strengthened with modern educational practices to cope up with the challenges of the time. As part of inclusive education, Madrasa educations cater the needs of the underprivileged and unprivileged sections of the society. Government of India's initiatives to enhance the quality of madrasa education, lags behind without proper mechanism in monitoring and supervision. Proper mechanism should be employed to ensure the proper execution of the various programmes in the field of minority education. Moreover, community initiative has its own importance in coping the madrasa education with modern educational practices [Mohammed Basheer K. (2013:102)].

The Islamic formal education was established, developed and spread out to the whole world including India during the Abbasid period and as such this period is called as the Golden age in the Islamic History. The Arab Muslims came to India in the form of Traders, Sufi-Saints and Invaders. Besides their vocation, they rendered the best services for propagating Islamic concept among the Indians and tried their best to impart Islamic knowledge side by side with Arabic Language and Literature so that they can understand the Qur'an and Hadith. To impart the knowledge of Qur'an and Hadith, they established Islamic Institutions in different parts of India [Khatun, J. (2016:81)].

The madrasa is one of the many institutions which have seen recurrent attempts at reform in Muslim societies during the nineteenth and twentieth centuries. Since the eleventh century, when it first emerged as the principal institution of higher Islamic learning, the madrasa has undergone many changes, adapting in varying degrees to local cultures and changing times [Zaman, M.Q. (1999)]. "Madrasas in India appear to be caught between the need to maintain their identity as centres of Islamic studies and culture and to remain relevant to the present-day needs of the communities they serve" [Nair, Padmaja

(2009:1)]. Madrasas and schools of Islamic thought in India, "felt threatened by changes in the system of education introduced by the British and their graduates' loss of access to coveted government jobs. Post-Independence madrasas appear to have lost much of their status as a sought after mainstream educational institution. Their subsequent course of development has been based on a perceived need to protect their image as 'religious' educational institutions, as well as to establish their relevance in contemporary society" [Nair Padmaja (2009:21)].

"The outcome of Muslim political socialization was a discourse that strengthened and legitimized the existing social and political order. Imitation, respect, and obedience to authority-religious or political-became a necessary part of Muslim cultures. Finally, these traditions and values, customs, and knowledge gave rise to a strong cultural and political identity. To be a Muslim meant to identify oneself with symbols of social-political obedience and to extend loyalty to traditional authority systems. As a result, the imposition of colonial rule created a serious threat to these religiously oriented identities and loyalties" [Talbani, A. (1996:72)]. "Islam is a religion that puts emphasis on the overall human life. It covers all aspects of the physical body, the soul or the spirit, the emotion and the intellect with the sole purpose of producing individuals who are able wholeheartedly enslave themselves to the Allah almighty in all sectors of their lives" [Abd Rashid, A. & Mamat, A. (2013:178)]. Islam presents many comprehensive senses which cover all systems of life and it has no elements of stagnation. The State and politics, according to Islam, are only an effort to realize the spiritual in human organization [Abd Rashid, A. & Mamat, A. (2013)].

Moreover, Abd Rashid, A. & Mamat, A. (2013:182) stated that the duties of Muslim leaders (through education) is to establish justice. He said: "every leader is ordered to be concerned with the importance of justice throughout his power to rule the Islamic society. The establishment of justice encompasses all spheres of life and runs through the entire community alongside the process of law and judgement. In the comprehensive sense of a Muslim's life and his social relations, the ideal type of justice which he should practice is far beyond a reciprocal concept such as returning bad for bad as well as good for good. This means that Islam encourages and educates a Muslim to act justly to everyone, even to those who create hatred and who are at enmity with him. In this regard Allah says in the Qur'an (5:8): "O you who believe! Stand out firmly for Allah as just witnesses; and let not the enmity and enmity of others make you avoid justice. Be just: that is nearer to piety; and fear Allah. Verily, Allah is Well-Acquainted with what you do."

The creation of a good environment of the Islamic society relies upon the individual goodness which is a crucial element of the whole well-being of the state. Therefore, to attain goodness and to reject bad behaviour needs a great individual effort to strive and purify the sole and this is promoted through right education which seeks justice, harmony and peace among people. The responsibility of the Islamic education is crucial in its efforts to uproot corrupt behaviour and to promote good character within man; particularly through believing in Allah, promoting good qualities, curbing any incentives which may expose to evil, and implementing the Islamic educational system. These are all done in order to inculcate good values and at the same time to disseminate knowledge of sciences [Abd Rashid, A. & Mamat, A. (2013)].

References

Abd Rashid, A. & Mamat, A. (2013). Educational view of the Islamic leadership: are the Islamic leaders performing their responsibilities? *International Journal of Humanities and Social Science,* 3(3), 178-185.

Abdul Waheedu K. (2003). Influence of Islamic Philosophy on the Theory and Practice of Education. Ph.D. thesis in Education. University of Calicut, India.

Afzal Ahmad (2017). A Study of Madrasa Education in modern Perspective of Azamgarh and Jaunpur Districts. Ph.D. thesis in *Education.* Veer Bahadur Singh Purvanchal University, Jaunpur (U.P.), India.

Ansari, M.A. (2016). Modern Education in Madrasas: A Perspective Study of Dar Al-Uloom Deoband. *Asia Pacific Journal of Research.* Volume I, Issue XLIV. pp. 101-8.

Anwaruddin Sardar M. (2012). Islamic Education and Modernity: An Uneasy Alliance? *The Independent* (A national newspaper in Bangladesh). October 1, 2012.

Anzar, Uzma (2003). Islamic Education: A Brief History of Madrassas With Comments on Curricula and Current Pedagogical Practices. https://www.researchgate.net/publication/264868678_Islamic_Education_A_Brief_History_of_Madrassas_With_Comments_on_Curricula_and_Curren t_Pedagogical_Practices.

Asimov, M.S. and Bosworth, C.E. (1998)., *History of civilizations of Central Asia,* Vol 4: The Age of Achievement A.D. 750 to the end of the fifteenth century, Part One: The Historical, Social and Economic Setting. Paris: UNESCO Publication.

Asimov, M.S. and Bosworth, C.E. (2000). *History of civilizations of Central Asia,* Vol 4: The Age of Achievement A.D. 750 to the end of the fifteenth century, Part Two: The achievements. Paris: UNESCO Publication.

Breen Damian (2018). *Muslim Schools, Communities and Critical Race Theory: Faith Schooling in an Islamophobic Britain?* London: Palgrave Macmillan.

Cook, B.J. (1999). Islamic versus Western conceptions of education: Reflections on Egypt. *International Review of Education*, 45(3-4), 339-358.

Dar Al-Ifta Al-Missriyyah (2018, July 24), *The Theory of Islamic Education.* Retrieved from (http://www.daralifta.gov.eg/Foreign/ViewArticle.aspx?ID=114&CategoryID=3)

Daun Holger and Arjmand Reza (2018) (Eds.) *Handbook of Islamic Education.* Cham, Switzerland: Springer.

Etheredge Laura S. (2010). *Islamic history*. New York: Britannica Educational Publishing.

Fatah Yasin R.F.B. and Jani Mohd. Shah (2013). Islamic Education: The Philosophy, Aim, and Main Features. *International Journal of Education and Research.* October 2013, Vol. 1 (10) pp. 1-18.

Hefner, R.W., and Zaman, M.Q. (Eds.). (2007). *Schooling Islam: the culture and politics of modern Muslim education* (Vol. 37). Princeton University Press.

Hilgendorf Eric (2003). Islamic Education: History and Tendency. *Peabody Journal of Education,* 78(2), 63-75.

Hiskett, M. (1974). Traditional islamic and modern Western education in tropical Africa: The problems of integration. *World Development*, 2(2), 41-43.

Jimba, Moshood Mahmood M. (2016). *Al-Azhar University's Role in Educating Nigerians: A Case Study of the Ilorin Al-Azhar Institute.* In Lo, Mbaye and Haron, Muhammed (2016) (Eds.) Muslim Institutions of Higher Education in Postcolonial Africa. Basingstoke, Hampshire, U.K.: Palgrave Macmillan.

Kazmi Yedullah (2003). Islamic Education: Traditional Education or Education of Tradition? *Islamic Studies* 42:2 (2003) pp. 259-288.

Khatun, J. (2016). Islamic Education in India with Especial Reference to the Women Sector of India. *International Research Journal of Interdisciplinary & Multidisciplinary Studies* (IRJIMS), 2(3), pp. 80-86.

Mohammed Basheer. K (2013). Future of Indian Madrasah Education in The Globalized World. *SRJIS*, September-October, 2013. Vol. (2)3 : 95-104.

Nair, Padmaja (2009). The State and Madrasas in India. The Religions and Development, Working Paper 15: Birmingham, UK: University of Birmingham.

Noaparast, Bagheri Khosrow (2001). Islamic Education. PhD. thesis, N.S.W. University. Australia.

Panjwani Farid (2004). The 'Islamic' in Islamic Education: Assessing the Discourse. *Current Issues in Comparative Education,* Vol. 7(1) : 19-29.

Sall, Mamadou Youry (2016). Scientific Profiles and Potential of Al-Azhar's

African Graduates: A Statistical Analysis. In Lo, Mbaye and Haron, Muhammed (2016) (Eds.) *Muslim Institutions of Higher Education in Postcolonial Africa.* Basingstoke, Hampshire, U.K.: Palgrave Macmillan.

Sulaiman, K.D.O. (2017). Islamic Perspectives on Western Education. *INSANCITA*, *1*(2), 185-198.

Talbani, A. (1996). Pedagogy, power, and discourse: Transformation of Islamic education. *Comparative education Review*, 40(1), 66-82.

Tan Charlene (2014). (Ed.) *Reforms in Islamic Education.* London: Bloomsbury Academic.

Tan Charlene and Salleh Hairon (2014). Curriculum and Pedagogy of Islamic Education. In Tan Charlene (2014). (Ed.) *Reforms in Islamic Education.* London: Bloomsbury Academic.

Tan, Charlene (2014). *Reforms in Islamic Education: International Perspectives.* London: Bloomsbury Academic.

Wani, H.A. (2016). Madrasah Education in India: A Need for Reformation. *Atikan,* 2(2) : 235-252.

Yaman, Basyir and Gultom Fades Br. (2017). Islamic Education System: Implementation of Curriculum Kuttab Al-Fatih Semarang. *International Journal of Educational and Pedagogical Sciences,* 11(12) 2017, pp. 2783-9.

Zaman, M.Q. (1999). Religious education and the rhetoric of reform: The madrasa in British India and Pakistan. *Comparative Studies in Society and History*, 41(2) : 294-323.

7

Dower (*Mahr*) in Islam: A Critical Analysis

Shah Raziq Khalid

Introduction

The *mahr* is meant to offer the bride a financial security within and after the marriage. It is a divine order by the Almighty Allah. The giving of *mahr* to the bride is an important and mandatory part of the Islamic terms of marriage.[1] The amount of *mahr* is not legally specified, however, a moderation in tandem with the existing social model is strongly recommended. According the Islamic rules, the *mahr* may be paid earlier to the bride as soon as possible at the time of marriage or deferred[2] to a later date or a compromise of both.

It gives the women their dowries willingly as an obligation); but if they, by their own free will, give up to you a portion of it then you may enjoy it with pleasure.[3] And a marriage ceremony means that one nuptial party proposes the '*Ijab*' (proposal willing consent to enter into marriage and the other party expresses '*Qabul*' (acceptance of the responsibility at the time of marriage ceremony. The word *mahr* is derived from the Arabic word. (Hebrew *mohar*, 'bridal gift' originally ''purchase-money'' which properly means ''friendship'' then ''present'' a gift given as a result of a marriage contract, as according to the Muslim law, the gift which the bridegroom has to give to the bride when the contract of marriage is made and which becomes the property of the wife.[4]

In the Holy Qur'an, it has also been referred to as *al-sadaq*, *al-saduqah*, *al-nihlah*, (*al-ajr*, *al-faridah* and *al-'aqd*. (It is a prerequisite for a marriage as mentioned throughout the Qur'an. The woman may choose to willingly forfeit anything as a reciprocity of the believing man who must offer the dowry with sincere intentions.

In *Shariat* Law, *mahr* is a gift from the husband to his bride at the time of marriage. The terms 'dowry'[5] and bride gift are sometimes used to translate *mahr*. In Islamic marriages, such assets brought into the union by the wife may only be accepted by the husband after the *mahr* has been paid by him to her. In the event that the marriage of the contract does not contain an exact or specified *mahr*, the husband must still pay the wife an equitable sum of money. The requirement of a *mahr* is mentioned several times in the Qur'an and as a Sunnah.[6]

The '*mahr*' is the payment of an agreed sum of money from the intending husband to the intended wife. It is often paid (at least partly) in advance, and should be completed at the wedding. This money belongs exclusively to the bride, and is hers to keep should her husband later divorce her. The *mahr* does not mean so much as a deterrent for the husband to divorce; but seeking a large '*mahr*' is not in keeping with the principles of Islam. Neither is the paying of it to the bride's father of family leader, nor not agreeing to pay it at all. The question of '*mahr*' should never be used as an opportunity as a means to insult a woman, or keep her 'prisoner', or force her to remain unmarried. (2:229, 236-7; 4:4, 19-21, 25). The bride's family should certainly not pay dowry to the husband or his family, the practices of which had been abolished by the Prophet (SAW).[7] *Mahr* in Islamic Law refers to the gift that must be given by the husband to the wife at the time of wedding.[8]

According to Islamic Family Law (Federal Territories), it is stated that the *mahr* refers to a payment from the husband to the wife that is legally due at the solemnization ceremony, either in the form of money actually paid or recognized as a credit with or without security, or as something that, according to Islamic law, has a monetary value.[9]

Mahr in the Holy Qur'an

Islam has made the determination and presenting of the '*mehr*' to the woman on marriage an absolutely obligatory condition of '*Nikaah*' between a man and a woman. Islam has not specified the exact amount of '*mehr*' to be presented, but rather any amount of '*mehr*' which is mutually agreed between the two parties: either proposed by the groom and accepted by the bride or demanded by the bride and accepted by the groom, regardless of, however, big or small it may be, would suffice to fulfil the obligatory condition of '*Nikaah*'.

Every Law and Command of the Creator is full to the brim with wisdom, and so is the command and condition of paying the *Mehr* to the bride. There are many reasons, wisdoms, and benefits of this condition of *Mehr* for the woman, and in the protection of her rights.

The man who proposes is sincere and is willing to show his sincerity by paying an agreed amount as a gift to his bride.

> *O you who believers! When believing women ask for asylum with you, you shall test them. Allah is fully aware of their belief. Once established that they are believers, you shall not return them to the disbelievers. They are not lawful to remain married to them, nor shall the disbelievers be allowed to marry them. Give back the mahr (dowries) that the disbelievers have paid to them. You commit no error by marrying them, so long as you pay them their due dowries.*[10]
> *Allah (SWT) says,*
> *So, you shall obtain permission from their guardians before you marry them, and pay them their due mahr (dowries) equitably.*[11] *Mahr only for the bride, Allah (SWT) says,*
> *So, you give them their bridal due (as) on obligation. And (there is) no sin on you concerning what you mutually agree of it (dowry) from beyond the obligation. Indeed, Allah is All-knowing, All-Wise.*[12]

Allah (SWT) has given permission to sexual intercourses with each other by giving the *mahr*.

> *O you who believers, when believing women (abandon the enemy and) ask for asylum with you, you shall test them. Allah is fully aware of their belief. Once you establish that they are believers, you shall not return them to the disbelievers. They are not lawful to remain married to the disbelievers, nor shall the disbelievers be allowed to marry them. Give back the dowries that the disbelievers have paid. You commit no error by marrying them, so long as you pay them their due dowries. Do not keep disbelieving wives (if they wish to join the enemy). You may ask them for the dowry you had paid, and they may ask for what they paid. This is Allah's rule; He rules among you. Allah is Omniscient, Most Wise.*[13]

Mahr (dower) is that amount which is paid by the husband to his wife at the time of *nikah* (marriage) or agrees to pay afterwards. *Mahr* is the term in usage to express the payment, the Qur'an has not used this word, and instead it has used the word *nehlah* to clarify that this amount is not in lieu of anything else except a specific gift to wife and not remuneration (4:4). Its payment is compulsory. In this regard an example of honeybee has been quoted in the holy Qur'an so far as payment of *mahr* is concerned, when the honeybee expels honey it does not expect any return for it.

If the amount of *mahr* has not been fixed at the time of *nikah* the payment will be acceptable by mutual consent. Since the payment has to be made necessarily, it has to be fixed as per the husband's capacity to pay it. Therefore, the amount could be anything, even a heap of gold (4:20).

***Mahr* in Sunnah**

The Dower (*Mahr*), according to the pre-Islamic customs, was to be paid to the father or guardian of the bride (wife), the action of which amounted to a sale, but in Islam, the dower becomes payable only to the bride and the idea of sale disappeared.[14] The Prophet (SAW) set the highest examples of all good principles for his ummah in that regard, so that a clear understanding of the basic principles would be implanted in the society, and the spirit of simplicity in applying them would spread among the people. Our beloved Prophet (SAW) has explained the full right to the woman in *Sunnah*. The following speech from the *Hadiths* will, Allah willing, enable us to understand the word *mahr* as per *Shari'ah's* laws. The relevant words have been highlighted for emphasis: In the *hadith* of 'Uqbah ibn 'Aamir (RA.), the Prophet (SAW) said:

> *The best dowry for woman is that which is easy*[15] *and he (SAW) said; the best of mahrs is the simplest (or most affordable).*[16] *Once a woman offered herself to the Prophet (SAW) for marriage. However, one of his Companions desired to marry her, thus, the Prophet (SAW) said regarding the mahr: Bring something, even if it be an iron ring. When he could not find even this, the Prophet (SAW) then married her for the dowry so that the man, from this example, would teach other believers whatever concept of the dowry in the Qur'an that he knew. Narrated from Abdullah Ibn Abbas (RA.) what Hazrat Ali (RA) said: I married Fatima (RA) and said 'O*

> *messenger of Allah, let me go ahead with the marriage. He said: 'Give her something.' I said: 'I do not have anything.' He said: 'Where is your Hutami shield, I have it with me.' He said, give it to her.*[17]

Whoever thinks of increasing his daughter's *mahr* and asking for more than the daughters of the messenger of Allah were given when they were the best women in this world in all aspects – then he is an ignorant fool. This applies even if one is well off and can afford it. With regard to one who is poor, he should not give a *mahr* greater than he can afford to pay without any hardship.[18]

The Methods of *Mahr* Payment

There are two principal methods of *mahr* payment according to Islamic scholars. (a) By Specified *Mahr* or *Mahr e Mosawamah*: This method has been agreed upon by the parties at the time of marriage.[19] Specified *Mahr* or *Mahr e Musawamah* can further be divided into two categories:

(i) *Prompt or Mahr-e-Mu'ajjal*: This *mahr* is payable immediately[20] upon the marriage under the following circumstances:

Only after the payment of dower can the husband enforce his conjugal rights and, if the marriage is consummated, then the wife cannot refuse cohabitation (intercourse) after that.

- The wife has a right to refuse cohabitation (intercourse) with the husband until she is paid the *mahr*;
- The period of limitation on demand and refusal of a dowry and any part of it is three years;
- A Prompt dower (*mahr*) does not become differed after consummation and the wife has the right to demand and sue (petition) [21] for it any time; and
- If the wife is a minor, the guardian can refuse to allow the wife to be sent to the husband until the *mahr* is paid.

(ii) *Deffered or Mahr e Muakkhar*: This type of *mahr* is payable upon dissolution of a marriage either by divorce or by death of a husband.[22] Its promise to pay does not make the full amount of *mahr* any less legally required.[23] There are differences between the nature of *mahr*, definition of proper contract and conditions of enforceability depending on the regional fiqh and school of Islamic Jurisprudence.[24]

(iii) *Customary or Mahr e Misil*: This type of *mahr* is not fixed in the marriage contract or even if the marriage has been contracted on the condition that the wife will not claim any *Mahr*, but the wife is legally entitled to a Proper Dower.[25] The amount of monetary value of the dowry is to be settled based on the bride's father's family. It is regulated with reference to the following factors:

- Age, beauty, fortune, understanding and virtue of an intended wife;
- Circumstances of the time;
- Economic condition of the intending husband;
- Social position of the intended wife's father; and
- Female paternal relations.

The Philosophy of *Mahr*

The payment of *mahr* has a deep symbolic philosophy. In Arabian world, there are various interpretations of *mahr* in relation to the marriage contracts, highlighting the differences between Maliki, Hambali and Hanafi religious philosophies respectively.[26] The word *mahr* does not appear in the Qur'an, however, the word *Sadaq* has been employed. There is no minimum amount of monetary value set for a *mahr* although various Sunnah suggest that it should not be excessively low. No specific amount of monetary value has been determined for the Sadaq, it is a matter that is decided by a mutual agreement between the woman and the man. Imam Baqir has stated:

> *Sadaq is something that the betrotheds agree upon, whether slight or considerable.*[27]

Imam Zafar Sadiq has pointed out that Hazrat 'Ali (RA) had declared:

> *I do not like mahr to be less than ten (10) dirham.*[28]

If the *mahr* was agreed to be paid on demand, the woman may request it before the consummation of her marriage. If the husband has the means to pay for it, he must do so. If he declines, the wife may abstain from sexual relations with him. This refusal is not considered *nushuz*[29] and thus her husband cannot withhold the financial support from her. The Hanafi School requires two witnesses on the documents for a *mahr* contained in the marriage contract to be valid, while the Maliki School holds that witnesses are only needed at the marriage's publication but not in the document.[30] The philosophy that the future owner of the *mahr*, regardless of the type of property, is only the wife. No one has the right to use or take possession of her property without her consent; not even her father, mother, or husband. The profits of a woman's properties, which she got as a *mahr* also belong to herself.

The Prophet (SAW) has stated:

> *Surely Allah will forgive any sin on the Day of Judgment save the sin of one who misappropriates the mahr of a woman or the wages of hired person, or who sells a free person (as a slave).*[31]

Conclusion

The *mahr* is one of the wife's rights that is sincerely given by the husband to the wife, without exception, as an expression of his love and responsibility. In Islam, the concept of *mahr* is more effective, comprehensive, vital and sacred than any other religions. It is one of the fundamental rights of every woman. *Mahr* is not only considered to be a trust, a sacred responsibility, which is to be performed in conformity with the provisions of the Qur'an and Sunnah; but the dispensation of *mahr* also constitutes one of the most important acts of devotion. It is intended to please the wife, so that she feels appreciated and more willing to bring and share a new life with the husband. Nevertheless, Islam recommends moderation and not setting a rate that is too high or low. The Prophet (SAW) has encouraged us to simplify the giving of *mahr*.

Notes

1. Al-Qur'an Al-Kareem.
2. Abdul Ohab Khallaf, *The Venture of Islam Conscience and History in a World Civilization* (University of Chicago, Vol. 3, 1958).
3. Altaf Hossein, *Islamic Jurisprudence and Muslim Law,* (Dhaka: City Law Books, Nilkhet, 5th ed. 2003 1st in 1996).
4. A. Fyzee, *Outlines of Mohamedan Law* (Oxford University Press, 14th edition 1984, 1st in 1949).

5. Allama Abdul Aleem Siddiqui, *Roots of Islamic Juriprudence* (Cairo: Daar al Ma'arif, 1998).
6. Brown, Driver, Briggs, Gesenius (1952). *The NAS Old Testament Herew Lexicon*. Oxford University Press. Retrieved 2014-09-06.
7. Delong –Bas, Natana J, (2004). *Wahhabi Islam: From Revival and Reform to Global Jihad* (First ed). (New York: Oxford University Press, USA. 1998).
8. *E.J. Brill's First Encyclopedia of Islam* (New York: Oxford University Press, USA.1993).
9. F.B. Tayabji.(1968). *Muslim Law* (Bombay: N.M Tripathi,1968).
10. Ibn Manjur, *Lisan al-Arab,* (Cairo: Dar al-Hadith, 2003, vol. 8).
11. Imam Abu Dawd, 2125 and An-Nasai. 3375. Also classed as Sahih by al-Albaani in Sahi an-Nasa'i, 3160.
12. Ibn Taimiyah said in his book *Majmu al-Fatwa*, 32/194.
13. Long Georg, Donatio propter Nuptias in William Smith, *A Dictionary of Greek and Roman Antiquities,* (London; John Mare Murray, 1875).
14. Maududi, Abul A'la, *The Meaning of the Qur'an,* (Lahore: Islamic Publications Ltd., Pakistan, 1988).
15. Ortolan, *Explanation Historique des Institutes,* Vol. 1, (London: Atlantic Highlands: Humanities Press. 1968).
16. Roqaiyyah Waris Maqsood, *A Basic Dictionary of Islam* (New Delhi, Goodword Books, Nizamuddin Market, India).
17. Taha Jabeer Alwani, *Source Methodology in Islamic Juris prudence,* (London, The International Institute of Islamic Thought, 3rd edition 2003, first edition in 1990).
18. F.B. Tayabji. (1968). *Muslim Law (Bombay:* N.M. Tripathi, 1968) p. 56.
19. A husband can settle any amount as dower to his wife, even if that leaves nothing to the heirs but he cannot settle for less than 10 dhirham in Sunni Law. The Shia Law, has no minimum.
20. A formal written request, typically one signed by many people, appealing to authority with respect to a particular cause.
21. Fyzee, Outlines of Mohamedan Law (Oxford University Press, 14th edition 1984, 1st in 1949) p. 169.
22. Jamal al-Din al-Asmawi, Nihaya al-Sawal fi Sharh Minhaj (Egypt: al-Maktaba al-Mahmudiyya al-Tijara, II, 1340H) pp. 233-234.
23. Lindsey E. Blenkhorn, Note, Islamic Marriage Contacts in Amirican Courts; Interpreting *Mahr* Agreements as Prenuptials and Effects on Muslim Women, 76 S. Cal.L.REV. 189, 210-11.
24. Allama Abdul Aleem Siddiqui, Roots of Islamic Juriprudence (Cairo: Daar al Ma'arif, 1998), p. 56.
25. Muhammad Yahya ibn Shaykh Aman, *Nuzha al-Mushtaq* (Cairo: Matba' Hijazi, 1370 H / 195) p. 598.
26. Shaikh Al-Hur, *Wasa'il ush-Shi'ah,* (Delhi: Chilti Qadr, Vol. 21), p. 240.
27. *Ibid*, p. 253.
28. Nushuz is when a spouse does not perform his or her obligatory marital duties towards the other.

29. Mona Rafiq, Rethinking Islamic Law Arbitration Tribunals: Are they Compatible with traditional American Nations of Justice. 28 wis. In't *Law Journal*, 108, 138-39 (2010).
30. Majid Khadri, *An Introduction to Ash Sahfis al – Risala*, (Beirut: Dar al-Ilmi lil-Malayen, 37th ed. 2003), p. 962.
31. Tahir Mahmood and Dr. Saif Mahmood – *Introduction to Muslim Law*, Universal Law Publishing Co., p. 162.

8

Women in the Light of Islam: As Child and As Daughter, As Sister and As Wife

Gulshana Wani and *Zaffar Ahmad Nadaf*

Islam deals with women in a comprehensive way in the context of her relationship with Allah, her Creator and Lord, with herself as a part of humanity, and with man, her partner and natural spouse in the family. During the presentation below, keep in mind the rights that other societies grant them in comparison to the rights to which Islam has entitled women. It is noteworthy that Islamic teachings are attentive to the needs and rights of the weaker gender throughout her life, as a daughter, sister, wife, mother, and as a member of the Islamic society.

Equality of Man and Woman in Islam and Their Complementary Nature to One Another

In one sense, equality between men and women is possible and reasonable because they are both human, with similar souls, brains, hearts, lungs, limbs etc. In another sense, equality between men and women is impossible and an absurdity due to their natural differences in physical, mental, emotional and psychological qualities, inclinations and abilities. Between these two we must tread to illuminate how they are equal, and how they are complimentary.

If total equality between all members of the same gender is impossible due to natural differences in strengths and other qualities, regardless of whether the gender is masculine or feminine, then it is definitely impossible between the two genders. Allah, the Exalted and Almighty, says in the *Glorious Qur'an*: *And of everything we have created pairs, that you may remember (the Grace of Allah).[51:49]*

Even atoms exhibit this dual quality mentioned, with interrelated and complementary roles played by the positive and negative particles and ions, yet each is an integral part of the whole system of the so called binary basis of all life. Most living beings have male and female sexes for reproduction. As the science of biology teaches us, all mammals have similar traits in their molecular and glandular structures that determine differences in gender. These basic physical, psychological and sexual traits have their definite effects on other spheres of life.

It is natural for a man to need and find fulfilment with a woman and for a woman with a man, since they are created one from the other and for one another. They both are inseparably bound to each other. Neither can they find fulfilment except when in the company of the other as legal and honourable mate and spouse, as Allah (SWT) says in His *Majestic Book, the Qur'an,* mentioned in the two verses' *Mankind! We have created you from a male and female, and made you into nations and tribes, that you may know one another. Verily, the most honourable of you in the Sight of Allah is the believer who has Taqwa (piety and righteousness) and loves Allah most. Verily, Allah is All-Knowing, All-Aware.[49:13]*

In many instances Islam treats women as equal to men. Some of them are given below. In the coming sections we will expand on these themes in various contexts throughout the book.

1. Both the male and the female are equal in terms of their humanity. Islam does not categorize women, for instance, as the source of evil in the world for some "original sin" that caused Adam (PBUH) to be dismissed from Paradise, or to be the cause of evil in the world by setting loose a Pandora's Box of vices, as some other religious doctrines and fables teach. Allah, the Exalted and Almighty, states in the Glorious Qur'an: *O mankind! Be dutiful to your Lord, Who created you from a single person (Adam), and from him (Adam) He created his wife (Eve), and from them both He created many men and women. [4:1]*

Allah also states in the Glorious Qur'an: *Does man think that he will be left neglected without being punished or rewarded for the obligatory duties enjoined by his Lord (Allah) on him? Was he not a mixed male and female discharge of semen pouring forth? Then he became a clot; then (Allah) shaped and fashioned (him) in due proportion, and made him into two sexes, male and female. Is He not able to raise to life those who are dead? [75:36-40]*

Allah illustrated in the verses that He created both sexes from one single source. There is no difference between the two sexes in terms of qualifications in humanity, and each complements the other as the two genders of the species. Islam has abolished and abrogated all the previous unjust laws that demoted women as inferior in quality and nature. The *Prophet of Allah* ﷺ said: *Verily, women are the twin halves of men.[Abu Dawood: 234, Tirmidhi: 113]*

2. Equal religious duties and rituals are required from both women and men. Testimony of Faith (*Shahaadah*), Prayer (*Salah*), Charity (*Zakah*), Fasting (*Saum*), and Pilgrimage (*Hajj*) are equally required of both genders. In some cases the requirements are a bit easier on women to alleviate their special cases of hardship. For instance, in consideration of her health and physical condition, menstruating woman or woman in the state of postnatal bleeding and recuperation are absolved from the duty of the prayers and fasting. She is required to make up the days of fasting missed due to menses and postnatal bleeding, but not her prayers, as that would be too burdensome. *Sheikh Muhammad Mutawali ash-Sha'raw said: "From the very beginning of creation, the male has been distinguished and differentiated from the female. One completes the other. Based upon this we believe that such a precise division in terms of the sexes does indeed entail two different missions in life, otherwise, there would be no need for such differences in the sexes. This indicates that each sex has its own merits, while both are human beings. We can easily recognize the difference between day and night, although both help us realize one basic reality about time. The daytime grants us the ability to seek our daily provision, while the night grants us peace to rest. Man and woman, in this aspect of difference, very much resembles the case of daytime and night-time. There are certain things that are required from man only, based on his natural preparation. Similarly, there are certain things that are required from woman only, based on her natural preparation. Yet both are human beings who share many common characteristics."*

3. Allah, the Exalted, says in the *Glorious Qur'an*: *The believers, men and women, are helpers, friends and supporters of one another. They enjoin all that is good, and forbid what is evil, establish prayers, give the Zakah* (Charity), *and obey Allah and His Messenger. Allah will bestow Mercy on them. Surely Allah is All-Mighty, All-Wise.[9:71]*

Both, males and females, have similar rewards for obedience and penalties for disobedience in this world and the Hereafter. As stated by Allah in the *Glorious Qur'an*: *Whoever does righteous acts, whether male or female, while he is a believer, verily, to him We will give a good life, and We shall pay them certainly a reward in proportion to the best of what they used to do.[16:97]*

And the *Lord Most Majestic* says: *Surely for men who submit to Allah and for women who submit to Allah, for believing men and for believing women, for devout men and devout women, for truthful men and truthful women, for steadfast men and steadfast women, for humble men and humble women, for charitable men and charitable women, for fasting men and fasting women, for men who guard their chastity and women who guard their chastity, for men who remember Allah much and for women who remember Allah much, for all of them Allah has prepared forgiveness and a mighty reward.[33:35]*

4. Women have the same moral obligations and are entitled to the same general rights as men in guarding chastity, integrity and personal honour and respect etc. No double standards are allowed. For instance, those who falsely accuse a chaste woman of adultery or fornication are publicly punished, just as if a man is slandered. Allah, the Exalted, states in the Glorious *Qur'an*: *And those who accuse chaste women, and produce not four witnesses, flog them with eighty lashes, and reject their testimony for ever. Indeed, they are those who are liars, rebellious and disobedient to Allah.[24:4]*

5. Women are equally qualified and allowed to engage in financial dealings and property ownership. According to Islamic law women can own, buy, sell and undertake any financial transaction without the need for guardianship, and without any restrictions or limitations—a situation unheard of in many societies until modern times.

6. Islam indicates that a man who honours, respects and deals with women justly and integrally, possesses a healthy and righteous personality, whereas a man who mistreats them is an unrighteous and unrespectable man. The Prophet of Allah said: "*The most complete of the believers in faith, is the one with the best character among them. And the best of you are those who are best to your women."[Tirmidhi, 1162]*

7. Islam entitles women to the same rights as men in terms of education. The *Prophet of Allah* said, as reported and authenticated by the scholars of prophetic traditions: *Seeking knowledge is compulsory for each and every Muslim (i.e. both male and female). [Ibn Majah, 224]*

Muslim scholars collectively agreed that the word "Muslim" when used in revealed scriptures includes both male and female, as we indicated in parenthesis. Thus, Islam entitles women to the same right of education in order to understand the religious and social obligations and obligated them both to raise their children in the best manner, in accordance with the right Islamic guidance and means of education. Of course, women have certain obligations in bringing up their children that are commensurate to their abilities and men have complementary obligations to finance, protect and maintain according to their added responsibilities in the family unit. In any case due to the stronger position of the male parent in the family, he is burdened with the overall responsibility of the family and accorded greater reward accordingly.

The *Prophet* said: *Whosoever takes care of three daughters and trains them well and marries them and treats them with the best of manners, will have the reward of Paradise.[Al-Bukhari in Al-Adab Al-Mufrad 92]*

About female slave girls, the *Prophet of Allah* said: *Whoever has a female child with him (under his guardianship from slavery), and trains her in the best behaviour, and teaches her well, and then frees and marries her, will have a double reward [Bukhari 97; Muslim 154; Tahirkheli, 2016]*

8. Men and women have similar obligations and responsibilities to reform and correct the society to the best of their capability. Men and women shoulder the responsibility of enjoining good and forbidding evil equally, as Allah, the Exalted, states in the *Qur'an*: *The believers, men and women, are helpers, supporters, friends and protectors of one another, they enjoin all that is good, and forbid all that is evil, they offer their prayers perfectly, and give Zakah (Charity) and obey Allah and His Messenger. Allah will bestow Mercy on them. Surely Allah is All-Mighty, All-Wise.[9:71]*

9. Men and women have set and determined rights to receive their fair share of wealth, just as they are obliged to give *Zakah* (obligatory Charity) according to the set calculation. All Muslim scholars unanimously agree upon this. A woman has her set share of inheritance, as will be discussed in more detail later, which was a right unthinkable in many societies. *Allah (swt) says*: *There is a share for men from what is left by parents and those closely related, and there is a share for women from what is left by parents and those closely related, whether the wealth be small or large: a legal mandatory share.[4:7]*

10. A woman, just like a man, can give someone the right of seeking refuge and security among the Muslims. *Allah, the Exalted, says: And if one of the polytheists seeks refuge, give him until he hears*

the words of Allah, then take him to his place of security.[9:71]

The Messenger of Allah ﷺ *said: and the protection of Muslims is one, and the least among them can give protection; and whoever usurps the right of a Muslim then the curse of Allah and His angels and all the people is upon him, and no repentance or ransom will be accepted from him. [Bukhari, 3008]*

This is also proven by the famous story of *Um Hani* (Mother of Hani) when she gave protection to a polytheist who sought refuge with her on the day of the conquest of *Makkah* after her relative threatened to kill that person (for some past enmity) so the *Messenger of Allah* said, *We protect and give asylum to whom you protect and give asylum O Um Hani. [Bukhari, 350]*

These are just some of the rights, mentioned here as examples in a summarized way to indicate the comprehensive nature of the Islamic jurisprudence.

Women as Infants, Children and Daughters

Allah, the Exalted, states in the *Glorious Qur'an* concerning the necessity and importance of the preservation and care of new born children, the very first right of the child: *And kill not your children for fear of poverty. We provide for them and for you. Surely, such a killing is a great sin.[17:31]*

The aborting of the foetus and killing of children for any reason is the greatest of the sins, punishable severely by Allah and the Islamic legal system. Islam requires the parents to give their children beautiful names, take proper care of them, take care of all their needs, provide for them reasonably in accordance with the parent's income, and ensure a decent, respected and honourable life for them. And the *authentic prophetic tradition says*: *Verily Allah has prohibited for you to be disobedient and ungrateful to your mothers or to bury your daughters alive.[Sahih Al-Bukhari: 1407 & Sahih AL-Muslim: 593]*

Thus they have the right of blood money if killed, as it is reported by Aishah, (pbuh): *Two women from the Huthail tribe fought and one threw a stone and killed the other and that which was in her womb, so the Prophet judged that the blood money of the foetus is a slave boy or girl, and the blood money of the woman (100 she-camels) was to be paid by her clansmen. Sahih Al-Bukhari: 3512 & Sahih Al-Muslim:1681*]

Allah, the Exalted, states in the *Glorious Qur'an: Mothers shall nurse their children for two whole years, for those parents who desire to complete the term of suckling, and the father of the child shall bear the cost of the mother's food and clothing on a reasonable basis. [2:233]*

Care and guardianship of children is the most important right after the right of (milk) nursing by the mother. The mother is entitled to the custody of the child, son or daughter at the early stage of life, between the ages of one and thirteen or fourteen. This applies particularly in cases of divorce due to essential differences between parents. Islam entitles the mother to her child's custody during early childhood because she, generally, is more caring and attentive to the child's needs. Amr bin Shu'aib related that a woman came to the *Prophet* complaining about her husband saying: My womb held my baby as a foetus, my breast nursed the baby as an infant, and my lap carried the child for a long time. Now the father divorced me and he wants to rip the baby away from me! *"He* said: *You deserve the child's custody more as long as you do not remarry.* [*Abu Da'wood: 2276 & others* and verified as correct]

Abu-Bakr (pbuh) the first rightly guided Caliph passed verdict in favour of 'Asim's mother, the wife of Umar binal-Khattab who later became the second Caliph (pbuh), when Umar divorced her. *Abu-Bakr* (pbuh) is reported to have said: *Her smell, and the way the mother smells her child, and her kindness is better for him than you. Parents are obligated to treat all their children mercifully and with compassion. Abu Hurairah* (pbuh) reported: *The Messenger of Allah* ﷺ kissed Hasanibn Ali (his grandson) in the presence of *Aqraibn Habis al-Tameemi* who said, *I have ten children and I never kissed any of them.* Upon that he looked at him and replied: *Whoever does not have mercy will not receive mercy.* [*Sahih Al-Bukhari: 5651*]

Islamic law stipulates that parents must care and pay attention to their children, especially girls for their special needs. The *Prophet* also said: *Whoever supports two girls till they attain maturity, he and I will come on the Day of Resurrection like this.* The Messenger of Allah then joined his fingers to illustrate this. [*Sahih Al-Muslim: 2631*] And he said: *He who has three daughters and exercises patience with them, feeds them, clothes them according to his means, with due attention, they will become like barrier between him and the (Hell) fire on the Day of Requital.* [*Ibn Majah* and verified]

Islamic laws and teachings mandate that parents raise their children with the best manners and offer them a sound, beneficial and healthy education. The *Prophet of Allah* said: *It is enough sin for a person to neglect those for whose care he is responsible.* [Ṣaḥi¯ḥ Muslim: 996]

Ibn Umar (pbuh) reported that the Messenger of Allah said: *Each one of you is a shepherd and each one of you is responsible for those under his care. A leader is a shepherd and is responsible for his citizens. A man is a shepherd of his family and is responsible for them. A woman is a shepherd in her husband's home and is responsible for whatever is under her care. A servant is a shepherd of his master's wealth and is responsible for whatever is under his care. Each one of you is a shepherd and each one of you is responsible for whatever is under his care.* [Sahih Al-Bukhari: 853 & Sahih Al-Muslim: 1829]

Islam commands justice in all matters and this general ruling is applied to all children regardless of their sexes. Allah, the Exalted, states in the *Glorious Qur'an*: *Verily Allah enjoins justice and the doing of good, and liberality to kith and kin, and He forbids all shameful deeds, wickedness, and injustice and oppression. He admonishes you that you may take heed.[16:90]*

Aishah, the wife of the *Prophet* and the mother of the believers (pbuh) said: *A poor woman came to my door carrying two little girls. I offered them three dates (i.e. since I had nothing else). She gave each of her two girls a date, and lifted the third one to her mouth to eat. Both her daughters urged her to feed them more, so she split the last date into two pieces and gave one half to each of her two daughters. I admired what the woman had done and told the story to the Prophet of Allah* who said upon hearing it: *Verily Allah obligated paradise for her due to this act of hers; or liberated her from the Hellfire due to this act of hers. And in another authentic narration he said at the end: Whoever is tested by trials in caring for these daughters, they will be a cover for him from Hellfire.* [*Bukhari & others*]

Islam calls for material and emotional justice and fair treatment from both parents to their children, regardless of their sexes. A male child is not to be given special preference over a female child, or *vice versa.* The *Prophet of Allah* said to one of his companions who had given a present to only one of his children: *Did you give all your children like this? He said: No. He said: Fear Allah and be just with all of your children. [Muslim]*

Islam emphasizes the importance of taking care of the orphans. Being an orphan has a great negative impact on the mental, spiritual and emotional status of a child. This state may lead an orphan to deviation or corruption at times, especially if the orphan exists in a society that does not give him due care, fulfil his needs and be kind and merciful to him.

Islam pays special attention to the welfare of orphans, males and females alike. Islam requires that the immediate relatives of that orphan take good care of him/her. If there are no relatives, then it becomes the responsibility of the Islamic State to take care of them, manage their affairs and provide them with care. Allah, the Exalted, states in the Glorious *Qur'an*: *As for the orphans, do not treat them with harshness. [93:9]* Allah, the Exalted, also states in the *Glorious Qur'an*: *Verily, those who unjustly eat up the property of orphans, they eat up only a fire into their bellies, and they will be burnt in the Blazing fire![4:10]* The *Prophet of Allah* said: *Verily I declare the gravity of the rights of the two weak persons: the orphan and the woman.*[*Haakim: 211 & Tabarani*] Here he indicates the great sin to perpetrate any harmer injustice to these two, who, according to their natural weakness in the society, often are neglected or denied their rights.

Allah's Prophet also said: *Avoid the seven cardinal sins that cause destruction. The companions asked: O Prophet of Allah! What are these sins? He said: To associate others in the worship of Allah, to practice sorcery, to kill a human soul for no just reason, to deal with interest, to devour the wealth of an orphan, to flee from the battle field, and to accuse the innocent, chaste, believing women with adultery.* [*Bukhari & others*]

Many other prophetic statements have been reported as urging believing Muslims to sponsor orphans, take good care of them, be kind to them, and demonstrate love and affection for them. For instance he said ﷺ:*"I and the guardian of an orphan are like these two in Paradise.* He then indicated with his index and middle fingers. [*Bukhari & others*] He ﷺ is also reported to have said: *Whosoever places his hand over the head of an orphan, placing it there only for the sake of Allah* (with true mercy and affection), *Allah will record the good deeds for that person according to the number of hair, that person's hand wipes of the orphan's head, and whoever does good to an orphan girl or boy of whom he is the guardian, I will be with him in Paradise like this.* He then joined his index and middle fingers. [Tirmidhi but with weak chain of narrators].

Islam cares for welfare of those illegitimate children who, through no fault of theirs, are left without any acknowledgement from their parents. The Islamic government is required to take care of such children, exactly as any other orphan so that they may become, by the will of Allah, normal and beneficial members of the society. As the Prophet of Allah ﷺ said as a general ruling of benevolence: *You have reward for (doing well to) every living being. [Bukhari & others]* Islamic jurisprudence obligated the fathers (or guardians) to ask the opinion of the daughters when it comes to marriage, as her opinion is an essential condition for the validity of the marriage. She is free from any coercion, and may accept the person or reject a proposal. The *Prophet of Allah* said:

A divorcee or widow should not be married without her permission and a virgin girl must not enter wedlock until she approves. They asked: *And how does she approve O Messenger of Allah? He* said: *She stays quiet* (i.e. out of shyness but doesn't indicate disapproval). [*Bukhari & others*] Imam Ahmad and others report that *Aishah* (pbuh) said: A woman came to Allah's Prophet and said, *O! Prophet of Allah*! *My father offered me in marriage to his nephew to elevate his social status. Allah's Prophet* returned the matter to her hands, to accept and approve the marriage or to reject. The woman said: *I approve now of what my father has done, but I wanted to teach other women that their fathers have no right in this* (to force them to marry whoever they want) [Musnad Ahmad: 25027]. This is because daughters are precious, as the Messenger of Allah ﷺ said in a verified tradition: *Do not force the daughters and girls for they are precious and delightful companions.* [*Musnad Ahmad:17411*]

Women as Sisters

Brothers are responsible to treat their sisters with utmost care and concern for their welfare, honour and respect. If for any reason the father, grandfathers or uncles are not available to care and maintain for the mother and the daughters, this responsibility falls on the shoulders of the brothers when they come of age to fulfil to the best of their abilities.

The *Prophet of Allah* said: *Whoever has three daughters or three sisters, and fears Allah in their guardianship, will be together with me in Paradise like this*. He indicated with his index and second fingers. [*Ahmad & others* and verified by some]

Women as Wives

Allah, the Exalted, says in the *Glorious Qur'an*: *Among His signs is that He created for you wives from among yourselves, that you may find tranquillity in them, and He has put between you affection and mercy.* [30:21]

One of the great signs of the Benevolence, Mercy and Power of Allah, the Exalted, is that He created for mankind mates, one from the other, so that they are comforted, satisfied and assisted by one another.

The *Prophet* emphasized the importance of the marriage bond when he said in a verified tradition: *Whoever marries has completed half of his religion so let him fear Allah in the remaining portion. [Tabrani and verified]* The basic foundation of the society is the family, and the husband and the wife are co-partners in that family upon which a Muslim home is established. For the success of the family and the tranquillity of the home, Islam grants each spouse certain rights and duties. We will only focus on the rights of the wives in the following section.

Dowry

A dowry is the right of every bride at the time of marriage. A marriage contract is not considered legal and complete unless and until a dowry has been specified. This right cannot be forfeited, even if the bride approves, until after the marriage contract is completed. The dowry belongs to the woman entering marriage, and she has the freedom to do whatever she wants with what she owns after the marriage contract is fulfilled. Allah, the Exalted, states in the *Glorious Qur'an: Give the women whom you marry their dowry with good heart. If they remit any part of it to you, of their own good pleasure, take it and enjoy it fully without fear of any harm.[4:4]*

The husband is not allowed to take anything back from the dowry if he decides later to divorce her; as Allah, the Exalted, states in the *Glorious Qur'an*: *If you intend to replace a wife by another and you have given one of them a huge sum of gold as dowry, take not the least of it back; would you take it wrongfully without a right and with a manifest sin. And how can you take it back while you have entered with intimate relationship unto each other, and they (the wives) have taken from you a firm and strong covenant?[4:20]*

This verse indicates, significantly, the sacredness of the marriage vows and the intimacy of the marriage relationship, as well as the right of retaining the dowry gift in case of divorce. Allah, the Exalted, also states in the *Glorious Qur'an: O! you who believe! You are forbidden to inherit women against their will, and you should not treat them with harshness, that you may take away part of the dowry you have given them, unless they commit open illegal sexual intercourse. Live with them honourably; if you dislike them, it may be that you dislike a thing and Allah brings through it a great deal of good.[4:19]*

This verse ensures the wife's rights and complete justice even if the man dislikes her for any reason. This is also mentioned in an authentic prophetic tradition wherein *Abu Hurrah* (pbuh) reported that the *Messenger of Allah* said: *A believer must not hate a believing woman (i.e. his wife): if he dislikes one of her characteristics, he will be pleased with another.* [*Sahih Al-Muslim:1469*]

Financial Support

The husband must give honourable and sufficient sustenance to his household according to his status and means. *Allah, the Exalted,* says: *"Let the rich man spend according to his means, and the man whose resources are restricted, let him spend according to what Allah has given him. Allah puts no burden on any person beyond what He has given him. Allah will grant after hardship ease." [65:7]*

If a sufficiently rich man refuses to spend on his family in accordance with his level of means, and the wife was able to take a portion of his wealth. She may take that which satisfies her essential needs and that of her children, avoiding wastage and extravagance. *Hind bint Utbah* came to the *Prophet* complaining about her husband, Abu Sufyan, saying*: My husband is a miser and does not spend enough on me and his children. He replied: Take whatever suffices you and your child within proper bounds. [Sahih Al-Bukhari: 5049]* If a husband came under heavy financial strain and was incapable of fulfilling his family's financial needs, or if he left his wife for an extensive period of time, whereby the wife was harmed due to that absence, the wife is entitled to seek court intervention, if she desires to annul that marriage, as indicated by the verdicts of the jurists in Islamic jurisprudence.

The Prophet of Allah explained these rights when he said: *Fear Allah in (the affairs of) women for you have taken them by the oath of Allah, and made their intimate relations legal by the sacred word of Allah: your right is that no one you dislike should (be allowed to enter) sit on your bed (or cushions), and if this happens then you may hit them lightly, and their right is that you feed and clothe them within proper bounds. [Muslim & Abu Da'wood]*

The Prophet said to his companion *Sa'adibn Abi Waqas* (pbuh): *No amount you spend on your family seeking reward from Allah but that He will reward you even if it is a bite of food that you put in your wife's mouth.* [Sahih Al-Bukhari H:2592 & Sahih Al-Muslim H:1628]

Justice, Equality and Fairness

Men who are married to more than one wife are required to act with justice, fairness and equality in dealing with them. This includes provision, clothing, housing and sharing his time, concerns and intimate relations. *Allah, the Beneficent, says*: *And if you fear that you shall not be able to deal justly with the orphan-girls, then marry (other) women of your choice, two or three or four, but if you fear that you shall not be able to deal justly (with them), then only one or (the captives and the slaves) that your right hands possess. That is better to prevent you from doing injustice. [4:3]* The *Prophet of Allah* said: *He who has two wives and leans to one as opposed to the other will come on the Day of Resurrection with one of his sides fallen.* [*Tirmidhi, Hakim & others* and verified]

This indicates that the husband must demonstrate justice, fairness and equality amongst all his wives. He is warned of this dire punishment of paralysis and deformity in the hereafter, just as he paralyzed and deformed the rights of one of his wives in this world. It is unlawful for a man to mistreat his wife in any fashion with abuse, hardships, harassment, undue burdens, insults, beatings abuse to her wealth and funds, forbidding her from lawful outings, etc. in an attempt to force her to pay all that she possesses as ransom to her husband so that he may release her through divorce. Islamic laws do permit the husband to impose certain restrictions upon the wife who displays some immoral and shameful conduct, dishonourable to him and his family, and harmful to the entire society and social order. The purpose of these restrictions is to seek her to return to proper behaviour. Those who continue to act indiscreetly, leading to suspicion of actual infidelity may be offered divorce, just as she may seek *Khula*; wherein she asks for dissolving the marriage contract due to his misbehaviour.

Protection and Preservation

A husband must protect and prevent his wife and children from any possible harm or immorality to the best of his abilities. *Allah, the*

Exalted, says: *O! you who believe! Save yourselves and your families from a Fire whose fuel is Men and Stones, over which are (appointed) angels stern (and) severe, who disobey not the Commands they receive from Allah, and do what they are commanded. [66:6]*

All that protects from unlawful and shameful deeds is commendable, but extremism is not. *He* also said: *There is a kind of jealousy that Allah loves and a kind which He hates: the kind that he loves is in the doubtful acts, and the kind he hates is in the acts without any doubt.*[*Ahmad, Abu Da'wood & Nisa'e*]

Certain types of jealousy are acceptable and commendable, and others are not, as the *Prophet of Allah* explained above, and in a verified tradition *he* said: *Verily Allah gets jealous and the believer gets jealous and the jealousy of Allah is to see a believer doing unlawful acts. [Sahih Al-Bukhari H: 4925 & Sahih Al-Muslim H: 2761]* And he said: *Three persons do not enter Paradise: the disobedient one to his parents; the one without commendable jealousy (about his wife); and the women who act (and dress) like a man. [Ahmed and verified]*

Companionship, Care and Intimate Relationship

A husband must live with his wife honourably, kindly and with respect. He must maintain a decent, clean and acceptable appearance when he relaxes in his household, just as he likes his wife to do for him at home, since this is only mutual respect and decency to another. The *Prophet of Allah* said, encouraging and explaining the comprehensive principle about good character and behaviour: *The most complete believers are those with the best characters, and the best of you are those who are best to their womenfolk. [Tirmidhi: 1162 & Ibn Hibbaan]*

The *Messenger of Allah* used to mend his own clothes or shoes and help his wives with their daily chores. His wife *Aishah* (pbuh) was once asked: *What did the Messenger of Allah use to do while at home?* She responded: *He used to serve and assist his household, and when he would hear the call to prayer, he would leave the house* (for worship). The *Messenger of Allah* was always pleasant, kind and caring to all, and would occasionally play and joke politely with his family members. *The Prophet of Allah* said: *Everything without containing the remembrance of Allah is just amusement and play except four: to joke and play with one's wife, to train one's horse, to walk between two destinations, and to learn swimming.* [Nasa'e: 8939]

This tradition indicates that most pastimes and amusements are built merely for play, a waste of time and are, therefore, without reward, except these mentioned above which are useful, lawful, and fulfil valid beneficial purposes. *Allah's Prophet* also is well known for being cheerful and decent in joking with his family and playing with them. An example of this fun pastime is when Aishah (pbuh) the mother of the believers, said: Allah's *Prophet raced with me and I won the race before I grew and gained weight. After I became a bit older and put on weight he raced with me again and he won. The Prophet of Allah said to me upon winning the race: This (win of mine makes up) for that (win of yours).[Ahmad: 26320 & Abu Dawood: 2578]*

The *Messenger of Allah* is reported to have sat in the house for a short while with his family, talking to them, giving them company and showing kindness, before going to sleep, and after offering the late evening prayer. In the authentic traditions we find that *Ibn Abbas* (pbuh) narrated: I slept at the house of Maymunah (his aunt and the Prophet's wife) one night—when it was her night turn to see the Prophet's worship in night prayer. He talked with his wife for a period of time, and then slept. Later in the night he awakened and prayed what Allah had written for him.

Allah, the Exalted, states in the *Glorious Qur'an*: *Indeed in the Messenger of Allah you have a good example to follow for whoever has hope in (the Meeting with) Allah and the Last Day, and remembers Allah much. [33:21]*

Hence, *Allah's Prophet* is the best example to follow for all of us, the believing Muslims. Muslims ought to follow the pattern of Allah's Prophet in all of their affairs, personal and public, throughout their life. All the secrets of the wife should be kept and preserved and her shortcomings hidden. No private affairs should be made public or shared as a conversation item, even among the closest friends. The *Messenger of Allah* said: *One of the worst people in the sight of Allah on the Day of Resurrection is a man who has intimate relations with his wife, or a wife who has the same with her husband, and then one of them discloses that privacy to others. [Sahih Al-Muslim: 1437]*

It is the right of the married woman to spend the night with her husband and have sexual fulfilment, satisfaction, and gratification. This right is one of the most emphasized rights in Islam, equal to the need of man to have his fulfilment. The husband is required and obliged by Islamic law to fulfil the sexual rights of his spouse, to ensure the satisfaction of the spouse so as to prevent her from being inclined towards shameful acts, may Allah forbid. A spouse, as any other female, has a great need for being loved and cherished, cared for, and fulfilment of her natural and physical rightful desires.

Islam forbids husbands from engaging themselves in matters of physical worship and devotions, like prayers and fasting, in a way that may detract them from attending to their spouses (physical, sexual and social needs). In a famous incident *Salman Al-Farisi* (pbuh) reported: "I went to visit my brother in faith, *Abu-Darda* (pbuh) and upon arrival; I was greeted by his spouse *Um Darda* (pbuh) who was in an unkempt state. Seeing that, I asked her, *'What is the matter with you; why are you in this state and not attentive to your husband?'* She said: *'Your brother, Abu-Darda has no interest in this world and its affairs. He spends his nights praying and days fasting!'* Upon the arrival of Abu-Darda, who welcomed Salman and offered him some food, Salman said: *'Why do not you eat with me?'* Abu-Darda said: *'I am fasting'*. Salman said: *'By Allah you must break your fast and eat with me.'* Abu-Darda broke his fast and ate with Salman. Salman spent that night with Abu-Darda, and Abu-Darda got up during the night to offer some night prayers whereupon Salman stopped him from doing so, saying: *'Your body has certain rights upon you, your Lord has certain rights upon you, and your family has certain rights upon you. Fast some days and break the fast on others, approach your spouse (for marital relations). Grant everyone their due right.'* Just before the break of dawn, Salman permitted Abu-Darda to get up and offer prayers. Both of them rose, performed ablution, offered prayers and then headed to the Masjid to offer *Fajr* (dawn) prayer. Upon finishing the prayer with the Prophet of Allah ﷺ Abu-Darda reported to the Prophet about the incident. The *Prophet of Allah* said: *'Salman has spoken the truth.' [Sahih Al-Bukhari: 1867]*

Considering the needs of his wife, a husband should not be away from home for an extended period of time. *Caliph Umar ibn Al-Khattab* (pbuh) after consulting with his *daughter Hafsa* (pbuh) about the length of the period a woman can patiently bear her husband's absence, set this period six months.

Abdur-Razaq and others narrate a famous story that: "*Umaribn al-Khattab* (pbuh) was making night rounds when he heard a woman lament:

The night has grown long, and its end is dark and black,
I am sleepless since I have, with whom to play, no lover,

If there was not (the Lord) whose Throne is above the Heavens,
The sides of this bed, would roll, shake and quiver!

In the morning he went to her and asked her the reason for her poetry, and she answered that her husband had gone with the soldiers on a long campaign. Umar then conferred with his *daughter Hafsa* on how long a woman can be patient for her husband to return. After some moments of hesitation and embarrassment, in which he convinced her that this question was for the general good of the Muslims, she replied "six months." After this, Umar would close a campaign within six months so that they could return to their wives within that time.

This period is approximate since circumstances may allow it to be less, or force it to be more. She may tolerate the absence of her husband for more than six months; or she may demand him to come back before that time. The husband may not refuse or deny his spouse's legitimate request unless he has a valid excuse. A husband must not make any financial decisions on behalf of his spouse unless she gives him such permission. The husband has no right to take any of his spouse's financial assets without her approval. He must also consult his spouse in the major household decisions, children's affairs and other mutual affairs. It is not wise to dictate a man's opinion upon the other members of the family without listening to the spouse's opinion, as long as her opinion is wise and correct.

Allah's Prophet gave us a practical example in this matter. On the Day of the Pact with the Quraish tribe, the Prophet ﷺ commanded his companions to shave their heads and to exit the state of '*Ihraam*', but they were slow and did not hasten to fulfil his command. Um Salamah (pbuh) his wife, recommended that he do so himself and then go out before his companions. Allah's Prophet acted upon the recommendation of his wife, doing what she suggested, and when the companions saw his action they all hastened in obedience. A husband must avoid counting every innocent mistake his spouse may make. For instance, the Prophet of Allah said: *A husband may not come to his home from a journey late at night* (i.e. without announcing his arrival in advance). *[Sahih Al-Bukhari: 4948 & Sahih Al-Muslim: 715]*

This recommendation is given so that the husband may not find his spouse in an unprepared state, which might become a reason for his displeasure. Of course with the modern facilities, now-a-days husbands have the ability to inform their wives well in advance, whether the arrival is during the daytime or late in the night. It is the obligation of a husband to be kind, attentive, sharing and caring with his spouse. He must deal with her with honesty, decency, patience and care, and must take into consideration her human nature. Women appreciate being loved tenderly and well taken care of. A husband must demonstrate his affection, love, appreciation, caring, consideration and genuine keenness to his spouse.

The system of divorce in Islam is designed to protect the rights and interests of the women, and allow ample opportunity and time for reconciliation. We will discuss in more detail below, but here we only mention that in divorce, as in marriage, one must act decent with civil behaviour to assure the right of both parties, as *Allah, the Most Wise*, says: *Divorce is two times: then one may retain with goodness* (and reasonable terms), *or let go with goodness* (and reasonable terms). [2:229]

Conclusion

Islam is the eternal divine message of Allah, the Almighty and Exalted, to all mankind, delivered by the Prophet and *Messenger of Allah*. Some have believed in the Message of Islam and followed it, while others disbelieved in it or refuse to follow. Allah (swt) declared that all human beings are dignified and honoured more than other creatures of Allah, as He stated in the *Glorious Qur'an*: *And indeed We have honoured the children of Adam, and We have carried them on land and sea, and have provided them with lawful good things, and have preferred them above many of those whom We have created with a marked preference. [17:70]*

Allah (swt) also declared another major principle: that all men are created equal in terms of original creation. He stated in the *Glorious Qur'an*: *O mankind! Be dutiful to Your Lord, Who created you from a single person (Adam), and from him (Adam) He created many men and women; and fear Allah through Whom you demand your mutual (rights), and (do not cut the relations of) the wombs (i.e. kinship). Surely, Allah is Ever an All-Watcher over you. [4:1]*

Based on the previous principles, all men and women are equal in terms of humanity and basic values, obligations and responsibilities. All men and women are created equal in the sight of Allah. Their differences in race, language, livelihood and geography etc. have no relationship to increase or decrease this honour. True distinction among them is based on their God consciousness, commitment to Islam, the revealed religion of Allah, and their level of practice and application of its principles in their own daily lives. Allah (swt) stated this in the Glorious Qur'an when He said *Mankind! We have created you from a male and a female, and made you into nations and tribes, that you may know one another. Verily, the most honourable of you in the Sight of Allah is the one who is most pious and righteous. Verily, Allah is All-Knowing, All-Aware. [49:13]*

Therefore, true honour of any person in the Sight of Allah is not on the basis of colour, social status, sex, race, strength, health, dignity or wealth. The only measure of distinction in the Sight of Allah is strictly on the basis of piety, faith and the performance of good deeds. Similarly, *Allah's Prophet* was also reported as saying *people, your Lord is one and your father is one. There is no superiority of an Arab over a non-Arab or non-Arab over an Arab, nor of a red person over a black, or a black person over a red, except by piety. [Ahmad and verified]*

References

Al Mustadrak Al Sahihain Al Imam Hakim Jild (1 to 6) H: 211, Shabeer Baradars, Urdu Bazar, Lahore.

Ibn Majah, SunanIbnMa¯jah H: 224.

Musnad Ahmad H: 25027; H: 17411; 26320.

Nasa'e H: 8939.

Qur'an [16:90]; Surah 16 An-Nahl Ayah 90; Ayah 97.

Qur'an [17:31]; Surah 17 Al-Israa Ayah 31; Ayah 70.

Qur'an [2:229] Surah 2 Al-Baqara Ayah 229; Ayah 233.

Qur'an [24:4] Surah 24 An-Nur & Ayah 4

Qur'an [30:21]; Surah 30 Ar-Rum & Ayah 21.

Qur'an [33:21]; Surah 33 Al-Ahzab & Ayah 21; Ayah 35.

Qur'an [4:1]; Surah 4 An-Nisaa Ayah 1; Ayah 3; Ayah 4; Ayah 7; Ayah 10; Ayah 19; Ayah 20.

Qur'an [49:13]; Surah 49 Al-Hujurat & Ayah 13.

Qur'an [51:49]; Surah 51Az-Zariyat & Ayah 49.

Qur'an [65:7]; Surah 65 At-Talaq & Ayah 7.

Qur'an [66:6]; Surah 66 At-Tahrim & Ayah 6.

Qur'an [75:36-40]; Surah 75 Al-Qiyamat & Ayah 36-40.

Qur'an [9:71]; Surah 9 At-Tauba & Ayah 71.

Qur'an [93:9]; Surah 93 Adh-Dhuha & Ayah 9.

Sahih Al-Bukhari H: 1407; H: 1867; H: 2592; H: 3512; H: 4948; H: 5049; H: 5651; H: 853; *H: 4925*; H 3008; H: 350; H: 97.

Sahih Al-Bukhari in Al-Adab Al-Mufrad H: 92.
Sahih Al-Muslim H: 1628H: 593; H: 1681; H: 715; H: 1829; H: 1437; H: 1469; H: 2631; H: 996; *H: 2761*; H: 154.
Sheikh Muhammad Mutawali ash-Sha'rawi.
Sunan Abu Dawood H: 2276; H: 2578; H: 234.
Tahirkheli, S.K. (2016) *Woman's Status & Islam*, Shamsi Publishers.
Tirmidhi, Vol. 1, Book 7, Hadith 1162; H: 113.

9

Islamic Education under the Great Mughals (1526-1857 A.D.)

Mohammad Hanif Ahmad

Introduction

The Mughal rulers comparatively showed greater interest in education than Turks and Afghans. Zahir-ud-din Muhammad Babar, the founder of the Mughal Empire, was a scholar of Arabic, Persian and Turkish. He is rightly regarded as the 'Prince of autobiographers and is stated to have invented a new type of hand writing, called Babari script in 1504 A.D., after his own name. He cultivated the art of poetry from an early age and is mentioned as the author of a collection of Turkish poems many of which are quoted in his '*Memoirs*'.

However, great might be the reputation of Babar's Memoirs for its accuracy, it is certainly not when it says that 'Hindustan had no College'. Babar was interested in paintings, and took with him to India all the specimens of paintings and manuscripts he could collect from the library of his ancestors (the Timurids). Some of these were taken back to Persia by Nadir Shah after the sack of Delhi. These manuscripts exercised considerable influence on the art of India. We learn from the *Tawarikh* of Saiyid Maqbar Ali, a minister of Babar, that the Public Works Department of the time which continued through the reign of the succeeding Mughal emperors was entrusted, among other duties, the building of *Maktabs* and Madrasas. That education received attention of the government is evident from it being made an item of duty of the state. Babar also established a Madrasa in the locality of Aziz-ullah in Jaunpur. During his reign from 1526-30 A.D., Amir Rahim Dad established a Madrasa at Gwalior. His premature death at the age of forty eight soon after he subjugated India, did not give Babar much time to do something for the advancement of education.

Babar was succeeded by his son, Nasir-ud-din Muhammad Humayun, who was also a great scholar. We do not have much information about the education of Humayun, but he followed the tradition of his father. He loved to study astronomy and geography and wrote dissertations on the nature of the elements. We hear of a Madrasa built by Humayun at Delhi, of which Savant Sheikh Husain was a teacher. Madrasat-uz-Zainiyya was built on the bank of the Yamuna, opposite Agra, to perpetuate the memory of Sheikh Zain-ud-din, who died in 1534 near Chinnar and was buried within the precincts of a Madrasa founded by him. Another great Madrasa connected with Sheikh Farid-ud-din bin Masud, was founded by Masud-ud-din Nur-ud-din.

The famous Humayun's Tomb, in the vicinity of New Delhi, was at one time used as a place of instruction. It once housed a Madrasa fulfilling a task beyond the one for which it was built.

The Sur Interregnul (1540-56 A.D.)

Sher Shah, the founder of Sur Dynasty, who deposed Humayun and ruled for four years, did much for the promotion of education in his dominions, notwithstanding the short duration of his reign. Sher Shah Suri used to visit Monasteries and Madaris and associated with learned doctors and Sheikhs for self-improvement. One such Educational Institution that he had opened, was the Shershahi Madrasa at Narnaul. It was located in one of the biggest buildings in the city. His successor, Jalal Khan, whose royal title was Islam Shah and also Balim Shah, followed in the footsteps of his father. The eminent scholars, Sheikh Abdullah Sultanpuri, Makhdum-ul-Mulk and Sheikh Abul Hasan Kamboh, were his constant companions.

Madris were also established by the nobility and the gentry. By the time the Mughals regained power, a large number of *Maktabs* and Madris had come up in various parts of the Mughal Empire. Each mosque had a *Maktab* attached to it in which pupils learned by heart some portions of the Qur'an, Kalima and the three R's. (Reading, Writing and Arithmetic). Many scholars taught students in their own houses.

Mughal Dynasty (Resumed)

Akbar's reign marks a new epoch for the system of education in *Maktabs* and Madaris. The monarch was sincerely eager to further the education of the Hindus and the Muslims alike. They were encouraged to study in the same *Maktabs* and Madaris. He also introduced changes in the modes of study and in the curriculum etc. The success of these measures gave his historian, Abul Fazal, ample reason to feel proud of the fact that 'although all civilized nations had schools to educate their youth, Hindustan was particularly famous for its seminaries. Akbar introduced the following methods of teaching and learning to improve the then existing system.

A boy had to pass through three stages before he could to read and write without difficulty. He was first taught the Persian alphabet along with accents and marks of punctuation. As this was mastered, which did not take more than two days; he was taught the combinations of two letters. After a week, he had to read short lines of prose or verse containing religious or moral sentiments, in which those combinations frequently occurred. The students tried to read these themselves with occasional assistance from the tutor. Then for a few days, the master taught them a new hemistich and in a very short time the boys were able to read with fluency. The teacher gave the young students four exercises daily, viz., (i) the alphabet, (ii) combinations; (iii) a new hemistich or distich; and (iv) to repeat of what they had read before. This method proved very successful. What would have usually taken those years was now accomplished in a few months. The curriculum was so modified as to enable the students to acquire education according to their particular aims and ambitions.

Ain 25 of the '*Ain-i-Akbari*', which is devoted to the organisation of elementary education for children, runs as follows:

> "In every country, especially in Hindustan, boys are kept for years at *Maktabs*, where they learn the consonants and vowels. A great portion of the life of the students is wasted by making them read many books. His Majesty orders that every school boy should first learn to write the alphabet, and also learn to trace their several forms. He ought to learn the shape and name of each letter, which may be done in two days. Then the boy should proceed to write the joined letters. They may be practiced for a week after which the boy should learn some prose and poetry by heart and commit to memory some verses to the praise of God, or moral sentences, each written separately. Care should be taken that he is to understand everything himself, but the teacher may assist a little. He then

> ought, for some time, to be daily practiced in writing a hemistich or a verse, and will soon acquire a current hand. The teacher ought specially to look after five things: Knowledge of the letters; meanings of words; the hemistich; the verse and the former lesson. If this method of teaching were adopted, a boy will in a month, or even in a day, what it took others years to understand, so much that people will be quite astonished. Every ought to read books on morals, arithmetic, the notation peculiar Arithmetic, Agriculture, geometry, astronomy, physiognomy, household matters, the rules of Government, medicine, logic, the Tabi-i-Riyazi and Ilahi science, and history; all of which may be gradually acquired. In studying Sanskrit, students ought to learn *Veyakaran, Niyai Bedanta* and *Patanjali.* No one should be wed to neglect those things which the present time requires regulations shed a new light on *Maktabs* and cast a bright over Madrasa..."

The Emperor was not satisfied with these healthy educational reforms and increased the number of educational institutions in his Empire by continually giving employment to a number of hands in erecting fortifications and palaces, Madrasas and mosques. Abul Fazl founded a Madrasa at Fatehpur Sikri which I known as Madrasa-i-Abul Fazl. A big Madrasa was founded at Fatehpur Sikri by Akbar. A contemporary observer says, Akbar on his return from Ajmer made Fatehpur his Capital and built many buildings there, including Madaris, *khanquahs* etc. It appears that were several other Madaris in the city founded at the instance of Akbar. Agra was also a famous seat of learning and celebrated centre of education. There were several Madaris, where several Chers brought from Shiraz, the famous centre of Muslim learning, to teach.

While speaking of the *Maktabs* and Madaris of those days, should not lose the sight of educational work done by the distinguished learned men who taught their people at their homes. It is supplemented, as already pointed. The educational work led by the educational institutions, and provided scope for higher studies. This system of imparting education has been in vogue since distant times, especially for those branches of the arts and sciences which *Maktabs* and Madaris generally made no provisions of, for example music, painting and the other arts, the various industries, studies higher branches of a subject and so on.

During Akbar's reign, as also during the reigns of his predecessors, the promotion of education found its supporters not only in the emperors, but also in private individuals belonging to the nobility or the middle classes. A Madrasa called *Khairul-Manzil* was built by Maham Anaga in the year 1561. Although the Madrasa is now in ruins, its dilapidated cloisters are still there. It stands almost in front of the Western gate of Purana Quila and near the supposed site of the Western gate of Sher Shah's Delhi. Besides this Madrasa of Mham Anaga, there was another one of Khwaja Muin. Here Mirza Mughis Samarqandi taught for three years from 1571. Another Madrasa was founded by Ala-ud-din-ul-Lari at Akbarabad, and was *Madrasa-i-Khas*. Mir Jumla founded a great Madrasa in Delhi, known as *Madrasa-i-Mir Jumla.* All Madrasas in Delhi were not residential.

Akbar's systematic and deliberate policy of protecting Hindu learning is evident from the generous provisions he made for educating Hindu youth in their own culture in the Madaris, along with the Muslim boys. This apart, he initiated discussion in *Ibadat Khana* with the orthodox Hindu learned men, published translations of Hindu classics and scriptures, exhibiting his profound appreciation of the value of Hindu culture, his zeal for its propagation, State patronage bestowed on distinguished Hindus for their efficiency in the fine arts such as music and painting, further confirms his policy of protecting and propagating Hindu learning and culture.

Soon after his accession to the throne, Jahangir, like his father repaired and reconstructed moribund *Maktabs* and Madrasas. In 1623 Muhammad Safi, Diwan of Suba of Gujarat founded a Madrasa at Habalpur besides Saif Khan's Madrasa. Under Jahangir, Agra retained its importance as a centre of education, as achieved Akbar. *Tuzuk-i-Jahangiri* says: 'The inhabitants of Agra exerted selves greatly in the acquirement of crafts and the search after learning. Various professors of every religion and creed have taken up their abode in the City.'

The French traveller Bernier, who visited India in seventeenth century, draws a depressing picture of the state of education in Hindustan, which seems somewhat exaggerated. He states: A gross and profound ignorance reigns in those states. For is it possible that there should be academies and Madaris bounded? Where are such founders to be met with? And if there any, whence were the scholars to be had? Where are those having means sufficient to maintain their children in Madaris? If there were, who would appear to be so rich? And if they would, where are those benefices, preferments and dignities that require knowledge and abilities and that may animate young men to study.

Though Shah Jahan's reign may not be distinguished for any special educational progress, yet Bernier's statement does not seem to describe the real state of affair. Shah Jahan made distinct and important contribution to education, viz. the foundation of a Madrasa at Delhi in the vicinity of famous Jama Masjid. Carr Stephen records:

> "To the South of the Jama Masjid (of Delhi) was the imperial Madrasa and to the north was imperial dispensary; both buildings fell into ruin long before the rebellion of 1857 and levelled with the ground soon after that event. They were built into the mosques in 1650 A.D."

Shah Jahan repaired the ruined Madrasa, named *Dar-ul-Baqa* and also appointed a few distinguished learned men as teachers. Maulana Muhammad Sadr-ud-din Khan Bahadur, the Chief Justice of Delhi, was appointed as the head of the Institution. Two other Madrasas were founded, one by his wife, Fatehpuri Begum, another by Akbarabadi Begum. The Madrasa founded by his elder daughter, Jahan Ara Begum, in the mosque of Agra achieved its importance and continued to function and prosper even in later times. There was a Madrasa meant only for girls, named *Madrsa-e-Banat* at Fatehpur Sikri near the Royal Palace.

Aurangzeb (1658-1707 A.D.), the last of the great Mughals, allowed an educational policy in keeping with his general policy of governing the Empire and also in the interest of his co-religionist promoted Madrasa education earnestly, diffused Islamic learning throughout his vast Empire and enunciated his own theory of Royal education which emphasized the importance of general knowledge—i.e. sincerely and earnestly endeavoured to foster the education of Muslim youth and appointed and supported teachers in different parts of his Empire for the purpose. Stipends were also given in proportion to their progress in education. He issued orders to Makramat Khan, the Diwan of Gujarat, as also to other diwajan in his dominion, to give pecuniary help from the State treasury, with the sanction of the teachers of Madrasa and of the sadar of the place to all students, good and bad, who could read the *Mizan* and the *Kashshaf*. He also ordered that three teachers for Ahmedabad, Patna and Surat, and forty-five students for Ahmadabad added to their existing numbers there. Aurangzeb also founded and promoted many Madaris. Among them the one at Firangi

Maha assumed importance. It also appears that Akram-ud-din Khan Sadr built a Madrasa in 1697 in Ahmedabad at an expense of Rs. 124,000 appealed to Aurangzeb for help. In response, the Emperor ordered the revenues of Sundra Village (in Pargana Sanoly) and Siha village (in Pargana Kari) to be earmarked for the maintenance of the Madrasa. Likewise, Imperial Farmans were issued to other provincial governors to take interest in the education of their subjects. Besides, Akram-ud-din Khan Sadr, others also established private Madaris. Qazi Rafi-ud-din Muhammad founded one in Bina close to Qazi-ki-Masjid which bears an inscription dated 1670 A.D.

During Aurangzeb's reign Sialkot was a renowned seat of Muslim learning. Learned men from various parts of the country flocked to this place. Maulvi Abdullah taught here in a Madrasa set by his father Maulvi Abdul Hakeem, himself an eminent teacher. The reputation of Sialkot as a place of learning went back to the reign of Akbar. This was possibly the reason why the town specialised, among others, in the paper industry. Sialkot was known especially for the Mansinghi and the silk paper which had a good texture and was clean durable.

The system of instruction followed in the *Maktabs* and Madaris founded by Aurangzeb must have been based on his own concept of education. He pleaded for a broad humanist approach, of which history, geography, the language of the surrounding nations, their forms of government, manners and customs, must find a suitable ace in every curriculum to be prepared for Madrasa education, the religious elements in vocational education for scholars was yet another objective proposed by Aurangzeb. Different in outlook and character, as he was from others, Aurangzeb advocated those very reforms in education which continue to engage attention of scholars even today. Probably political expediency influenced his outlook, and perhaps the curricula were also framed with political expediency mind.

The Mughal Empire began to disintegrate with the death of Aurangzeb. Works of public utility by emperors and private individuals declined after Bahadur Shah came to the throne, even though he was well educated and fond of the society of learned men. Ghazi-ud-din constructed a Madrasa near the Ajmeri Gate of Delhi. He taught there and was later buried there.

In 1722, during the reign of Emperor Muhammad Shah (1719-48), Nawab Sharaf-ud-Daula constructed a Madrasa and a (mosque close to each other in the Dariba Market of Delhi. It was Madrasa Radatmand Khan. He also founded another Madrasa in this market. There was also another one near the mosque of Bulbuli Khana. Nadir Shah, who invaded India in 1739, carried away with him the celebrated Imperial Library of Delhi along with enormous treasure to Persia. This Library had been built up and preserved by Mughal Emperors as their most precious possession. Ironically, some of these valuable books were later sold at ridiculously low price in Persia.

Hasan Raza Khan, the Minister of Asaf-ud-Daula of Awadh, founded a Madrasa at Farrukhabad. During Shah Alam's reign Maulana Abdul Wahid Khairabadi was a teacher there. A Madrasa as established by Nawab Alivardi Khan in Hoogly (West Bengal) in 751 with a '*Wakf*' of 10,000 Bigha landed property. Ghazi-ud-din Khan established a Madrasa during the time of Alamgir II (1754-59). Nawab *Itimad-ud-Daula* Fazal Ali Khan, then a Minister at the Court of the Nawab of Lucknow, gave a sum of Rs. 1,70,000.00 to the East India Company for its maintenance. But the Company misappropriated the funds for establishing an English teaching school.

It needs to be noted that Madaris, did not exist only as government institutions. Muslims established and maintained Madaris on their own as well, charging a religious duty. It is well known that Islam enjoins the pursuit of knowledge as a religious duty upon every Muslim— man and woman. In the wake of the Muslim conquest, therefore, there also came preachers of Islam and religious enthusiasts, and mosques sprang up for observing congregational and other religious rites. These mosques also served as *Maktab* and Madaris in which the rituals of Islam and the recitation of the Qur'an were taught as an essential part of religious observances. The Imam of a mosque in addition to his duty to lead prayers, imparted free instructions to boys and girls. This marked of free education among Muslims. Some Arabic scholars began imparting instructions in the higher branches of Islamic studies, either in a Mosque or at home, without seeking any remuneration or charging fees from students. As they became popular, ambitious students from surrounding parts of the country gathered around them for higher studies. Noblemen and wealthy persons often engaged such scholars to teach their son's along with other students of the locality. Sometimes Madrasas were started under state patronage through grants of land and other allowances. Apart from these Madrasas of medieval India, there were many others, but detailed information about them is not available.

Alongside these Madaris, there existed in Medieval India many other seats of learning where facilities were provided for studying Hindu religion and culture. Such institutions were mostly at Banaras,

Nadia, Mithila, Tirhut, Mathura, Prayag (Allahabad), Hardwar, Ujjain, Ayodhya, Madurai and Tanjore. In almost all these seats of learning Sanskrit grammar, literature, system of Hindu Philosophy (*Darsana*) and Hindu religious scriptures were taught. Bernier writes about Banaras, which he visited in the seventeenth century: 'Banaras is a kind of University, but it has no college or liar classes as in our universities, but resembles rather the schools of the ancients, the masters being spread over different parts of the town in the private houses.'

Madaris, where in a number of cases even Hindus were educated, thus, appear to have existed alongside Hindu centres of education as a distinct system in the cultural fabric of India. Their importance and significance can be gauged from the fact that European Universities were modelled after the Madaris as developed in the Muslim countries as well as in India.

References

Carr Sephen: *Archeology of Delhi*, p. 255

Concise Encyclopedia of Islam, Stacey International, London, p. 245.

Francis Bernier: *Travels in the Mughal Empire 1656-1668 A.D.* A revised editor based on Irving Broke's translation by Archibald Constable and Company. 1891 p. 210.

H.G. Keene: *Fall of Mughal Empire*, Reprint, 1972, p. 23.

H.M. Elliot and John Dovvson: *History of India As Told by Its Own Historians*; Vol. Ill, p. 63. *Tarikh-i-Farishta;* English translation by John Briggs, Vol. I, p. 61.

Khurshid Ahmad, *Muslim Tradition in Education,* Islamic Publications Ltd., Shah Alam Market, Lahore, 1982, p. 45.

Kuldip Kaur: '*Madrasa Education in India*', Centre for Research in Rural and Industrial Development; Chandigarh, Twenty-First Century India Society Printing Press, August 1990.

Mohammad Shahidullah: *A Brief History of Madrasa Education in India*; Calcutta Madrasa College Bicentenary Celebrations, Calcutta, February 12-13, 1985, p. 6.

Mujibur Rehman, *History of Madrasa Education*, Calcutta, 1977, p. 62.

Tarikh-i-Farishta; (Briggs), Vol. I, p. 132. N.N. Law: *Promotion of Learning in India*; Delhi, Reprint, 1977, p. 14.

Tarikh-i-Farishta; (Briggs), Vol. I, p. 200.

Tuzuk Jahangiri or Memoirs of Jahagir from the first to twelfth year of his reign; translated by Alexander Roger and edited by Henry Bever, p. 7.

Yusuf Husain Khan: 'The Educational System in Medieval India'; *Islamic Culture,* April, 1956, p. 107.

10

Islamic Education Through Modern Teaching Methods in Jordan

Ahmad Mahmoud Ali Al Ghzawi

Introduction

The era of the knowledge revolution, with its vast evolution in communication, education technology, computerization of curricula, the spread of the Internet, and the satellite world, has contributed to the rethinking of strategies of teaching. With the tremendous developments in the world of knowledge, the adoption of modern and diverse teaching strategies has become a goal of the development of the educational system in general, and students in particular, turning from passive recipient of knowledge to a strategic participant and active in the educational learning process. Modern teaching strategies are in line with cognitive development following the transformation that the cognitive school led by its theories. The most harmonious and realistic with the needs and abilities of students at different levels of knowledge (Qatami, 2012).

The use of teaching strategies is a qualitative leap in the world of modern education, especially after the transformation of educational thought, from focusing on the role of the teacher as a conveyor of knowledge to his role as facilitator and moderator. The old methods of indoctrination, filling students' brains with information. As the horizons of knowledge widened, and the world turned into a small village thanks to the explosion. Knowledge and technology, which necessitated the use of more modern and effective methods, which contribute to the development of thinking and self-development to serve the objectives of the stage, and meet the needs of students and communities (Jaber, 2010).

A strategic word refers to a plan of action that is designed to achieve pre-defined goals that allow for the achievement of desired goals. It is a method of teaching based on a set of skills that the teacher should master in order for him to succeed in his task and in turn. Each strategy of teaching includes a number of teaching methods. The more the teacher mastered it, the more effective the strategies of modern teaching (Zaytoun, 2003). A. Zaytoun refers to several modern strategies of teaching, each based on a theory, such as direct teaching strategy, lecture-discussion strategy, cooperative learning strategy, constructive learning strategy; (Weil & Calhoun, 2009) (other set of teaching strategies), strategy of inquiry, strategy of induction, strategy of discovery, strategy of dispersion of the Diaspora; creative thinking, strategy of role play, strategy of technical learning. The theories of learning play an important role in the acquisition of trends, starting from the theories of classical conditioning, which believe the importance of repeating the association for a certain period with the use of reinforcement, as the basis to create new links, and to learn. The theory of procedural conditioning demonstrated the importance of reinforcement tables in shaping behaviour and learning new responses. Cognitive social learning theory is no less important than its predecessors in acquiring trends by observing the behaviour of the role-model and the importance of alternative experiences in acquiring trends (Abu Alam, 2014).

The trends have received considerable attention, not only to represent them as contradictory parties, but because they are very important in guiding behaviour and predicting how to behave towards the internal and external vents of the individual. The trend in favour, negativity, approval, or opposition is one of the cognitive states of motivation that direct and predict behaviour in the future. The science of the teacher's attitudes towards teaching strategies modernity reveals the reality of the actual use of it, and identify the positive outlook contributes to the success of the education system, and achieve the objectives of the development of various aspects of the educational process, learning and improvement (Majidil and Sharia, 2012).

Direction: Self-reliance depends on what the person experiences, and can eventually lead to a change of direction. It is known as (Krech & Cru Sheffield, 2011) a stable organization of emotional, emotional, cognitive and cognitive processes towards the subjects of his or her own world. It is clear to the researcher that the trend: acquisition of self-organization, has relative stability, beliefs that the individual believes about a subject, or attitude, and prepares to respond to a response to his satisfaction. Trends are an exciting force in an individual's personality, characterized by a degree of stability that reflects in one way or another the decisions of his life and affect many aspects of his life (Faqih, 2009). Trends are characterized by principles governing the formation and philosophy of the individual towards specific themes, or society (Swift, 2010).

Trends also grow through socialization. They represent the general framework of human life in different societies. Culture also contributes to drawing the boundaries of the process of social interaction by holding members in certain directions as the basis for formulating expectations that facilitate the process of social interaction. Psychological effects of the society and culture, in the sense that the individual acquires from his culture and society the psychological trends appropriate to the different subjects, whether its own or others, or things (Alsaid, 2008).

That the process of social interaction trends grow by direct exposure to the subject direction, or through interaction with others who carry the same direction, which explains the negative trends towards a subject, and shows through the experience gained during dealing with these persons, or subjects (Ross, 2008).

And parents contribute to the methods of social upbringing in the formation of positive trends or negative, the patriarchs are creating negative attitudes of their children towards the environment in which they live, namely oppression and oppression, and create mental configurations saturated with intolerance, intellectual closure, psychological fragility, unconventional ideas. (Swift, 2010)

Learning theories play an important role in the acquisition of trends, based on the theories of classical conditioning, which believe in the importance of repeating the association for a certain period of time with the use of reinforcement, as the basis to create new links, and to learn. The procedural theory of procedural importance showed the importance of reinforcement tables in shaping behaviour and learning new responses. The theory of social learning is no less Cognitive is important for its predecessors in acquiring trends through the process of observing model behaviour and the importance of substitution experiences in acquiring trends. (Abu Alam, 2014)

(Campbell) pointed out that there is a term used by psychologists to describe social motives such as trends, values, acquired motives. Trends can be modified on the condition that they are individual, and if they are associated with religious values it is difficult to change them, and need strenuous efforts.

In addition, the psychological trend is linked in a way that is coordinated by values relating to the individual's idea of oneself, where more complex efforts are required to try to change them. The change of direction takes a conscious dimension by changing one's beliefs or emotional element, if one changes easy to change the other (Swift, 2010).

In the field of pedagogy, pedagogical scholars invest in learning trends as an educational goal, to achieve many modifications in behaviour to conform to the higher educational goals in order to prepare a generation capable of giving, contributing to human development and achievement. The teachers have positive attitudes towards modern teaching strategies that contribute to the improvement of educational systems and their components, and facilitate the psychological adjustment of many variables, based on modern teaching strategies (Ministry of Education, 2006).

Positive attitudes of teachers are transmitted to students through the process of social interaction and through the role-model. Teachers' statements alone are not the only variable in the upbringing of students, but the actions and trends also contribute to students' behavioural and attitudes towards different subjects, working to raise their motivation and develop their love or hatred of the methods of teaching used, and their reflection on the final outcome of the educational process.

The Study Problem

Recent challenges in the field of educational development have led to a change in the role of the school and the teacher. The transformation from the teacher's being the focus of the learning process to the students. The learner has become a strategic partner in the learning process. This shift in educational thought was accompanied by a development in the methods of learning. The revolution began with the actual call to change the teaching strategies used, based on memorization and indoctrination, with modern strategies that serve between exhibitions and supporters. And the importance of the role played by trends in the formation of human thought, and identify expected behaviours, and formation of different reactions, this study was to investigate the attitudes of teachers towards modern teaching strategies in Jordan by answering the following questions:

1. What are the attitudes of Islamic education teachers towards the use of modern strategies in Islamic schools?

2. Are the trends of Islamic education teachers different from the use of modern strategies in Islamic schools according to gender and experience?

The Importance of Studying

This study draws on the importance of the sensitivity of the subject, its relevance to the preferences and decisions on the most important topics at the level of the individual and the community, and the educational policy and its relation to the behaviour of both the teacher and the learner within the classroom, and the impact on the outputs of the educational process. Their findings are opposed. This study acquires practical importance by providing information in the process of improving and developing the concepts related to the attitudes towards teaching strategies, which are the core of the success of the education system or its failure as a whole, and building programmes that contribute to avoiding the dangers of neglecting such a topic.

Objectives of the Study

1. Identify trends of Islamic education teachers towards the use of strategies in modern teaching in Islamic schools.
2. The impact of variables (gender, experience) on the trends of Islamic education teachers towards the use of modern teaching strategies in Islamic schools.

Definition of Terms

Modern Teaching Strategies: A set of steps or methods used by the teacher within the classroom to achieve desired goals (Zaytun, 2003).

Trends: A response from an individual to a subject. The response may be positive or negative depending on the experience of the previous individual (Pickens, 2013). This study is measured by the degree to which the teacher is on the scale of trends towards the use of modern teaching strategy.

The Limits of the Study

1. *Spatial Boundaries*: This study was conducted in Jordan.
2. *Time Limits*: This study was conducted in the academic year (2017-18).

3. *Scientific Limitations*: The study used a measure of the trends of Islamic education teachers towards the use of modern teaching strategies, which the researcher built after studying the standards in the previous literature and the indications of sincerity and stability.

Previous Studies

Omolara (2015) aimed at revealing teachers' attitudes towards the use of cooperative teaching strategies in social subjects, which consisted of (345) teachers and teachers from the city of Illoren, Nigeria, the study used the trend scale of the researcher. The teachers towards the cooperative learning strategy were positive, and there are differences of statistical significance towards the use of cooperative learning strategy due to gender variable, scientific qualification, years of experience, specialization.

Chemwei & Somb (2015) conducted a study aimed at investigating teachers' attitudes towards the use of cooperative learning strategies in language poetry, and the sample consisted of (312) teachers. Improvement in the skills of verbal and formal creativity, and verbal and formal skills of students, and the results of the study showed that there are no significant differences in the attitudes of teachers towards the use of strategies is attributed to the gender variable, specialization, qualification and experience. Maito & Ochiel (2013) conducted a study aimed at investigating teachers' attitudes towards the use of the science inquiry strategy in teaching national culture in Kenya. The study sample consisted of (455) teachers and teachers of the two basic stages in secondary school in Siaya City. The results of the study showed that teachers' attitudes towards using the scientific survey strategy are positive and that there are no statistically significant differences in trends teachers toward the use of strategy are attributed according to the variable of experience, gender, qualification.

Odiri (2011) presented a study aimed at investigating teachers' attitudes towards the use of discovery strategies, problem solving, creative model (in social studies material). The sample consisted of (820) teachers and teachers of the basic and secondary stages in the city of Silay in Nigeria. The results of the study showed that teachers' attitudes towards the three strategies were positive, and did not reveal the results of the study of the existence of significant differences in the attitudes of teachers towards the three strategies attributed to the gender variable, experience, qualification, specialization.

Khleifat (2010) studied the goal of revealing the attitudes of physics teachers in Jordan towards the teaching and evaluation strategies included in the science curriculum, and the impact of gender, scientific qualification, and teaching experience on their attitudes towards those strategies. The study sample consisted of (304) teachers and teachers who study the science curriculum in the capital Amman. Results showed the study is equal to the percentage of negative and positive attitudes of teachers towards teaching and evaluation strategies (33.55%). The percentage of those with neutral attitudes reached 32.90 per cent. There are also no statistically significant differences in teacher attitudes due to the gender variable and scientific qualification. The results of the study also revealed the existence of statistically significant differences in trends. Teachers are attributed to the variable of experience and to the benefit of females.

Comment on Previous Studies

It is noted through the review of previous studies that it was unanimously agreed that teachers' attitudes towards the use of modern teaching strategies were positive, except for the study of Khleifat, (2010), whose results revealed equal proportions of the attitudes of physics teachers towards the teaching and evaluation strategies included in the science curricula. Most of these studies focused on one or more of the modern teaching strategies [Odiri, 2011; Standslaus, Chemwei & Somb, 2015; Maito & Ochiel, 2013; Omolara, 2015)].

Most of these studies were conducted in non-Arab environments, with the exception of Khleifat (2010). These studies are insufficient to show teachers' attitudes towards the use of modern teaching strategies in Arab environments, especially Jordan. The effect of the following variables is gender, experience, qualification, and specialization.

The difference in the results of the previous studies is the actual justification for conducting this study. The Jordanian society is a developing society that needs further studies on different segments to confirm each other or to indicate the differences between them. Also, the scarcity of studies in the Jordanian environment that dealt with this subject. The current on the other hand that it addressed the attitudes of teachers of Islamic education towards the use of all modern teaching strategies in the classroom.

Methodology of the Study

Use the descriptive approach, for suitability for study purposes.

Study Society

The study community is composed of all teachers and teachers in Directorates of Education in Jordan and affiliated to the Ministry Jordanian Education.

The Study Sample

The sample of the study consisted of 1120 teachers. The percentage of females was 60. The percentage of males was 40. 448 were teachers, 672 were teachers from the directorates of education. Teachers were randomly selected to ensure all members of the population were represented in the sample, according to the study variables.

Study Tool

To achieve the objectives of the study, use the measure of trends of Islamic education teachers towards modern study strategies. After the researcher studied the measures of trends used in the subject of the study, the researcher developed a measure suitable for the purposes of the study and the scale of (25) paragraph. The validity of the scale was verified by presenting it to ten of the faculty members of the Jordanian universities specialized in psychology and teaching methods. They were asked to indicate the clarity of the paragraphs, the correctness of the linguistic formulation, the appropriateness of the scale of the study sample and any other observations they consider appropriate. The researcher adopted a ratio of (80%) as the criterion for accepting the paragraph. Based on this criterion, the scale has maintained all its paragraphs of 25 paragraphs.

Stability of the Scale

The stability of the scale was verified by applying it to (60) teachers and teachers from outside the study sample, and calculating the internal consistency coefficient, using the coefficient of the Cranach Alpha for the standard paragraphs, and the value of the stability coefficient (87%).

How to Correct the Meter

The scale is in the final form of (25) paragraphs, and the answer was given by five levels. It was strongly agreed and was given (5) degrees, OK was given (4) degrees, neutral and given (3) OK and given two degrees, not strongly agree and given one degree.

Study Procedures

After the measure was prepared to collect the data, the sample was selected accurately, and then the scale was applied to the sample of the sample (1120) teachers and teachers, and by the same researcher during the academic year 2017-18, the answers were completed and data were entered into the computer and analyzed according to the study questions.

Study Variables

The study included the following variables:

Independent Variables

- *Sex: male – female*
- *Academic Qualifications: BA-Postgraduate Studies,*
- *Experience (1-5), (6-10), (11-15), (16-20), (21+).*

The dependent variable: trends of Islamic education teachers towards the use of modern teaching strategies.

Statistical Processing

To answer the first question, the arithmetical averages, standard deviations, frequencies and percentages were used. In order to answer the first and second hypotheses, the arithmetical averages, standard deviations, and binary variance analysis were used.

Results

First: Results related to the first question: What are the attitudes of Islamic education teachers towards the use of modern teaching strategies in Jordanian schools? To answer this question, the computation, standard deviations, frequency and percentages of teachers' scores were extracted on the scale as a whole, as shown in Table 10.1: Shows the arithmetical averages and standard deviations of teacher scores on the scale as a whole.

Table 10.1

Paragraph number	*Arithmetic average*	*Standard deviation*
1	4.3	0.86
2	4.2	0.87
3	4.3	0.87
4	4.1	0.9
5	3.7	1.27
6	4.2	1
7	2.5	1.3
8	3.5	1.4
9	3.5	1.3
10	3.7	1.3
11	3.8	1.3
12	3.9	1.1
13	2	1.3
14	3.7	1.5
15	4.2	1.5
16	3.3	1.4
17	3.4	1.5
18	4.2	1.1
19	3.6	1.4
20	3.9	1.2.
21	4	0.9
22	4.1	0.9
23	3.8	1.1
24	4.2	1
25.	4.2	1
26	3.8	0.41

Table 10.1 shows that the total arithmetic mean of teachers' attitudes towards the use of modern teaching strategies was (3.8), and the arithmetical averages for paragraphs ranged from (2) of paragraph 13 states: I am happy to use modern teaching strategies as it promotes initiative and commitment among students. And (4.3) of paragraphs (1), which states: It is felt that teaching's modernity enhances students' ability to communicate and communicate effectively with the subject strategies and paragraph (3) which states: I believe that modern teaching strategies address the weaknesses of students in the schools of Jordan.

To determine the level of teachers' attitudes towards the use of modern teaching strategies, the researcher saw that half a standard score is taken above the total arithmetic mean of teacher attitudes towards the use of modern teaching strategies (3.8 + 0.21 = 4.01) as well as half a standard deviation below the total arithmetic mean is (3.8 – 0.21 = 3.59). To determine the levels of direction, and to ensure no overlap between these levels. Therefore, the following criteria were adopted to judge the level of teachers' attitudes towards the use of modern teaching strategies: Negative trend (1-3.58), Neutral direction (3.59–4), Positive direction (5-4.0). Table 10.2 shows levels of teachers' attitudes towards the use of modern teaching strategies in Jordan.

Table 10.2

Trend level	*Duplicates*	*Percentage*
Positive direction (54.01)	325	29
Negative trend (3.581-)	353	31.5
Natural (4.39)	442	39.5
Natural (4.39)	1120	100

Table 10.2 shows that the proportion of teachers with positive attitudes towards these strategies was (29%). The proportion of teachers with a negative attitude towards these strategies was (31.5%). The proportion of teachers with a neutral attitude towards these strategies reached (39.5%).

Second, the results related to the second question: Are the attitudes of the Islamic education teachers different towards the use of modern strategies in Islamic schools according to gender and experience?

Table 10.3 shows the arithmetical averages and standard deviations of teacher scores on the scale as a whole, by gender variable, experience.

Table 10.3

	Variable	*Arithmetic average*	*Standard deviation*
Gender	Male	3.72	0.41
	Female	3.81	0.40
Experience	(1-5)	3.84	0.39
	(10-6)	3.73	0.45
	(15-11)	3.8	3.36
	(20-16)	3.74	0.42
	More-(-21)	3.8	0.46
	Total	3.8	0.41

Table 10.3) shows that there are apparent differences in teachers' average scores on the scale as a whole to find out the significance of these differences, use 2-Way ANOVA Table 10.4 illustrates this.

Table 10.4: The analysis of the binary variance shows the differences between the arithmetic averages on a scale trends as a whole, by gender variable, experience, and interaction between them.

Table 10.4

Source variance	*Sum the squares*	*Degrees of Freedom*	*Average the squares*	*Value of f*	*Level Significance*
Gender	4.152	4	4.152	25.422	*000
Experience	1.311	4	0.328	2.006	0.091
Gender Experience	2.39	7	0.597	3.685	*0.006
Wrong	181.28	1110	0.163		

Table 10.4 shows that there is a statistically significant effect at the level of significance (α = 0.05) due to the gender variable. The differences were in favour of females, with an average of (3.81) and males (3.72). There is no significant statistical effect at the significance level) = (0.05) is attributable to the variable of experience. The table also shows a statistically significant effect at the level of significance (α = 0.05) due to the interaction of sex and experience, where the value of (f = 3.69) (1) Effect of interaction.

Discussion of Results

Discussion of the results of the first question: The percentage of teachers with a positive attitude was 29 per cent. This percentage is small compared to other percentages. This result can be explained in the light of the fact that the shift in the use of modern teaching strategies was surprising. Teachers in advance of the importance of these strategies, and their role in the success of the educational process of learning, and we are talking about trends previously painted as relatively stable, and because of the impact on the performance of the teacher (Latchanna, 2009).

The result of this category was linked to other personal variables such as preconceptions about the teaching profession and the extent to which they are convinced, such as a profession that achieves individual ambition, saturation of motivation, and love of development, contributes to positive attitudes towards the use of teaching strategies.

They also agreed with the results of the study (Odiri, 2011, Omolara, 2015) and differed with the study (Khleifat, 2010), which revealed the equal level of attitudes of teachers of physics towards the use of teaching strategies and evaluation included in the curriculum of science.

The percentage of those with a negative attitude was 31.5 per cent. This result can be explained within the long period of time for adopting traditional strategies in the teaching process and is a decisive factor in influencing their direction. Fear of failure to use what is new is an important aspect of retaining traditional methods and resisting change, and is a fear of failure to use what is new. The results of this study differed with the result of the study (Chemwei & Somb, 2015; Selma, 2009; Standslause, Maito & Ochiel, 2013).

As for the ratio of neutrals, it was their ratio (39.5) can be explained in light of role theory (ABU Ghazal, 2014). The importance of isolation and the absence of the important role represented by the direction of the teacher in the educational system is a success for the preparation of future generations.

Discussion of the second question: Are the trends of Islamic education teachers different from the use of modern strategies in Islamic schools according to gender and experience?

The results of the study show that the use of modern teaching strategies varies according to gender, and results are in favour of females. This is explained by Gilgan's theory that female attitudes differ in their nature from male attitudes, and that females are more prone to care and attention issues, while males are more likely to focus on relationship and rights (Cobb, 2001).

The results also revealed an effect on the interaction between experience and gender in the use of modern teaching strategies. Females were higher than males at all levels regardless of the number of years of experience. The importance of the role they occupy, and educational and psychological literature suggest that females are more inclined to issues related to care and attention to others, which paved the way for the superiority of females to males in the use of modern teaching strategies (Gilligan, 2007).

Recommendations

Based on the study results, the researcher recommends the following:

1. The importance of the Jordanian Ministry of Education should be on importance teachers' attitudes towards the use of modern teaching strategies.
2. Further studies on teachers' attitudes towards the use of modern teaching strategies.

References

Chemwei, B. & Somb, A. (2015). Teacher perspectives and experience with use of cooperative learning in poetry classroom settings. *International Journal of Current Research,* 6(4): 6141-6153.

Cobb, N. (2001). *The Child.* California: Mayfield Publishing Company,

Gilligan, C. (2007). *In a Different Voice: Psychological Theory and Woman.* Cambridge: Harvard University Press.

Jaber, Abdel Hamid, (2010). *Teaching and learning strategies.* Cairo: Arab Thought House.

Joyce, B., Weil, M & Calhoun, E. (2009). *Models of Teaching (8).* New Delhi.

Krech, D & Crutchfield, R. (2011). *Theory and Problems of Social.* New York: McGraw-Hill Book Co.

Majidil, Abdullah and Al-Shurai, Saad, (2012) *A Comparative Field Study Faculty of Education*—Kuwait University and Faculty of Education Hasaka—Euphrates University is a model. *University of Damascus Journal* 28 (4): 17-57.

Ministry of Education, 2006. *Education strategies and learning.* Amman: Training, Rehabilitation and Educational Supervision Department.

Mr. Abdel Halim, (2008). *Social and media psychology.* Cairo: House of Culture Printing and Publishing.

Odiri, O. (2011). The Influence of Teacher's Attitude on Students Learning of Social Studies in Nigerian Secondary Schools. *Journal of Research in Education and Society,* 2(1): 15-37.

Omolara, Sh. (2015). Teacher's Attitudes: A Great Influence on Teaching and Learning of Social Studies. *Journal of Science and Education,* 42(1): 131-147.

Pickens, J. (2013). Attitudes and Perceptions. *Journal of Personality and Social Psychology,* 71(2): 230-255.

Qatami, Youssef, (2012). *Teaching strategies.* Amman: Dar Ammar for Publishing, Distribution and Printing.

Ross, E. (2008). The Present Problems of Social Psychology. *American Journal of Sociology,* 10(4): 456-472.

Swief, Mustafa, (2010). *Introduction to social psychology.* Cairo: The Anglo-Egyptian Library.

Zaytun, Hassan, (2003). *Teaching strategies Contemporary vision of teaching methods.* Cairo: The World of Books.

11

Women, Qur'anic Injunctions and Indian Nation-State

Iftekhar Ahmed Ansari

In the present century the provision and enjoyment of Human Rights by citizens are taken as an accepted standard to measure the level of development across the nationalities. Since the Magna Carta in England in June 1215 C.E., and the Bill of Rights there in 1689 C.E., the journey of Human Rights travelled from Declaration of the "Rights of Man and Citizen in France" in August 1789, to "Universal Declaration of Human Rights" by the General Assembly of the United Nations in 1948. On 15th August, 1947 India as well incorporated these Human Rights in the part third of its Constitution which came into force on 26th January, 1950.

Qur'anic Perspective

The concept of Human Rights in Islam is as old as the religion itself. The study of Qur'an and preaching (*sunna*) of Prophet Mohammad (PBUH) is evidence that Islam stands for upholding of Human Rights and Human Values.

According to the Qur'an, dignity of the children of Adam is a divine bestowal, which is to be secured by all means, including the law and the state authorities, and is to be defended by all forces.

> "*We have conferred dignity on the children of Adam, and borne them over land and sea, and provided for them sustenance out of the good things of life, and favoured them far above most of our Creations.*" (Qur'an 17:70)[1]

Concept of Equality

Defending the human rights of any human being is a religious duty for a Muslim, who believes that any oppression is an obstruction of God's will and plan in His creation. Moreover, a Muslim believes that God has created all mankind equal as human beings, and no one can claim superiority in this respect, whatever his/her ethnicity, family, wealth or gender may be. The Qur'an teaches:

> "*O humanity! Be conscious of your Lord, who has created you out of one living entity, and out of it created its mate, and out of the two spread abroad a multitude of men and women.*" (Qur'an 4:1)[2]

Before Islam, it was a prevalent belief that Eve was responsible for tempting Adam to eat from the forbidden tree. The Qur'an assigns equal responsibility to both of them, clarifying that the temptation came solely from the devil:

> "*But satan caused them both to stumble therein, and thus caused the loss of their erstwhile state." (2:36)*[3], "*and thus be (Satan) led them (both) with deluding thoughts."* (7:22)[4]

Both realized their sin and offered their repentance to God:

> "*The two replied: O our Lord! We have sinned against ourselves, and unless You grant us forgiveness and bestow Your mercy upon us we shall most certainly be lost."* (7:23)[5]

Islam does not consider woman a mere shadow or an extension of a man, always following him. She has her full individual freedom and responsibility to the belief in the message of God and in practicing its obligations:

> "*Now whenever God and his Apostle have decided a matter, it is not for a believing man or a believing woman except to obey in so far they themselves are concerned."* (33:36)[6]
> "*And thus does their Lord answers their prayer: I shall not lose sight of the work of any of you who works (in My way) be it man or women: You are members, one of another."* (3:195)[7]

In the Society

The relationship between men and women and between parents and children represents the model relationship in society:

> "*and (those true servants of the Most Gracious) who pray: O, Our Lord! Grant that our spouses and our offspring to be a joy to our eyes, and cause us to be foremost among (model for) those who are conscious of You.*" (25:74)[8]

The precedence of a man's responsibility cannot give him any justification for a general claim of social prominence and leadership everywhere, and does not establish a rule for every social institution:

> "*Men shall take care of (and full responsibility for) women with what God has bestowed on the former, and with what they spend out of their possessions (on women whom they are responsible for).*" (4:34)[9]

There are people who try to find a support for restricting woman's activities to only the family in Qur'anic Verse that addresses the Prophet's wives, "And abide quietly in your home" (33:33)[10]. But those should not ignore that it was a special rule for the Prophet's wives because of their special situation, as suggested clearly in the previous verse: "O wives of the Prophet! You are not like any of the (other) women." (33:32)[11]. Accordingly, the prophet's wives could not marry after the Prophet, and they had to observe special restrictions that are not applied to others (e.g. 33:28-30, 50-53)[12].

Education and Work

Islam secures women's rights in education and work. The Prophet responded positively and instantly to a woman, asking him to appoint a certain time to teach the Islam regularly. Some women reported the Prophet's traditions (rawiyatal'hadith). Muslim women also made their contributions in various fields, such as: literature, arts and artistic crafts (e.g. fashion, decorated textiles and rugs, cuisine, perfumes, hair-dress etc.), and Sufism (e.g. famous poet Al-Khansn in early Islam, famous sufi Rabi'a d. 801). As early as the time of the Prophet, they accompanied men in the battlefield, where they treated the wounded, and participated sometimes in fighting the enemy when this became necessary. In Muslim Spain "Andalus", several women were famous as physicians in various specializations, including optometry and surgery.

An Independent Legal Personality with Full Equal Rights

Islamic law gives women full independent legal personality. She can maintain her maiden name after marriage, and she can enjoy independence in relation to earning money and spending it:

> "*Men shall have a benefit from what they earn, and women shall have a benefit from what they earn.*" (4:32)[13]

So, the Qur'an explains the women's rights of inheritance as independent individuals, as it has been mentioned previously.

Considering two women equal to one man as legal witness for a credit provides a special case not a general rule—as the prominent jurist, Ibn al-Qayyim (d.1356) rightfully pointed out. The Qur'an is clear on the rule and gives strong reason for that special case:

> "*O You who have attained to faith! Whenever you give or take credit for a stated term, set it down in writing...And call upon two of your men to act as witnesses; and if two men are not available, then a man and two women from among those who are acceptable to you as witnesses can be called upon. So that if one of them should make a mistake the other could remind her...*" (2:282)[14]

Equality in Political Matters

Islam teaches equality in political matters as well. Any human being cannot decide arbitrarily and independently a matter that concerns others and not himself or herself alone, nor claim if he or she does so, an immunity from accountability. The Qur'an makes "shura" or "participation with others in making a decision that concerns them." Both men and women have the equal right and obligation to participate in deciding who will be their leaders and representatives, as required in a democratic system in our country.

In assuming the role public responsibilities women are equal to men as Qur'an explicitly states: "And the believers, both men and women, are in charge of (and responsible for) one another: they all enjoin the doing of what is right and good and forbid the doing of what is wrong and evil..." (9:71).[15] In Islam, women may be members of the parliament, ministers, judges, and military and police officers.

The concept of Human rights as a benchmark for the development of humans across the globe in the present century has to travel a very unchequered path. Since the Magna Carta in England in June 1215 C.E., and the Bill of Rights there in 1689 C.E., several national documents have been issued in the West to give concrete shape to the concept of Human Rights, the culmination of which came out in the provisions about human rights in the "Declaration of Independence of the United States" in July 1776 and in the first ten amendments of the U.S. Constitution which became known as the Bill of Rights, adopting the name of the English Bill, the "Declaration of the Rights of Man and Citizen in France" in August 1789 following the famous French Revolution. At the end of the Second World War, an international effort was made to bring out the "Universal Declaration of Human Rights" by the General Assembly of the United Nations in 1948. In the subsequent years, other national documents and provisions followed in this direction. The Indian nationhood which came into being after years of struggle against colonialism on 15th August, 1947 incorporated these Human Rights in the Part Third of the Constitution of India which came into force on 26th January, 1950. In response to this trend, other international documents from the United Nations followed, such as the "International Covenant on Civil and Political Rights" and the "International Convention on Economic, Social and Political Rights", which were both approved by the General Assembly of the United Nations in December 1966 and made effective from July 15, 1967. In India, all the citizens of the country irrespective of caste, colour, sex, religion or region are equal sharer of Human Rights as given in the fundamental rights from article 14 to 32 of the Constitution.

Human Rights of Muslim Women in India: Constitutional Provision

The independent India sensitive to the concept of individual liberty, as such, soon after the declaration of Human Right Charter in 1948, India became signatory to it. The makers of our Constitution adopted Fundamental Rights to safeguard individual liberty and also ensured (together with the Directive Principles) social, economic and political justice for every citizen irrespective of caste, creed, sex or colour. So, the Constitution of India has embodied a number of Fundamental Rights in Part III of the Constitution, which are to act as limitations not only upon the powers of the executive but also upon the powers of the legislature. To this effect, the Supreme Court and the High Courts are made constitutionally competent enough to declare a law unconstitutional and void so far as it is in contravention of Fundamental Rights. These fundamental rights are in conformity with the universal declaration of human rights. Article 14[16] of the Constitution provides Equality Before Law and Equal Protection of Law, Article 15[17] prohibits discrimination against any citizen in any matter at the disposal of the state on any of the specific grounds, namely religion, race, caste, sex or place of birth. Article 16[18] is restricted to one aspect of public discrimination, namely, employment under the state. Article 17[19] abolishes Untouchability; Abolition of titles was effected through Article 18[20].

Apart from the rights flowing from the above prohibition, certain positive rights are conferred by the Constitution in order to promote the ideal of liberty held out by the Preamble. The foremost among these are the six fundamental rights in the nature of 'freedom' which are guaranteed to the citizens by Article 19[21], they are—(1) Freedom of speech and expression. (2) Freedom of assembly. (3) Freedom of association. (4) Freedom of movement. (5) Freedom of residence and settlement. (6) Freedom of profession, occupation, trade or business. Protection in respect of conviction for offences (Art. 20); Freedom of person (Art. 21); preventive detention (Art. 22); Right against exploitation (Art. 23); Prohibition of employment of children in factories etc. (Art. 24); Freedom of Conscience and free profession, practice and propagation of religion (Arts. 25-28); Cultural and educational rights (Arts. 29-30).[22] Besides, articles 32 and 226 ensure implementation of these above mentioned individual and human rights of the citizens through the constitutional remedies for enforcement of fundamental rights through writs and judicial processes such as *habeas corpus*, *mandamus*, prohibition, *certiorari* and *quo warranto*.

Despite the constitutional prohibition of any discrimination on the ground of sex and its subsequent reiteration in the 1966 UN Covenants on Human Rights and the 1979 UN Convention on the Elimination of All Forms of Discrimination against Women which have been ratified by the Government of India in 1979 and 1992 respectively, women are facing many disabilities and innumerable forms of discrimination. In spite of Qur'anic injunctions and constitutional provisions making no difference between the male and the female, in practice, scene is just the opposite. The concept of human rights is totally alien to Muslim women though they enjoy a better legal/theoretical position than their

Hindu counterparts. So far as giving share in landed property to women in India, Muslim women's rights are given a go by. It is held more in breach than in practice. Landed property is a sole prerogative of males only. Muslim male resent any attempt to deprive them of their land property right even when Qur'anic injunctions are invoked and attempts are made to enforce Shariah rules on giving inheritance rights to women. When our founding fathers were debating the adoption of Muslim Personal Law (Shariah) Application Act, 1937 in the Federal Assembly, there were entranced opposition to it from the landowning class of Punjab on the ground that the Bill would ruin agriculturists. Finally the Act was passed, which emphatically abrogated prevailing customs or usage concerning inheritance rights, *inter alia*, it explicitly excluded them from its purview agriculturally and, the devolution of which would continue to be governed by local customs. While the Act meant to extend women's property rights, it hardly served that purpose. It only served the political purpose of affirming Muslim identity.

The light of dawn on Indian Independence could not remove the corrosion of 1937 Act. The southern states of Tamil Nadu and Andhra Pradesh amended the same in 1949 to include agricultural land into it, followed by Kerala in 1963. Other states like Assam, Maharashtra, Gujarat and Bengal, had no strong preference of custom even before the Act was passed; so the Shariah rules could be applied to agricultural land as well. In several north-western states such as Uttar Pradesh, Punjab, Himachal Pradesh and Haryana, the Act has not been amended to include agricultural land. Despite the land reform laws, customs still govern the succession of such land. Thus, in these states severe gender inequalities still persist.

The separation of Muslim personal law in a secular state has caused many problems for Muslim women. The case in point is the infamous Shah Bano Case (1985), wherein the rights of Muslim women for maintenance was subjugated under the pressure from conservatives and the Government of India passed the Muslim Women's (Protection of Rights in Divorce) Act, 1986 which granted less generous rights to women than prescribed by the Qur'an and the Islamic jurisprudence. Such a position has led to aggravation and confusion in already poor condition of Muslim women in India.

Another case in point is the divorce law for Muslim women. The passage of the 1956 Hindu Code Bill has separated legal provision of Muslim and Hindu women and raised the position of Muslim men by leaving intact the provision of unilateral divorce and polygamy which is not only against the spirit of Qur'anic teaching but as per the 1994 Allahabad High Court ruling also unconstitutional.

In the field of education as the biasness against Muslim women is prominent as revealed through National Sample Survey and Census of India conducted from time to time. Muslim women are more backward than their counterparts in other religious communities or their male co-religionists. According to Census Report 2001[23] in the state of Uttar Pradesh, out of total population of 166 million only 57.36 per cent were literate. Male literacy was 70.23 per cent and female 42.98 per cent. The differential between female and male literacy is very high. Among Muslims, it is even worse; the total literacy rate is 47.8 per cent. Out of which 57.3 per cent are male and 37.47 per cent are female, these figures are irrespective of the fact that the state boasts of 20 universities, more than 400 affiliated colleges, a number of medical colleges and several institutes for specialized studies and research. The scenario for Muslims in education is bleak and below average, to say the least.

It would not be wrong to say that Muslim community, to the larger extent; are to be blamed for the pitiable education condition of women irrespective of government apathy and neglect. There is a definite precedence given to religious education in comparison to formal education among the poorest sections of Muslims. Religious ignorance and obscurantist cultural ethos have given rise to self-destructive orthodoxy which combines to keep Muslims education backward. Even the drop-out rate among the Muslim girls is higher compared to Muslim boys owing to early marriage, *purdah* system and non-availability of girl schools.

Prof. Qamar Hasan and M.N. Khan[24] of A.M.U. did a comparative study of the educational and vocational intentions of the Hindu and Muslim students on the verge of completing schooling in Aligarh (Table 11.1).

All these studies show that Muslims were unable to take advantage of the educational facilities provided by private, local or government institutions due to acute poverty, religious orthodoxy and non-availability of facilities.

Table 11.1: Dropouts of Muslims and Hindus

Class	*Dropout*	
	Boys	*Girls*
Muslim	4.5%	5.7%
Hindu	Nil	Nil

Conclusion

It can be said that existence of a huge corpus of law and even the religion sanctions are useless unless those laws and religious preaching are understood in a right earnest and cultural orthodoxy and backward looking approach are given a go-by through a copious dose of secular and scientific temperament aided and abetted by formal education. Our religious texts are to be understood in proper spirit to avoid religious obscurantist only then complete gender justice as desired by constitution of India and the glorious Qur'an can be justified.

Notes

1. The Holy Qur'an, *Text, Translation and Commentary* by Abdullah Yusuf Ali, Kitab Bhavan, Second Reprint, 1991, New Delhi. p. 714.
2. *Ibid.*, p. 178.
3. *Ibid.*, p. 25.
4. *Ibid.*, p. 345.
5. *Ibid.*, p. 345.
6. *Ibid.*, pp. 25-26.
7. *Ibid.*, p. 174.
8. *Ibid.*, p. 943.
9. *Ibid.*, p. 190.
10. *Ibid.*, p. 1115.
11. *Ibid.*, p. 1115.
12. *Ibid.*, pp. 1113-1114, 1121-1124.
13. *Ibid.*, p. 461.
14. *Ibid.*, p. 189.
15. *Ibid.*, p. 113.
16. Basu, D.D. (1993). *Introduction to The Constitution of India.* Prentice-Hall of India, Pvt. Ltd., New Delhi, p. 87.
17. *Ibid.* p. 90.
18. *Ibid.* p. 92.
19. *Ibid.* p. 93.
20. *Ibid.* p. 94.
21. *Ibid.* pp. 95-102.
22. *Ibid.* pp. 102-115.
23. Census of India, 2001.
24. Prof. Qamar Hasan and M.N. Khan of A.M.U. did a comparative study of the educational and vocational intentions of the Hindu and Muslim students on the verge of completing schooling in Aligarh.

12
Basic Notion of Islamic State and Politics

Meraj Ahmad Meraj

Introduction

Islam is a religion that takes account of all aspects of human life including personal, social, economic and political relationships among people. Islamic political system is constitutional by nature founded upon the conditions underlined by the *Shariah.* Islam supports directly or indirectly the constitutional type of government which is the closest version of political systems to Islam as it held people accountable. It legislates that such relationships are to be conducted in accordance with God's command. In this regard, Islam does not allow its members to live in isolation from other people. A Muslim who believes in God and in what has been sent down through His Prophet is required to communicate with the people around him. He has to be sensitive to what happens to other members of his society. Islam views change, as an inseparable part of our life and it should be allowed to take its natural course at both the individual and societal level. In Islam, no change would take place in any society without changing what is within the heart, soul and mind of its individuals. Individuals are essential for the existence of a society and for the changes of all aspects of life. Therefore, Islam gives more emphasis to change the individual of a society internally and externally both materially and immaterially. Islam proposes such concepts and processes to change the internal and the external natures of human beings. The inner nature of human beings constitutes soul and mind, while the external nature includes physical appearance, activities and relationships with one another.

Islam is the first call for all social changes. Islamic approach for change should include all aspects of life: political, economic, social, and moral. The Islamic political system based on the principles laid by the Qur'an. This study now focuses on the practical application of these concepts to human society. This includes the elements of the Islamic political system, the management of wealth and its role in achieving social equity, and finally, the applications of Islamic principles in regard to human relations. The study also particularly examine how Islamic notion of the state, government and its economic policy were intended to solve the current social and economic disparities and create justice in human society.

The Concept of Islamic State

The Islamic State is based on the Islamic ideology of humanity and derives its strength solely from that ideology. It is its main cause of progress and prosperity and the basis of its existence. The Islamic faith *'Aqeeda'* constitutes the foundation of the State and running of the government. Therefore, nothing is permitted to exist in the State's structure, political system, accountability, or any other aspect connected with the State that does not take the Islamic faith *Aqeeda* as its source. The Islamic *Aqeeda* is also the source of the State's constitution and laws implementation. The Islamic State came into existence and established itself in a powerful fashion due to the strength of Islam. It consolidated large areas of the world in the space of less than a century despite the fact that horses and camels were its only means of transportation, and all its conquered peoples and nations embraced Islam within a short period of time, despite the fact that its means of communication were limited to the word of mouth and pen. Islam made all this possible by being the driving force behind the State. The Islamic vision of an Islamic State government and polity is not a dream, nor is it a figment of the imagination, for it had dominated and influenced history for more than thirteen hundred years. It is a reality; it has always been and always will be. The vital elements of its existence are far greater than can be ignored or fought against by anything or anyone. The enlightened people have adopted it and it is the wish of the *Ummah* which is eager for the return of the glory of Islam. Those who truly tread the path of the Islamic call to restore the Islamic State would be aiming to assume the authority in order to resume the Islamic way of life in the Muslim lands and to convey the Message of Islam to the whole world. Islam as the solution to the social, economic and political problems of Muslim-majority countries, justice and prosperity envisioned through the implementation of *Shariah* Law and the establishment of an Islamic State. Ibn Taymiyya stressed in his book '*al-Siyäsa al-Shariyya*' that the establishment of an Islamic state is a religious duty. Regarding the goals of an Islamic state, he said: "The greatest goal of the Islamic state is to enjoin good and forbid evil: for example, performance of prayer, payment of *zakat,* fasting, truth, honesty, obedience to parents, good relations with kinsmen, good conduct within the household, with neighbours and with members of the society."[1] Therefore, the establishment of a Islamic state with a just government which obeyed God's commands is essential for cause of ground level true reform, be it moral, social, economic or any other, could never be achieved while power was in the hands of corrupt people.[2]

The Primary Structure of the Islamic State

The state is a complex web of organs, institutions and processes that are supposed to implement the policies that are adopted through the political process of each society. It signifies the continuity of institutions like the judiciary and administrative agencies, as distinguished from the government or regime of the day which is the product of current politics.[3] A state is a political organization with a centralized government that maintains a monopoly of the legitimate use of coercive force within a certain territory. The state institutions include the executive, the legislature, the judiciary, the finance and military or religious organizations.[4] The social institution of state is to carry out all issues which relate to the lives of human civilisation as per the law. From time immemorial, man has been carrying out the affair of his daily life. Thus, the state maintains the law and order, the administration and all the institutions which relate to the social life. When Islam emerged as a political power, The Prophet of Islam ruled over both Muslims and non-Muslims and he managed their affairs from the first day herest his foot in Madina city. Once the Islamic State was founded, he set about forming an Islamic society in which the welfare of the people was properly catered for. The state is ruled by Islamic precepts and thus become an Islamic state. Unlike the modern state the Islamic state is different in its nature. Islam and the concept of the Islamic state based on the *Shariah.* The Islamic State is one which is administered on the basis of 'Islamic principles' laid down in the *Shariah.* Islamic state has to adhere too and abide by the laws of God. The type of theocracy with which the Europe is acquainted, is different from theocracy in Islam. In European theocracy a religious class or a class of priests, frames laws and associate themselves with God. Theocracy which Islam preaches does not involve any priestly class. It is in the hands of the Muslim and those men who run their affairs as per the laws of God and the *Sunnah* of the holy Prophet. In an Islamic State, the God is the supreme sovereign and the implementation of His commands is essential goal of Islamic state. The executive and the legislator will be constituted as per the opinion of the people after consultations. In matters where the guidelines are not available in the *Shariah,* such matters would be resolved through consultation of *Shura.* It is, in this sense, this form of government is actual democracy. It is theocracy because neither the religious classes nor the common Muslim can change or alter the laws of God.[5]

The Key Features of an Islamic State

- ***Khilafat*:** The Arabic word *Kalifa* is a verbal noun of Caliphate, meaning succeeding someone, represents. In Islamic jurisprudence terminology, Caliphate means to consider everybody under the Islamic jurisprudence perspective in their worldly benefits and interests as well as in relation to the Hereafter. He is in reality a vicegerent of the Law-maker in safeguarding the religious and worldly affairs. A caliph is a person who applies the Islamic jurisprudence and ruling the Muslims in their religious and worldly matters. A caliph is a person who safeguards the foundation of Islam according to its well-established and everlasting principles. A caliph is a person who establishes the *Shariah* and safeguards all the interests of Muslims. In fact, he is the selected elected person who executes the rules and laws in an Islamic State.
- ***Consultative Council*:** A *Shura* 'Consultative Council' elected by the people has to assist and guide the elected Amir. It is obligatory for the *Amir* to administer the state with advice of his *Shura.* The Amir can retain office only so long as he enjoys the confidence of the people and must resign when loses this confidence. Every citizen has the right to criticize the Amir and his decision-making policy. The *Amir* is to be held all responsible before the people. All reasonable means for the expression of public opinion should be available.
- ***Legislation*:** Legislation in the Islamic state should be within the limits prescribed by the Sharia law. The duty of ascertaining the intent of these commandments which are open to more than one interpretation should develop on people possessing a specialized

knowledge of the *Sharia* law. Hence, such matters may have to be referred to a sub-committee of the *Shura* comprising men who are experts in the *Sharia* law. A huge scope would still be available for legislation on questions not covered by any specific injunctions of the *Sharia* and the advisory council or legislature is free to legislate in regard to these matters.

- ***Sharia Law***: At Islamic Law, State and political authorities have a responsibility to both the human beings they are required to protect and assist and to God to ensure that the rights and obligations prescribed in the *Sharia* are not violated without justification. This is self-evident in the fact that in the *Qur'an* almost every prohibition pertaining to the regulation of inter-human relations '*mu'amalat*' is accompanied by a justifying clause. The door is wide-open to the adoption of anything of utility, of whatever origin, so long as it does not go against the texts of the *Qur'an* and the *Sunnah*."[6]
- ***Judiciary***: In Islamic state, the judiciary is not placed under the control of the executive. It derives its authority directly from the *Sharia* and it is all answerable to God. The Judges appointed by the government, but once appointed they will have to administer justice impartially according to the *Sharia* law. All the organs and functionaries of the government in the Islamic state should come within their jurisdiction, even the highest executive authority of the government will be liable to be called upon to appear in the court of laws as a plaintiff or defendant. Rulers and ruled are subject to the same law and there can be no discrimination on the basis of position, power or privilege. Islam stands for equality and thoroughly adheres to this principle in the social, economic and political realms alike.

Executive and Legislature in the Islamic State

The responsibility for the administration of the government in the Islamic State is entrusted to an *Amir* 'leader' who may be likened to the president or prime minister in modern democratic system. All adult citizen of the state are entitled to cast their votes to select their leader.[7] The essential qualification for the election of the *Amir* are that he should command the confidence of the largest number of people in respect of his knowledge and grasp of the spirit of Islam. He should possess the Islamic attribute of fear of God. He should be endowed with the quality of statesmanship. In short, he should be both able and vistous. The essential characteristic of legitimate Islamic government is that it is subject to and limited by *Shariah* law. The integral relationship between the *Shariah* and Islamic political life, because the *Shariah* is the foundation and the government is the guard. If something has no foundation, it is bound to fall into ruins, and if something has no guard, it will be lost and destroyed. Consultation is an important pillar of Islamic socio-political system. All the affairs of the Islamic state like its constitution, its administration, election of the members of the parliament, president and other offices must be on the basis of consultation.

The Purpose of an Islamic State

The very purpose of the establishment of an Islamic state is to develop a complete system of social justice for its people. To establish social justice and equality, to maintain the law and order and to restore peace and harmony is one of basic characteristics of an Islamic state. The Islamic state shall establish a government, which will promote the good and eliminate the evil. The chief characteristics of an Islamic state shall be the protection of the freedom of expression of its citizens and safeguard their interest. An Islamic state shall not be totalitarian and autocratic in its nature like the modern forms of government. There shall not be any dictatorship, which squeezes the freedom of its citizens.[8] The most fundamental principle based on which an Islamic state can be conceptualised is the sovereignty of the universe which belongs to God and God alone. To substantiate his argument the following Qur'anic verses could be cited: "All authority to govern vest only with Allah. He has commanded that you serve none but Him."[9] "His is the creation and His is the Command."[10] "Do they now seek a religion other than that prescribed by Allah even though all that is in the heavens and the earth is in submission to Him?."[11] An Islamic state must strive to remove oppression and establish peace and harmony on the earth. [12] The Qur'an and *Sunnah* constitute the supreme Law of the Islamic State. These laws were revealed by God upon His messenger, Muhammad, who explained these divine commandments through his words and deeds. The Qur'an says: "O, men! Follow what has been revealed to you from your lord and follow no masters other than Him."[13] "Take whatever the Messenger gives you, and refrain from whatever he forbids you."[14] According to Mawlana Mawdudi, sovereignty is purely and totally for God and His Messenger. This law

'Shariah' has been given by Allah to all of His prophets according to their needs. Therefore, the Qur'an and the Sunnah constitute the 'Supreme Law' in Islam. This law is unalterable. It is the 'final authority'. In Islamic state nobody can challenge the 'Supreme Law'.[15] For administrative purposes, Muslims elect the best person among them and places the custody of his vicegerency in his hands. In other words it can be said that Muslims place their vicegerency in such a person who could implement the laws of God. Thus the elected vicegerent is accountable to Allah on one hand and to the men for his deeds and actions on the other. The Qur'an therefore, says, "Allah has promised those of you who believed and those righteous deeds that He will surely empower them as the vicegerents in the land even as He empowered those that preceded them, and that He will firmly establish their religion which He has been pleased to choose for them."[16]

The state in Islam is not intended for political administration only or for the fulfilment through it of the collective will of any particular set of people. Rather, Islam places a high ideal before the state for the achievement of which it must use all the means at its disposal. The aim is to encourage the qualities of purity, beauty, goodness, virtue, success and prosperity. The Islamic state can, thus, plan its welfare programmes in every age in any environment.[17] The constant demand made by Islam is that the principles of morality must be observed at all cost and in all walks of life. Islam laid down an unalterable requirement for the state to base its politics on justice, truth and honesty. It is important to note that the purpose of *Shariah* in jurisprudential theory is to ensure the welfare of the people. The welfare of the people according to *Shariah* law can be categorised into three basic principles.

- (*Dharuriyat*) Necessities,
- (*Hajiyyat*) Needs, and
- (*Kamaliyat*) Luxuries.

According to Islamic principles, the law and policies of the government must be fulfil these interests, in descending order of importance, first necessities, then needs, then luxuries. It is the incumbent duty of the Islamic state to extend these rights to its citizens, either Muslims or non-Muslim without any discrimination of religion, nation, colour or race. The Islamic state must promote love and peace and restrain from oppressions. They should treat hostile powers on friendly basis.[18] An Islamic state is required to maintain honesty in all its transactions with other nations.[19] This Islamic State should be founded upon the Islamic concepts and emotions, grounded in the Islamic faith *'Aqeedah'*. The Islamic mentality nurtured by Islamic thought and rationally shaped by the Islamic ideology and method should be present in its citizenry. The incentives to adhere to the *Shariah* should originate from the inner self. This Islamic disposition would ensure the voluntary implementation of the system and its rules with passion, zeal and peace of mind. This State must be Islamic both at the level of the *Ummah* and that of the people in authority. It must be Islamic in all aspects of its life, securing the resumption of the Islamic way of life in a manner which would enable her to carry its Message to the whole world. The only way to establish the Islamic State is to carry the Islamic Message and to work towards the resumption of the Islamic way of life, which necessitates taking the Islamic countries altogether as one unit because the Muslims are but one *Ummah,* which represents a human group bound by one faith *'Aqeedah'* from which emanates her system. Any task carried out in any Muslim country, touching on the emotions and concepts should, therefore, have its effects in all the other Muslim countries. The issue is in fact the existence of the Islamic State which implements Islam as a system emanating from the Islamic faith *'Aqeedah'* a State which implements Islam according to the *Shariah* rules, since these are the rules of Allah. Thus, the Islamic way of life would initially be resumed at home and the Islamic Message would come to be conveyed to all the peoples abroad.

Fundamental Rights in Islamic State

The rights of citizenship in Islam are not confined to persons born within the limits of its state but are granted to every Muslim irrespective of his place of birth. A Muslim *Ipso facto* becomes the citizen of an Islamic state as soon as he enters in the territory of Islamic state with the intention of living there. He can enjoy with equal rights of citizenship with those who are its citizen by birth. Maulana Abul A'la Mawdudi observes that citizenship must be common to all the citizens of all the Islamic states that existing in the world.[20] Every Muslim must be regarded as eligible for the position of the highest responsibility in an Islamic state with distinction of race, colour or class.[21] Islam does not seek to restrict human rights or privileges to the geographical limits of its own state. Islam has laid down universal fundamental rights for humanity as whole which are to be observed and respected in all circumstances irrespective of whether a person lives on the territory of the Islamic state or outside it and whether he is a at peace with the state or at war. Islam never allows to oppress women, children, old people, women honour and chastity must be respected in all circumstances and hungry must be fed and the ill people must be treated medically.[22] Islam is the first religion to confirm the concept of universal fundamental rights. There are several Qur'anic verses which guarantee the life, honour, dignity, property, freedom of faith, right to criticism, freedom of speech, protection against injustice and discrimination against caste, creed and religion.

Non-Muslim Rights in Islamic State

The terms majority and minority are being used in modern democratic state. Islamic state being an ideological state such term cannot be used but they should be referred to as Muslims and non-Muslims. Islam clearly defines the rights of the non-Muslims living in an Islamic state. It is the duty of the Islamic state to protect their life, honour and dignity, freedom of religion, equality before the civil laws for both Muslims and non-Muslims, freedom in matters of personal law, liberty to carry out their religious rituals and maintenance of their religious places. Islam has given full human rights to the Non-Muslims who resides in an Islamic state and these rights must treated as essential fundamental rights from part of the Islamic constitution.[23] According to Islamic terminology the Non-Muslims who reside in the Islamic state are called *"Dhimmis"* 'the Covenanted' implying that the Islamic state has entered into a covenant with them and guaranteed their fundamental rights. The life, property and honour of *'Dhimmis'* must be protected and respected in exactly the same way as that of a Muslim citizen of the state. There is no difference in Muslim and Non-Muslim citizens in respect of civil or criminal law. The Islamic state has no rights to interfere with the personal law of Non-Muslims. They will have full freedom of conscience and belief and will have to perform their religious rites and rituals. Not only this, Non-Muslims had complete freedom to criticize the Islamic system while the civil law of the Islamic state has to be fully respected and all criticism has to be made within its constitutional framework. The Qur'an does not differentiate between the sanctity of a Muslim and that of non-Muslim. As the Qur'an repeatedly asserts, no human being can limit the Divine mercy in any way or even regulate who is entitled to it.[24] The nature of and grounds for political obligation in Islam is the establishment of an Islamic state.

The Law of the Islamic State

Shariah is the God's law. It is represented by a set of normative principles, methodologies for the production of legal injunctions, and a set of positive legal rules. *Shariah* encompasses a veriety of schools of thought and approaches, all of which are equally valid. Nevertheless, *Shariah,* as a whole, with all its schools and variant points of view, remains the way and law of God. Although politics and religion are inseparable in the teachings of Islam, and the establishment of the first Islamic state in Medina by the Prophet of Islam confirmed this—there are Muslims who are still at the crossroads of political issues. They believe that Islam should not be associated with social and political affairs. Therefore, Syed Qutb's critical discussion on the need to establish an Islamic community leading to the creation of a state, is to be seen to break the deadlock based on the belief that power wielded according to the *Shariah* of God brought more modesty into politics and more attention to justice in human society. Syed Qutb characterized religion as a way of life sent down by God to organize human affairs, and to guide people to a true path. It is not a mere emotional belief, cut off from the actual domain of human life, but the implementation of what God has revealed in the Qur'an, including the enforcement of *Hudud.* Had refers to any penalty that is not prescribed in the Qur'an and its enforcement is dependent on the discretionary power of the judge, as laid down in the *Shariah* law.[25] In the dictum of Muslim jurist, *Shariah* is considered the foundation of law and politics is its protector. Muslim jurist often assert that religion if the foundation and political authorities are its protector. Muslim jurist insist that the rulers ought to consult with jurists on all matters related to law, but jurist themselves never demanded the right of the rule the Islamic state directly. *Shariah* law fulfils the criteria of justice and legitimacy. It binds the governed and governor alike. Because it is based on the rule of the law and thus deprived human beings of arbitrary authority over each other, the caliphate system is considered superior to any other. The institution of the state is subordinate to the religious community and can be even considered to be its instrument because, in Islam, sacred law comes before any idea of social and political organisation.[26] In this context, Islamic law '*Shariah*' is not only a religious imperative but it also embraces the juridical, political and social dimensions of community life.

Sources of the Islamic Law *Shariah*

1. ***Kitab, The Qur'an:*** The Qur'an is the foremost and supreme

source of Islamic law. The Qur'an deals with number of subjects such as social, cultural, spiritual and moral levels. It deals with subjects not only at the given social but also at moral levels. Therefore, it is important to note that Qur'an has to be understood not only in the context in which the verses were revealed but also at different levels when these were expressed. Thus, Qur'an is the great source of law in all concerned period, time and place.

2. ***Sunna: The Tradition of Prophet:*** The second major formal source of Islamic law is the *Sunna.* This word means 'Practice', 'Tradition' or 'Precedent' and derives from stories that relate to the behaviour of the Prophet Muhammad and of his companions. These stories record the minutiae and detail of how the Prophet and his Companions sought to live their lives in accordance with the newly promulgated religious order propounded by the Qur'an. Particularly important amongst these stories are those which relate to the Prophet himself in which he is not infrequently being asked to arbitrate disputes or decide questions of law.
3. ***Ijma:*** **'Consensus':** The third source of Islamic law is *'Ijma'* which means 'consensus'. The technical term *'ijma'* comes from a root jama'a, that means "to bring together" and in the fourth conjugation, jama'a "to agree together." Thus, *Ijma* means literally "unanimous agreement" or "total consensus." *Ijma* also means consensus on rules of law claimed to be derived from either the Qur'an or the Sunna. *Ijma* may take one or two forms which are analytically distinct.[27]
4. ***Qiyas, Analogy:*** The fourth root of Islamic law is a system of logical reasoning called Qiyas. Qiyas, originally signified the derivation of rules of law by analogy with earlier rulings found in the either Qur'an or the Sunna. The oldest juristic analogies were rather crude. For instance an attempt to fix five dirhams (by analogy with five fingers) as the minimum value of stolen goods which could incur the Qur'anic penalty of amputation of the hand. But, later on, analogies became more sophisticated and the art of Qiyas developed into an elaborate system which included many other kinds of rhetorical argument besides analogy.[28]

Objectives of the Shariah Law

Islamic Law strives to fulfil with respect to the human life as well as the specific aims that particular legal injunctions have been set down in order to achieve. The general objectives of Islamic Law are those that aim at realizing the general human welfare, both in this world and in the hereafter. This is achieved by Islamic Law through the legislation of a body of legal injunctions. The specific objectives of Islamic Law are those that Islamic Law seeks to realize in a narrower domain of human activity, such as economics, family life, or the political order. This is achieved through specific legislation aimed at dealing with particular issues. There are many objectives of the *Shariah* which can be summarised as follows:

- The *Shariah* protects basic human rights for all members of the community irrespective of race, religion and culture. This protection is important to preserve a harmonious living in the community. Traditional scholars have classified these rights as faith *'Iman'*, life *'hayah'*, progeny *'nasab'*, property 'maal', and intellect '*aql*'. The protection of these five rights will ensure the freedom of faith and uphold the sanctity of life. It will also affirm and validate the importance of familial ties and protection of assets and uphold rational and true reasoning of the mind.
- The *Shariah* aims to establish justice between Muslims and the rest of humanity. Indeed, justice is the true essence of Islamic teachings which has been repeatedly mentioned in the Qur'an. With justice on earth, people will live in peace and harmony. The *Shariah* teaches that all human beings are equal and that nobody is superior above the other because of religion, race, wealth and family. This equality is among the key messages of Prophet Muhammad in his Last Sermon.
- The *Shariah* aims to provide benefits 'maslahah' for human beings and removing hardships 'al-usr' from them. Bringing about benefits and removing harm is essential in establishing a harmonious society. Protection of the basic rights mentioned earlier, brings benefit and violating them will cause hardships in the society. For example, adultery is prohibited as it violates the sanctity of the family while alcohol consumption has the potential to damage a person's intellectual capacity that could lead to the abuse of other people's right.

Shariah norms is worthy of consideration when determining the protection and assistance secured by forced migrants at Islamic Law. The principle of *maqasid al-Shariah* holds that the main objective of the *Sharia* is to promote human welfare.[29] *Maslahah* is understood by many of today's Islamic jurists to contain "the seeds of the future of the *Shariah* and its viability as a living force in society. [30] The doctrine of *Maslahah* can strike balance between the highly idealistic levels of expectation from the government on the part of the public and the efforts of the latter to identify more meaningfully with Islam.[31] The Qur'anic verse stating that "God has ordained a law *Shariah* and assigned a path '*minhaj*' for each of you."[32] It supports this theory, the path being the approach (purpose and objective) of how to interpret all norms presented in the *Shariah*. For example, the overarching and consistent message presented throughout the Qur'an is that human beings should enjoin "justice, charity, kindness and peace among men.[33] ... do what is right.[34] ... help one another.[35] ... and do good works."[36] The purpose of the Islamic Law is for humans to achieve happiness in this world and the hereafter, by following the law of adopting the good and neglecting the bad. Islamic law protects wealth and safeguards it from corruption so it can fulfil its necessary and indispensable role in the order of human life and facilitate the growth of civilization. Its place is just like that of the other necessities of life, for together they form the basis of human life and civilization. If they are not properly managed and preserved, the world would fall into ruin and the positive contributions of human civilization would come to a halt.

Implementation of Sharia Law

The *Shariah* laws would be effective only in an environment *'bay'a'* where there is Amir or *khalifa* who applied the law legitimately along with the governed, who accepted its application to their social and economic affairs. The original idea of Islam and the method by which this idea is implemented had become vague. The Muslims could not correctly perceive the Qur'an and the *Sunnah* and began to think that Islam was merely a spiritual religion. They began comparing Islam with other religions from a spiritual point of view, instead of looking at Islam as being an belief *'Aqeedah'* and a complete way of life. Only a clear understanding of Islam would bring back the Islamic State. The maintenance of the State would rely on its strength of safeguarding such a clear understanding, and the proper implementation of its *Shariah* at home and the conveyance of its Message of Islam to the world. Religion and politics are inseparable in the teachings of Islam since religious regulations, being related to the law and the administration of justice among the people according to God's command could not be established without an authority to uphold God's commands and apply them to the reality of human life. Authority over the affairs of the people is the greatest religious duty. In fact religion cannot be established at all without this authority because Allah has prescribed as a duty the enjoining of good, the prohibition of evil and the support of the oppressed. In the same way, all that He has prescribed in terms of fighting for His sake, the establishment of justice and the enforcement of the penal code cannot be implemented without power and authority."[37] The two central charges of failure have been political Islam's inability to provide an effective blueprint for an Islamic state based on a *Shariah* law code and the abandonment of the pan-Islamic or caliphate model in favour of acquiescence to a world order based on nation-states.[38] This is largely a failure only to the extent that it has not met the vision of Maududi and Qutb. The issue of an Islamic state based on the implementation of *Shariah* law has been so central to political Islam and continues to be a yardstick against which Islamic political parties in so called Islamic countries. Following Ibn Taymiyya's view, al-Mawdudi views that the realization of the objectives of the *Shariah* is simply impossible without the agency of the state and the power that it commands. In his view: Any reform, which Islam wants to bring about, cannot be carried out merely by sermons. Political power is essential for their achievement; the struggle for obtaining control over the organs of the state when motivated by the urge to establish the religion and the Islamic *Shariah* and to enforce the Islamic injunctions, is not only permissible but is positively desirable and as such obligatory."[39] The application of the *Sharia* must be approached in accordance with the spirit of justice, kindness and charity which God through the *Qur'an* has called for and the Prophet Mohammed (PBUH) through his actions, sayings and demeanour upheld throughout his life at all times.

The Political Dimension of Islam

Islam has established fundamental principles of state politics, whose application throughout the centuries has been based on the clear understanding of them, interpreting them and being bound by them. Islam was associated with power from the very beginning, from the first formative years of the Prophet and his immediate successors. This association between religion and power, community and polity, can already be seen in the Qur'an itself and in the other early religious tenets on which Muslims base their beliefs.[40] In an Islamic political system there is no place for monarchy or dictatorship.[41] The government of the righteous caliphs is a consultative government because all the four caliphs consulted the companions of *Madinah* in legislative, administrative, and all other matters of the state. The members of the consultative body were free to express their opinion whether for or against the caliph.

Principles of Islamic Political System

Islam and politics were inseparable and the struggle to gain authority *'Sultah'* is essential to enable people to follow God's way *'Manhaj'*. Many scholars strongly advocate that political power is necessary to enforce Islam fully in personal and social life. Scholars like al-Mawdudi, al-Ghazali and Ibn Taymiyya are of this opinion. These scholars outlined several characteristics and principles upon which the political system of Islam is based. They emphasize only the major characteristics which, according to them, are the most essential elements applicable to Muslims of this modern age who are facing social and political disparity. They held the view that the characteristics of Islamic politics are applicable in all circumstances of Muslims' lives, whether they were living in a society, a community or a state. Their views, in the political system of Islam, therefore, can be discussed under the following headings:

1. God's Sovereignty *(Hakimiyyat Allah).*
2. Caliphate or Imamat Government *(Hukumat al-Khilafawa al-Imama).*
3. Consultative Government *(Huumat al-Shura).*
4. Pledge of allegiance *(Bay'a).*
5. Obedience *(Tä a).*
6. Justice and Equality *(al-Adlwa al-Musawàt).*

1. God's Sovereignty (*Hakimiyyat Allah*): The idea of God's sovereignty is widely stressed on the doctrinal concept as well as on questions regarding the socio-political aspects of Muslim society, including the establishment of the Muslim community and the Islamic state. Islam is a religion of faith and practice *'Aqida* and *Sharia'* where both should run parallel in Muslim life. Therefore, it is obligatory for every Muslim to believe in the sovereignty of God since it is one of His attributes and His authority *'Uluhiyya'*. To put this belief into practice, Muslims have to refer to the *Shariah* of God to govern their daily lives. If one analyses the terminology of modern political science, the word sovereignty means a complete suzerainty. Though it has numerous definitions, all signify the highest governmental and legal authority of some sort.[43] The concept of sovereignty in modern political thought, defined it sovereignty as the supreme owner of the state over citizens and subject, unrestrained by law. Sovereignty has also been defined as the supreme political power in one whose acts are not subject to any other and whose will cannot be overridden.[44] These definitions show that if a person or an institution is to be "sovereign", then it would follow that the word of that institution or person is law. A "sovereign" has also an undisputed right to impose orders on people living under his or her rule, who are under an absolute obligation to obey any command from him, willingly or unwillingly. Islam by its very nature opposes to the idea that an individual or community had full power to legislate or claim absolute, permanent sovereignty, because only God is sovereign over the entire universe and so has the ultimate power.[45] This meant in an Islamic society, the political authority is subject to the divine laws *"Shariah."* Thus, an Islamic state has neither the independence to conduct its foreign policies, nor it has the exclusive right to lay down its domestic policies, for its authority is restrained by the *Shariah*. It became clear that the major struggle between Islam and human society is over the question of "sovereignty", in which people began to misuse its meaning and claim for themselves an attribute which belong to God alone. This sovereignty must, therefore, be manifested in the reality of human society. By doing so, people would have fulfilled their duty as God's servants in that they showed total respect for God as their Master, and their Ruler *'Amir'*. The sovereignty in God meant that people were God's vicegerents on earth, and their mission in life is to establish and carry out the commands of the Sovereign. In the context of state, this meant that the imam, or those who are in authority, has the power to lead their people and apply to them the law of *Shariah*. This is because only in the command and *Shariah* of God would people find justice in the real sense, since it was not influenced by any human desires. All people are equal and treated justly before the lawof God.[46] It is, therefore, logical that the *Shariah* is the only law to be followed and implemented in human society instead of man-made laws. Another important principle to be derived from the above is that no one had the right to claim absolute, permanent and indivisible sovereignty, because God was the only sovereign over the entire universe and had all the attributes of ultimate power. This implied that political authority is also subject to God's law, which provides its basis. Human beings as God's vicegerents have only one choice: that of exercising God's law. The power of exercising this trust was given only to the *Imam* who was chosen or appointed with the consent of all members of the community to judge with justice.[47] Therefore, it seems that the real holders of authority are the people, and the Imam is appointed by the community only for exercising the authority vested in them. This, in fact, is the most significant step towards a representative government which is commissioned to carry out God's mandate. It also implies that the leader has a right to be obeyed, as the above verse describes, as long as he does not deviate from the basic instruction of the *Shariah.* Al-Mawdudi held a similar view with Qutb that the political system of Islam was based on God's sovereignty, not man-made law. In addition, al-Mawdudi himself clearly indicated that the legislative sovereignty of God must become the foundation of the Islamic state, it is incumbent on every citizen of the Islamic state who claims to be a follower of Islam to accept the moral guidance of Allah and obey the commands and injunctions of God in socio-economic and political life as laid down in the Holy Qur'an and the Sunna of the holy Prophet.[48] Al-Mawdudi maintained that there were ten conditions regarding public affairs which are binding on the imam. They included:

- to guard the *deen* religion as it was established in its original form;
- to execute legal judgment between two contestants and bring them back to the path of God; and
- to establish the add punishments to maintain justice.

The Amir, on the other hand, will always remember his being merely a trustee to exercise God's trust in accordance with His *Manhaj.* Therefore, the Amir claims to absolute power will no longer be heard in human society, since all know that God's power overrules them. Thus peace and justice will be established.

2. Caliphate or Imamate Government ***(Hukumat al-Khilafawa al-Imama):*** According to Arabic lexicon, *Khilafat* means 'representation'. The word *Khalifa* (caliph) is a title given to the

Muslim leader, literary means successor or deputy. According to Islam, Man is the representative of God on the earth and His vicegerent. This is to say the virtue of powers delegated to him by God. He is required to exercise the God-given authority in this world within the limits prescribed by the God. There are many verses of the Qur'an which mention the role of human beings as God's vicegerents on this earth. The holy Qur'an says: "And (remember) when your Lord said to the angels: Verily, I am going to place (mankind) generations after generations on earth." They said: "Will You place therein those who will make mischief therein and shed blood, while we glorify You with praises and thanks and sanctify You." He (Allah) said: "I know that which you do not know."[49] One of the famous Qur'anic commentator and Islamic scholars Hasan al-Basri, viewed the vicegerency of Prophet Adam and his descendants as their role as God's successors to settle the earth and to rule it justly in accordance with God's command,[50] whereas Syed Qutb maintained that the concept of *Istihklaf* (the appointment of human beings as God's vicegerents) on this earth referred to people's capability to develop their lives here and reform them in accordance with God's command. It also referred to their capability to realize justice on this earth.[51] Syed Qutb views that the establishment of a *khilafat* government is necessary to achieve harmony throughout human society on this earth. The vicegerency of humankind entailed ruling this earth justly and making judgements in accordance with God's commands. The one who assumed this responsibility was known as the *khalifa* or Imam. The vicegerency of human beings and their duty to rule this earth were also related to the management of the universe. This meant that God created them and imposed upon them the divine duty to carry out His commands so that their lives would run in parallel with the rest of God's creation. Syed Qutb always reminded Muslims to study carefully the Islamic theory about the universe, life and humankind and their correlation before discussing other human social relations, because Islam and all it doctrines, legislation and ritual are built on this fundamental idea. Since the government itself represented Muslims in executing God's command, the *khalifa* or *Amir*, who is selected to lead the government, held the same responsibility. The only difference between the *khalifa* and other Muslims was that the former had the power to enforce the *Shariah* of God and punish those people who deviated from the right path and bring them back to the teachings of Islam. It is, therefore, mandatory that made the *khalifa* or the *Imam* eligible to be obeyed by all. The Obedience to the *khalifa* constituted a Qur'anic in junction. This is because after the Prophet there are only the Qur'an and his *Sunnah* as the main sources of legislation for Muslim society. The *khalifa's* role is to implement the *Shariah* of God as stated in the Qur'an and the *Sunnah* so as to maintain obedience to God and His Prophet. The term *Imam* to refer to those who led an Islamic government. The *Imam* is the one who led the people to the way of God, guided them to the right path and showed a good example to them in conduct and, more importantly, religious commitment. This clearly signified that only those who work for justice and execute the law of God are eligible to be *Imam,* not those who oppressed other people. The most important criteria in appointing the *Imam* is religious commitment and readiness to be a just *Imam,* not that of family ties and blood relations. Thus, faith *'aqida'* and justice are the most important criteria for the *Imamat,* so that any person coming to the post would be from among the God-fearing and ready to execute the *Shariah* of God in human affairs. In regard to the way the *khalifa* or Imam comes into being. Syed Qutb stressed that its appointment should be through the *Shura* system. This is because the holder of that post represented the whole Muslim community to uphold God's command and put it into the practice. Therefore, the appointment is subject to the will of the people, whose duty would be to supervise and observe their leader's application of the *Shariah.* It is not belligerent act to be permitted against the *khalifa* or *Imam* until he deviates from the basic instructions of the *Shariah.*[52] Since the government itself is based on *Shura* system and the Imam is appointed by a majority of *Shura* members, the emergence of another Imam within the same territory, assuming him to be a transgressor. The role of the Imam was to maintain justice, unity and solidarity among the members of the community and also to look after their welfare. It would be impossible to do this job effectively if someone else claimed to be imam. Once an *Imam* had been selected to lead the Muslims and had been given a *bay'a,* no other person could hold the post. Rather, the transgressor was to be fought to bring him back to obey the one Imam. Since *Shura* is one of the principles of the caliphate government, any matters concerning Muslims should be discussed first with the Imam, who would then decide how to proceed. The role of the Imam as being the focal point to which everyone referred their problems. It is then for the Imam to decide, after holding a counsel with the *Shura* members, what should be done to solve the problem. The post of Imam does not mean that one could act freely in the administration of the state. Rather, the

Imam should always have the consent of the people that he might act in accordance with their desires, enjoining good and forbidding evil, part of the purpose of human existence on earth as God's vicegerents.[53]

3. Consultative Government ***(Hukumat al-Shura):*** The institution of *Shura* is considered one of the most important principles in the political system of Islam. History has shown that *Shura* played an important role in the political development of the early Islamic state in Medina. The Prophet of Islam himself continually consulted his companions in almost all daily affairs of state which proves that no one in Islam has absolute authority over the affairs of the Muslim community. Although the Prophet received direct commands from God concerning the governing of the state, he was still required to consult his people on the conduct of his government. The Qur'an says: "to hold a counsel with other Muslims, and consult them about the affairs. Then when you have taken a decision, put your trust in Allah, certainly, Allah loves those who put their trust in Him." [54] Furthermore, many of the Prophet's sayings '*ahadeeth*' emphasize the importance of *Shura* and its contribution towards just and sound decision-making, as one can see from the following *hadith* in which the Prophet is reported to have said, after the revelation of the above verse: "Although Allah and His messenger are in no need of it consultation." "Allah has made it a mercy for my people; and whoever holds council among them, lie will not be deprived of right guidance and whoever neglects it will not be devoid of error."[55]

The institution of *Shura* began during the Prophet's time. The first verse to be revealed about the subject of *Shura* when the Qur'an said: "And those who answer the call of their Lord, and perform and who conduct their affairs by mutual consultation and who spend of what we have bestowed on them."[56] This means *Shura* is one of basic features of the Islamic way of life in general and is not confined to political activities. Every Muslim should discuss with others the problems of every aspect of life. To do so, Muslims need to understand fully the necessity of *Shura* and its position as one of the criteria of faith, so that mutual consultation will accord with Islamic principles.[57] The importance of *shura* in Muslim life, for its position had been mentioned together with performing prayer, which is an obligatory duty for every Muslim. The Qur'an already regarded *Shura* as one of the criteria of faith. In other words, there would be no perfection of individuals' faith unless they use the *Shura* in their affairs.[58] *Shura* comprises consultation and evaluation of opinions by members of society to reach the best decision on their affairs. In politics, both the imam and the governed are obliged to consult one another regarding administration of their state so that the decisions made are acceptable to all its citizens. If the *Shura* decision represents the majority voice in the Islamic political system, how does it compare with Western democracy, where the majority voice is only taken into account in decision-making process? Syed Qutb contends that *Shura* is instituted for the benefit of all Muslim affairs, where none of the *Shura* committee members had a personal interest in every decision made. In addition, these committee members were not allowed to dispute decisions that had already been made and agreed to by the majority. This phenomenon does not happen under the democratic system, since the parliament's voice, represented the interests of some capitalists or other influential figures who already controlled the government and all the members of parliament.[59] Al-Mawdudi argued that the general principles of Islam must be explained first so that Muslims would not have a vague perception of their own religion. Al-Mawdudi outlined two important facts that every Muslim should bear in mind: first, Islam was neither a religion mixed with other ideological beliefs nor the product of any human mind. It was a universal religion whose objective was to create and cultivate in humankind equality and Islamic attitudes. Secondly, the Islamic principles regarding every aspect of human society were interrelated on the basis of the oneness *tawhid* of God.[60] According to Syed Qutb, the Islamic political system based on *Shura* did not emerge from a vacuum. It came into being as a result of a well-trained and educated community, whose members had a strong faith in God. But the principle of *Shura* would not work effectively in a society based on un-Islamic principles, whose members knew nothing about that important element of Islamic governmental system and did not know how to choose a good leader to represent them.[61] Since *Shura* was based on co-operation, brotherhood and solidarity among Muslims, it would, therefore, prevent the exploitation of power by the mam, because any decision made by him represented the views of other people too. What was clear was that the principle of *Shura* signified that under an Islamic government there existed a means of a collective decision-making regarding the administration of the state.

4. Pledge of Allegiance *(Bay'a)*: *Bay'a,* is an Arabic word derived from the root *bay'a,* a technical term, it has been defined in various ways. Ibn Khaldun, for instance, defined it as a commitment to give obedience to the ruler.[62] *Bya'a* is also defined as taking an oath to observe what has been prescribed in the Qur'an and the *Sunna* of the

Prophet and to perform the duties required by them.[63] They agree to accept him as their *Amir* leader, to obey his orders and to work with him in protecting the state from its enemies. In fact, it was a kind of *bay'a* in Medina, when they accepted the Prophet (pbuh) as their religious and political leader and undertook to protect him from all his enemies.[64] The importance of *bay'a* in an Islamic government has been specifically mentioned in the Qur'an and *Sunna* of the Prophet (pbuh) for example, this verse of the Qur'an clearly says: "Verily, those who give pledge to you O, Muhammad, are giving pledge to Allah. The Hand of Allah is over their hands."[65] From the *Sunna* of the Prophet one finds that the Prophet himself practiced this principle, when, before migrating to Medina, he made an allegiance with the people of that city. In Medina, once the Islamic state had been established, the Prophet began to take allegiance with its citizens, including the people of the books—the Jews and Christians. These events prove that '*bay`a'* allegiance is an important element of an Islamic government since it indicated an agreement between the imam and the governed people to struggle together for the improvement in everyone's welfare. No Muslim becomes a *Khalifa* without the *Bay'a* and the Islamic State followed that rule until the last days of its reign. The application of the *Bay'a* is varied. In some cases, the *Khalifa* was given the *bay'a* directly. The Amir or Imam agreed to uphold God's command in his administration and to lookafter the welfare of his people in accordance with the requirement of the law of God. It is clear from the above principles of *bay'a* that the governed have to obey and assist the Amir or Imam in maintaining and protecting the state from external and internal attacks and to struggle together with him, to maintain the unity of all members within their boundaries, Muslim and non-Muslim. According to Syed Qutb, the '*bay`a*' in fact, is an agreement or a contract in Muslim society between Muslims themselves or between Muslims and people of other religious beliefs. In the context of the government, Syed Qutb viewed *bay'a* as an agreement between the imam and the governed, in which both agreed to work and co-operate for the betterment of their state and achieve God's blessings on all their affairs. The Imam agreed to follow God's defined law in his government, and the governed agreed to obey and co-operate with Imam. Obedience was required only for righteous deeds 'al-birr' and the fear of God *'al-taqwa'* and not for any wrongdoing.[67]

5. Obedience ***(Täah):*** One of the important characteristic of the Islamic government is obedience by the governed people to their *Imam.*

In this regard, obedience to the Amir or Imam becomes obligatory once the governed have given their allegiance to him. This concept is important because the existence of an Islamic State would be meaningless if its Imam ruled justly according to the *Shariah* law but there is no obedience from his people. The *Imam* constituted one of the religious obligations of every Muslim. The Qur'an first taught Muslims the particular importance of Imam and Islam. Then it described the system for managing their lives in accordance with God's command, and how it differed from that based on *Jahiliyya.* It is believed that obedience to the Prophet constituted one of the conditions of Imam and Islam itself. Ignoring this religious injunction would not only have prevented them from being true believers but also classed them with the liars in their declaration of faith. The Qur'an describes the nature of obedience in Islam: it is not merely obedience to any imam or ruler without certain limitations and conditions. Rather, it teaches Muslims a true form of obedience that brings a peace and harmony to both the imam and his people. More importantly, such obedience is in line with the requirements of Imam and Islam regarding the government. The Qur'an says: "O, you who believe! Obey Allah and obey the Messenger Muhammad and those of you (Muslims) who are in authority. (And) if you differ in anything amongst yourselves, refer it to Allah and His Messenger, if you believe in Allah and in the last Day. That is better and more suitable for final determination." (Both the Qur'an and the *Sunna* are therefore, reference by Muslims seeking God's guidance to solve problems that could not be solved with their own knowledge.[70] Moreover, by referring to the *Shariah* of God, Muslims would not lose their way in their search for the truth. It would be the role of the Qur'an and the *Sunna* of the Prophet to guide people and act as a final reference to unite everyone's opinion to reach a unanimous conclusion. The obedience to those in authority as the above verse describes, is conditional and would depend on how far the Imam followed the *Shariah* law in his government. There are several sayings of the Prophet which clearly showed that there is no absolute obedience to the command of the Imam. According to a *hadith* narrated by *Yahyä al-Qattän,* the Prophet said: "A Muslim must listen whether he likes it or not, unless he is commanded to disobey God."[71] In that case he must neither listen nor obey, The Imam's right to obedience existed when he followed the *Shariah* of God and the *Sunna* of the Prophet. The Imam and the governed needed one another in the administration of the government. There would be no just *Imam* if none of his people obeyed him. Nor could there be any justice for the governed and society as a whole if they are led by an unjust *Imam* who knew only how to oppress and exploit people for his own economic and political interests. Another important principle to be derived from the above discussion is the administration of an Islamic government is always overshadowed by God's *Shariah.* There is no room left for the Imam to act freely in administrative matters, since he was always required to follow the path '*Manhaj'* of God to govern human life as a whole.

6. Justice and Equality: ***(al-Adlwa al-Musawat):*** Equality is one of the most important characteristics of an Islamic government. The implementation of justice and equality was a religious duty for the *Amir* or *Imam* who would lose his right to the post if he did not fulfil that duty. In other words, the *Imam* has to be just in his government because performing justice is one of the conditions of the post. If he deviated, his right to the post would cease. Justice on the part of the *Imam* is also a religious duty in that it indicated the fulfilment of the allegiance that he has been given by his people. Therefore, any deviation would mean a breach of the agreement with the people who have given their allegiance. Islam clearly gives particular attention to justice in government and emphasizes the heavy responsibility borne by the Imam the aim of the criteria attached to the *imamat* was to create peace and harmony for all members of the community. These strict conditions would at least make the imam feel responsible for leading his people to the right path, following God's command, since he would know that *Imamat* itself was a trust that needed to be fulfilled in the right way, the *Imam* to play a vital role in maintaining justice and equality in the affairs of the people. Moreover, it is the power granted to the Imam that enabled him to direct the affairs of his people in line with God's command.[72] There is no discrimination in colour, family ties or race in their application of the *Shariah* law. This meant that no one was above the shad a law, not even the Prophet or his relatives. Justice in the administration—of the Islamic government also required the imam to be fair in passing judgment on his people and their activities. The *Shariah* laws must be applied to everyone impartially regardless of sex, colour, wealth, blood ties and even religious belief. Everyone became equal before the law. The Qur'an clearly states: "when you judge between men, you judge with justice."[73] The application of justice is not only a religious duty of the *Imam;* it also constituted a valuable attribute of a Muslims. Therefore, every Muslim, regardless of social status or personal circumstances was required in Islam to uphold justice, even to an enemy. Despite the fact that judgement according to the *Shariah* laws becomes a religious duty on the part of those holding authority, the role of the *Imam* in the Islamic state derived, in reality, from the role of humankind on the earth as God's vicegerent. In the context of a government administration, the *Imam* represents the whole Muslim community. This meant that the role of *Imam* includes working together with his people in realizing God's command and maintaining justice, brotherhood and goodness for all.[74] It is, therefore, the Imam's role to apply justice and equality and make this an obligatory duty to his people irrespective of their belief, race, and colour and so on. Justice on the part of the Imam also included justice in the enforcement of the *shariah* laws pertaining human transactions. In other words, it was the *Imam's* responsibility to monitor businesses run by people under his rule and ensures that they were in accord with Islamic teachings. Besides this, establishing justice in the governmental system is a religious obligation. The establishment of an Islamic state is a religious duty, it becomes the purpose and function of the state to maintain peace and order in the country and prevent people from wasting their energies in quarrelling etc. However, the real aim is to enforce the system of collective, social and economic justice prescribed in the Qur'an on human life as a whole. There is no room for act unjustly, even towards those who are his personal rivals or enemies. The Qur'an instructed him to do so by stating: "Do not let hatred of any people dissuade you from dealing justly. Deal just, for that is closer to Godliness."[75] The concept of justice broadly can be divided in two main categories:

- **Human Equality:** Human equality in Islam demands the assurance of an individual's rights, respect and honour as a human being, irrespective of race, tribe, language and faith. This returns on the basis of humankind as a whole who belongs to Adam and comes from dust. If Adam was honoured, then his children were all equal in every respect. To maintain the principle of human equality, Islam also demanded that Muslims not be suspicious of other members of society, Muslim or non-Muslim. "Indeed, some types of suspicion are sinful."[76] Therefore, equality in Islam apparently sought to assure an individual's right, honour and freedom in society. No one would be allowed to violate another's sanctity as all human beings were originally equal, coming from the single soul *'Nafsun Wahida'* irrespective of their colour, race or even sex.
- **Social Justice:** Justice plays a central role in the Qur'anic

discourse. The Qur'an does not define the constituent elements of justice. It emphasizes the ability to achieve justice as a unique human charge and necessity. In essence, the Qur'an requires a commitment to a moral imperative that is vague but recognizable through institution, reason and human experience. The Qur'an states that God created people different and grouped them into nations and tribes so that they would come to know one another. Muslim scholars reasoned that the expression "come to know one another" indicates the need for social cooperation and mutual assistance in order to achieve justice.[77] Islam laid certain responsibilities on individuals and society of mutual social care or social solidarity the principles of which were mercy, love and unselfishness. Social solidarity was not limited to the relationship and co-operation between individuals and society. Islam acknowledges the right of every individual to oppose an unjust ruler. It states that the Muslim has the right to be disobedient to an oppressive ruler and speak the truth to his face. Thus, the right of the individual to "command right and forbid wrong" is transferred to the office of the *Muḥtasib*, who is a public official supervises public spaces and inspects behaviour and in return receives a salary from the state. No adverse distinction in protection and assistance can be made which negatively discriminates amongst forced migrants on the basis of race, gender, creed or any other caste. The Qur'an entreats tolerance towards all beliefs, beseeching humankind to imbibe the maxim "you have your own religion and I have mine."[78] The Qur'an also states that "There shall be no compulsion in religion."[79] Justice demands that when the matter is collective in nature, all people involved in it shall be consulted and in case of their absence their authorized representatives shall be invited for talks.

Modern Democracy

Modern democracy is a system of governance with specific practices, strategies and rules. The members of that system treat each other as political equals, govern collectively, and have at their disposal rights, resources and institutions that guarantee their capacity for self-government.[80] In this political regime, the rulers are held accountable for what they do in the public sphere by citizens and citizens are political actors who act indirectly through the competition and cooperation of their elected representatives. Democracy does not ensure justice but it does establish a basis for pursuing justice and thus for the fulfilling a fundamental responsibility assigned by God to each and every member of the society. Democracy depends on the presence of rulers, i.e. persons who occupy specialised roles of authority and can give legitimate commands to others. What distinguish democratic rulers from nondemocratic ones are the norms that determine how rulers come to power and the practices that hold them accountable for their actions. Legal and political power is separated, and this separation constitutes the basis of the separation of powers that is one of the fundamentals of modern democracy.

The Concept of Democracy in Islam

The relationship between Islam and democracy in the contemporary world is complex. It presents a broad spectrum of perspectives ranging from the extremes of those who deny a connection between Islam and democracy to those who argue that Islam requires a democratic system. Some of the Islamic scholars believe that "democracy" is a foreign concept that has been imposed by the West. They argue that the concept of popular sovereignty denies the fundamental Islamic affirmation of the sovereignty of God. On the other hand, many prominent Islamic intellectuals and groups, however, argue that Islam and democracy are compatible. Some extend the argument to affirm that under the conditions of the contemporary world, democracy can be considered a requirement of Islam. In these discussions, Muslim scholars bring historically important concepts from within the Islamic tradition together with the basic concepts of democracy as understood in the modern world. Islam is not only a religion; rather it is a complete code of life. All aspects of Muslim society, individually or collectively, are covered by the social structure of Islam. The important manifestation of a political system is vindicated through the establishment of a state and the way of its governance. Our Holy Prophet (PBUH) established a state at Medina, of a unique type, based on consultation, justice, equality and accountability. After his passing his righteous successors maintained the same system of governance. The Holy Qur'an has mentioned the word *'Shura'* for governance. "They govern with mutual consultation." The essence of a true democracy is also consultation. The governing system of the Righteous Caliphs was the manifestation of this democracy. Today there is much talk about Western democracy, but the aforesaid democracy presented by Islam is more accomplished. Every person in the Islamic society enjoys the rights and powers of the caliphate of God and his in this respect, all individuals are equal. No one can deprive anyone on his rights and powers. The agency for the running the affairs of the state will be established in accordance with will of these individuals and the authority of the state will only be an extension of the powers of the individuals delegated to it. Their opinion will be decisive in the formation of the Government, which will be run with the advice and in accordance with their wishes. Whoever gains their confidence will carry out the duties of the caliphate on their behalf and whenever he losses their confidence he have to relinquish his office. In this respect, the political system in Islam is a perfect democracy in modern times.[81] Islam transcends time and space and that it accommodates all other ideologies and philosophies. Islam, as the last revealed message, is compatible with all ages and nations. The compatibility between democracy and Islam should express their arguments in a way that is understandable to the average believer. Democracy is not attained simply by making institutional changes or winning political elites over. Its survival depends on the beliefs and opinion of ordinary people. There are no other regimes in the history of the world that were so dependent on what the ruled thought about the rulers and the way they were ruled. No other political regime needs such strong feedback from the common man.

The Islamic caliphate is democratic in nature. The Islamic democracy works under the sovereignty of God and the supremacy of Shariah and implementation of His commandments, whereas the Western democracy is based on popular sovereignty and manmade laws. Therefore, there is no concept of monarchy, oligarchy or theocracy in Islam.[82] Islamic democracy is based on consultation because the Qur'an says, "And (Muslims) conduct their affairs by mutual consultation."[83] Islam is incompatible with democracy and modernity is false. As a religion, Islam contains democratic concepts such as *Shura*, and *Ijtihad*, while Muslims tend to strongly favour democracy over any other system. Since Islam supports democracy, and Muslims favour it, then Huntington's claim that Islam is resistant to democracy no holds water at all. In this complex context, it is clear that Islam is not inherently incompatible with democracy.

Islamic Democracy and Western Democracy

The modern concept of democracies does not necessarily follow one formula or aspect. Democracy may lead to a liberal system as well as it may lead to a socialist system. Or it may be a democracy with the inclusion of religious norms in the government. The Islamic tradition contains a number of key concepts that are presented by Muslims as the key to "Islamic democracy." Most Muslims would agree that it is important for Muslims not simply to copy what non-Muslims have done in creating democratic systems.

Islamic democracy is based on the principle of *Khilafat,* whereas the Western democracy is based on the concept of popular sovereignty. In Western democracy the people are severing, whereas in Islam sovereignty is vested in God and the people are His representatives. In Western democracy, the people make their own laws, whereas, in Islamic democracy, people are bound to obey the *Sharia* law. In Western democracy, the government undertakes to fulfil the will of the people, whereas in Islamic democracy, the government and the people alike have to do the will of God. Western democracy is a kind of absolute authority which exercises its powers in a free and uncontrolled manner, whereas Islamic democracy is subserveint to the Divine law of *Shariah* and exercises its authority in accordance with the injunctions of God and within the limits prescribed by Him. In Western democracy, the people are the source of law, and the law in turn ensures the fundamentals rights that protect the well-being and interest of the individual member of the sovereignty, whereas in Islam, God is the only sovereign and the ultimate source of legitimate law.

It is general belief that democracy poses a formidable challenge for the Islamic political notion. The Islamic scholars argue that law made by a sovereign monarch is the illegitimate because it substitutes human authority for God's sovereignty. But law made by sovereign citizen's face the same problem of legitimacy. They advocate that God is the ultimate source of legitimate law.[84] The traditions of Islamic political thought contain both interpretive and practical possibilities that can be developed into a democratic system. To be sure, these doctrinal potentialities may remained unrealized with will power and inspired vision, and a moral commitment there can be no democracy in Islam, but for Muslims, Islam is the authoritative frame of reference, can arrive at the conviction that democracy is an ethical good and that pursuit of this good not required abandoning Islam.[85] The Qur'an itself does not specify a particular form of Government, but it dies identify a set of social and political values that are central to a Muslim polity. In Islamic notion of politics, three values are some particular importance:

1. To pursue Justice through social cooperation and mutual assistance,
2. To establish a no autocratic, consultative method of governance, and
3. To institutionalize mercy and compassion in social interaction.

The concept of power in Islamic philosophy is according to which political power receives its legitimacy from religious law. Power, therefore, belongs to professional legal elites, the jurists. Theologians developed the principles of the Islamic doctrine of power and established the permanent connection between politics and theology—the classical Islamic philosophy; and these are indigenous concepts within the Islamic tradition. "Democracy pessimists" are quick to conclude that there is a cultural and religious gap between the original Islamic and modern democratic understandings of legitimate power.[86] Islamic democracy is not like the 'Western democracy' where people are free to legislate without any restriction. People are empowered to make laws, to amend the laws and to delete the laws from their constitution. But whereas 'Islamic democracy' firmly believes in the absolute sovereignty of God, where in the executive comes into existence through election.

Conclusion

Islam has a wide system that guides human being at every walk of life. It is much more gentle and rational religion. It has given some basic principles in the field of state, government and constitutional affairs pertaining to Islamic political order. The Islamic principles has given birth new social order, such as equality and liberty, social justice, religious freedom and freedom of expression which later adapted as fundamental human rights in modern age. These principles considered to be 'supreme values and have a great effect upon the formulation of the Islamic concept of state, its functions and characteristics of system of government. The Qur'an laid down the principle of consultation to guide the community's decision making process. Islamic political system is constitutional by nature founded upon the conditions underlined by the *Shariah*. Islam supports directly or indirectly the constitutional type of government which is the closest version of political systems to Islam as it held people accountable. The Islamic tradition of legal-political thought suggests ideas of representation, consultation and legal process, but the precise content of these ideas remains contested and provides no direct link between Islam and democracy. *Shura* is one of the key operation elements in the relationship between Islam and democracy. Hence, there is substantial similarity between Islamic political system and democracy.

Notes

1. Ibn Taymiyya, *al-Siyasa al-Sharia,* pp. 90-91.
2. *Ibid.,* 2: 878-879.
3. Gianfranco Poggi, *The State: Its Nature, Development and Prospects* Stanford, California: Stanford University Press, 1990, pp. 19-33; Graeme Gill, *The Nature and Development of the Modern State*. New York: Palgrave Macmillan, 2003, pp. 2-3.
4. Syyed Abul Ála Mawdudi, *Siyashi Kashmakash,* Vol. II, p.109. See also *Islami Riyasat*, pp.135, 57:25.
5. Syyed Abul Ála Mawdudi, *Islami Riyasat,* pp. 129-130.
6. Kamali, Kamali, M.H; *'Have We Neglected the Sharia Law Doctrine of Maslahah?', Islamic Studies, No.4, 1988.*
7. Syyed Abul Ála Mawdudi, *Islamic Law and Constitution,* translated by Khurshidahmad, Lahore, Pakistan, 1960, p. 73.
8. Syyed Abul Ála Mawdudi, *Islami Riyasat,* pp. 135-136.
9. The Qur'an: 3:38.
10. The Qur'an: 18:26.
11. The Qur'an: 12:40, 6:57.
12. Syyed Abul Ála Mawdudi, *Tafhim al-Qur'an,* Vol. I, p. 406.
13. The Qur'an: 7:3.
14. The Qur'an: 59:7.
15. Syyed Abul Ála Mawdudi, *Islam KisChizka Alambardar Hay,* p. 7. See also 4:65.
16. The Qur'an: 24: 55.
17. The Qur'an: 5:8.
18. Syyed Abul Ála Mawdudi, *Tafhim al-Qur'an,* Vol. II, p. 156.
19. *Ibid.,* p. 569.
20. Syyed Abul Ála Mawdudi, *The Islamic Way,* Markazi Maktaba Islami Publisher, New Delhi, 2009, p. 33.
21. Syyed Abul Ála Mawdudi, *Islamic law and Constitution*, translated by Khurshid Ahmad, Lahore, Pakistan, 1960, p. 160.
22. Syyed Abul Ála Mawdudi, *Fundamental Rights of Man*, Lahore, 1960, (quoted from, The Islamic way, Markazi MaktabaIslami Publisher, New

Delhi, 2009, p. 33.

23. Syyed Abul Ála Mawdudi, *Islamic law and Constitution*, translated by Khurshidahmad, Lahore, Pakistan, 1960, p. 139.
24. The Qur'an: 2:105, 3:74, 35:2, 38:9, 39:38, 40:07, 43:32.
25. Syeed Qutb, *Fi Zilal al-Qur'an,* Cairo, Dal al-Shuruq Qutub,17th ed. Vol. 2, p. 20-21
26. Al-Mawardi, *Kitāb al-A%kām as-Sulmāniyya,* ed. Enger (Bonn), 1853, pp. 2-3.
27. Blankinship, K.A., *The Constitution of Medina.* In *Medieval Islamic Civilization-An Encyclopedia,* 2001.
28. Brown, L.C., *Religion and the State: The Muslim Approach to Politics,* New York, Columbia University Press, 2000.
29. Hallaq, W.B.; *A History of Islamic Legal Theories* (1997), pp. 180-187; Masud, M.K.; Shatibi's *Philosophy of Islamic Law*, (1995), p.151.
30. Kamali, Kamali, M.H., *Have We Neglected the Sharia Law Doctrine of Maslahah?*, 27 *Islamic Studies*, No.4, 1988, p. 288.
31. *Ibid.,* p. 283.
32. The Qur'an: 5:48.
33. The Qur'an: 4:114, 2:195, 5:93, 63:10, 3:16, 64:16.
34. The Qur'an: 7:142, 2:237.
35. The Qur'an: 5:3.
36. The Qur'an: 2:112, 3:115, 3:136, 4:37, 4:124, 5:9, 7:42, 10:4, 10:8, 10:26, 11:11, 11:22.
37. Ibn Taymiyya, *al-Siysah al-Shariyyyah*, pp. 218-219.
38. Olivier Roy, *The Globalized Islam, The search for a new Ummah*, 1-2, Columbia University Press, 20.
39. Syed Abul-A'la al-Mawdudi, *The Islamic Law and Constitution,* trans. Khurshid Ahmad (Lahore: Islamic Publications, 1980), 165.
40. Bernard Lewis, *"The Return of Islam, "in Religion and Politics in the Middle East,* ed. Michael Curtis 'Boulder: Westview Press, 1981, p. 12.
41. Syyed Abul Ála Mawdudi *Islam ka Nazariyah-i Siyasi,* pp. 24-25. See also *Islami Riyasat,* pp. 373-375.
42. Syyed Qutb, *Fi Zilal al-Qur'an,* 2: 890, 902. See also 4: 2526.
43. Syyed Abul Ála Mawdudi, *First Principles of the Islamic State,* trans. Khurshid Ahmad, Lahore: Islamic Publication Limited, 1974, p.16.
44. Syyed Abul Ála Mawdudi *First Principles of the Islamic State*, p.18.
45. Syyed Qutb, *Fi Zilal al-Qur'an,* 4: 1990.
46. *Ibid.,* 2: 929, 948-951. See also 4: 2526.
47. *Ibid.,* 2: 688-689.
48. Syyed Abul Ála Mawdudi *Islamic State,* trans. Mazheruddin Siddiqi, Karachi: Islamic Research Academy, 1986, p.10.
49. The Qur'an: 2:30.
50. Abu Jafar Ibn Jarir al-Tabari, *Tafsir al-Tabari,* Beirut: Dar al-Kutub al-'Ilmiyya, 1997, 1: 233-238.
51. Syyed Qutb, *Fi Zilal al-Qur'an,* 4: 2529.
52. *Ibid.,*4: 1990.

53. *Ibid.*,6: 3510.
54. The Qur'an: 3:159.
55. Abd al-Qadir, *Awda, al-Islam waAwda al-Siyasia,* Beirut: Mu'assasa al-Risala, 1997, p. 194.
56. The Qur'an, 42:38.
57. Syyed Qutb, *Fi Zilal al-Qur'an,* 5: 3165.
58. Abd al-Qadir, *Awda, al-Islam wa Awda al-Siyasia,* Beirut: Mu'assasa al-Risala, 1997, p. 193.
59. Syyed Qutb, *Fi Zilal al-Qur'an,* 3:1754.
60. Syyed Abul Ála Mawdudi, *Nazariyyat al-Islam al-Siyasiy'a,* Jedda: al-Dar al Saudiyya, 1985, pp. 11-12.
61. Syyed Qutb, *Fi Zilal al-Qur'an,* 4: 2009.
62. Ibn Manzür, *Lisan al-'Arab,* 1: 299.
63. Abi Id, Arif Khalil, *Nizam al-HukmfIl-Islam,* Jordan: Dar al-Nafais, 1996, p. 248.
64. *Ibid.,* pp. 249-250.
65. The Qur'an: 48:10.
66. Abu Faris, Muhammad 'Abd al-Qadir, *al-Nizdm al-Siyasifil-Islam,* Dar al-Furqan, 1989, pp. 302-303
67. *Ibid.,* pp. 304-305.
68. Syyed Qutb, *Fi Zilal al-Qur'an,* 4: 2009.
69. The Qur'an: 4: 59.
70. Syyed Qutb, *Fi Zilal al-Qur'an,* 2: 687.
71. *Sahihal-Bukhari,* Hadith No. 663.
72. Syyed Qutb, *Fi Zilal al-Qur'an,* 6: 3017. See also 1: 327.
73. The Qur'an: 4:58.
74. Syyed Qutb, *Fi Zilal al-Qur'an* 1:327.
75. *Ibid.,* 2: 776.
76. The Qur'an, 49:12.
77. The Qur'an: 49:13.
78. The Qur'an: 109:6.
79. The Qur'an: 2:256.
80. Robert Dahl, *Democracy and Its Critics*, New Haven: Yale University Press, 1989.
81. M.A. Muatdar Khan, *Islamic Governance and Democracy,* Cambria Press, New York, 2009, p. 20.
82. Syyed Abul Ála Mawdudi, *Khilafatwa Mulukiyat,* pp. 33-34. See also *Tafhim al-Qur'an,* Vol. III, pp. 416-419.
83. Syyed Abul Ála Mawdudi, *Islam ka Nazriya Siyasi*, pp. 36-38.
84. M.A. Muatdar Khan, *Islamic Governance and Democracy,* Cambria Press, New York, 2009, p. 68.
85. Hamid Enayet, *Modern Islamic Political Thought*, Austin. University of Texas Press, 1982, p. 72.
86. Syed Khatab and Gray D. Bouna, *Democracy in Islam,* London and New York: Rutledge, Taylor and Francis Group. 2007, p. 29.

13

Significance of Seeking Education in Islam: With Special Reference to Women's Education

Firdous Ahmad Sofal

Introduction

The fact cannot be denied that in the world of today if a nation or a country does not emphasize and focus on educating its people then the future of such people is doomed and they can neither compete nor survive in the fierce competition this world has at present. Therefore, all the members of a nation have to strive and struggle towards knowledge and learning if a nation is to survive and be successful.

The importance of education is without doubt imperative for a nation, the second thing that is even more important than that is the equality in education where both men and women receive equal educational rights and facilities. The general perception of people about women in Islam is that they are considered the lesser being and that they have no right of being educated and striving for knowledge in Islam. This notion is wrong and women have the same rights towards education as men do. There have been great Muslim women in the history of Islam that standout as a true role model for Muslim women. The lines below firstly discuss the importance of learning and education in Islam and then discuss the equality of this opportunity in both the genders.

Islam is the only single religion in which the first direction of the Holy Scripture was revealed with the direction of education. Allah says in the Qur'an, "Read! In the Name of your Lord who has created (all that exists). He has created man from a clot (a piece of thick coagulated blood). Read! And your Lord is the Most Generous. Who has taught (the writing) by the pen. He has taught man that which he knew not." (Qur'an 96:1-5) The first word in Arabic "*Iqra*" is a command that means "read" and that includes the ideas of "learning", "exploring" and "seeking education." Education is the initial point of each human activity. Education is the main uniqueness of human being all over the creation. Allah honoured human being over all of His creations for the knowledge and wisdom. The first human being (Adam) in the world was recognized greatest by his knowledge to all creatures. The angels and Satan failed in the test of knowledge. Hence the vicegerency was assigned to Adam. Al Qur'an says, "And He taught Adam the names of all things; then He placed them before the angels, and said: "Tell me the names of these if ye are right." (Qur'an 2: 31) Al Qur'an further declares, "Allah will rise up, to (suitable) ranks (and degrees), those of you who believe and who have been granted (mystic) Knowledge. And Allah is well acquainted with all ye do." (Qur'an 58:11) Moreover, Allah sent many messengers including the last Prophet Muhammad in several eras with knowledge and wisdom in the world for showing the correct path to those who were a fidel from Islam. Allah says, "And to Lut, too, we gave Judgement and Knowledge, and We saved him from the town which practiced abominations: truly they were a people given to Evil, a rebellious people." (Qur'an 21:74) It is particularly mentioned that Allah honoured His apostle Muhammad with the knowledge, wisdom which; He taught it to Muhammad so that he might teach it to mankind. The Holy Qur'an says, "Allah did confer a great favour on the believers when He sent among them a messenger from among themselves, rehearsing unto them the Signs of Allah, sanctifying them, and instructing them in Scripture and Wisdom, while, before that, they had been in manifest error." (Qur'an 3:164) Most of the Prophet hunted to Allah for increasing their knowledge, i.e. Hazrat Ibrahim (A.) said-"O my Lord! Bestow wisdom (*Hukm*) on me, and join me with the righteous." (Qur'an 26: 83) Allah also taught teaching for increasing knowledge. Al Qur'an says, "O my Lord! Increase me in knowledge." (Qur'an 20: 114).

Historical Background

Historically women have been subjected to social injustice and educational dispossession. Before advent of Islam Arabs has engaged to infanticide the girl babies and Islam frequently recognize the dignity and rights of girls. Education is the prime human rights of human being after ensuring the right to life. Hence Allah firstly instructs the prophet to read and acquire knowledge as a divine guide. Islamic Education is one of the greatest schemes of education, which makes a decent presented person with all the potentials. In Islam, pursue knowledge is a holy duty. The significance of acquirement and broadcasting education has been highlighted constantly in the Qur'an and hadith, which are the decisive source of direction for Muslims. The Prophet (s.m) said, "Convey from me even an Ayah of the Qur'an." (Al-Bukhari, 1987). Girls or women are total half of population of every society; avoiding or treating them as less important does not survive in the Muslim society. Unfortunately by the weakness of Muslim with adverse and fallacious propaganda of opposition against Islam, accurate position of Islam towards girls' education is absent-minded. The specific objectives are from this study to recognize the Islamic approaches towards girls' education from the view point of Qur'an and hadith, to broadcast the genuine attitude of Islam about obtaining knowledge out of gender discrimination, and to explore the major barriers of girls' education in Bangladesh. Nik & Yaacob (2013) discussed about concept of education in Islam and Yasin et al. (2013) argued aim and objectives of education in Islam. Rayan (2012) mentions Islamic education from philosophical aspect. Abukari (2014) shows education of women from Qur'anic perspective. Al-Naquib Al-Attas (1979) and Al-Attas (1980) discussed on concept, aim and objectives of education in Islam.

Concept of Education from Islamic Perspective

The word 'Education' has been derived from Latin word: "educare, educere, educatum, educates" or "education" which indicates to lead pupils or pull out there dormant abilities (Alamgeer, 2010). The word "educare" means "to bring out" or "to nourish" where "educere" means "to lead out" or "to draw out", "educatum" means "act of teaching" or "training", "educates" means "to bring up, rear, educate" and "education" means "a breeding, a bringing up, a rearing" (Parankimalil, 2012). The Greek word "pedagogy" is also sometimes used for education (Parankimalil, 2012). Several scholars have attempted to define Education from their own approaches. According to Aristotle, "Education is a process necessary for the creation of sound mind in the sound body." According to Socrates, "Education is the mean that helps in searching the truth" (Imaillah, 1999). Imam Ghazali defines,

"Education is a process which enables an individual to distinguish between the true and the false, the good and bad and the right conduct and the evil doing." (Asif & Khan, 2010). The concept of education in Islam from the terminological and philosophical point of view, Al-Attas states, "Recognition and acknowledgement, progressively instilled into man, of the proper places of things in the order of creation, such that it leads to the recognition and acknowledgement of the proper place of God in the order of being and existence." (Al-Attas, 1980). Education in Islam is "an education which trains the sensibility of an individual, in such a manner that their attitude towards life, their actions, decisions and approach to all kinds of knowledge are governed by the spiritual and deeply felt ethical values of Islam" (Ashraf & Hussain, 1979). It is a mode of training the body, mind and soul through informing the knowledge of all kinds, i.e. fundamental as obligatory and specific as optional (WORLD-COME, 1977). It formulates human beings for complete life with no separation of this short-term life which ends with death, and the eternal life that begins after death (Sarwar, 2001). Education in Islam is not simply of obtaining intelligent knowledge but it is a process of decoration the nature and character of an individual so that they can jointly represent Islamic ethics, work as *khalīfatullāhfī al-ard* (vicegerent of Allāh on the earth) (Ashraf & Hussain, 1979), watcher of true, nobility and human greatness (WORLD-COME, 1977). In other word, education is "a method through which human beings are competent and organized in a concerted way to do their Creator's command in this life (*dunyā*) to be pleased in the life of hereafter (*ākhirah*)." (WORLD-COME, 1977). According to Al-Attas, the meaning of education is inherent in the associations of term "*tarbiyyah*", "*ta'lim*", and "*ta'dib*" taken altogether. Though all terms denote to education, *ta'dib* is more perfect and exact in understanding the concept of education (Daud, 1998). *Ta'līm*, from the root "*alima*" means to instruct, to teach, to train, to school, and to educate, which contains elements of knowledge through teaching and learning. *Tarbiyah*, from the root "*raba*" means to nurture, to bear, to feed, to foster, to nourish, to cause to increase growth, to rear, and to bring forth to mature produce, which denotes the method of education that gives stress on physical, intellectual, spiritual and ethical development of an individual in accordance with the will of Allah (Al-Attas, 1991). However, *tarbiyyah* is not suitable to carry the meaning of education from its terminological point of view. Because this meaning is not only applicable to human, but also to other species, such as animal and plants (Al-Attas, 1991). *Ta'dīb*, from the root "*addaba*" denotes to be cultured, refined, to discipline (Wehr & Cowan, 1979), well-mannered, implies the process of education that delivers emphasis on nurturing worthy human beings with decent codes of conduct accepted by Islam, so that he displays behaviour and position himself in the society with fairness and justice (Khamis & Salleh, 2010). The concept of education in Islam must takings into reflection of all the dimensions specified above (Yasin *et al.*, 2013). The word *ta'dib* is also used by the prophet (s.m) when he says, "My Lord educated (*addaba*) me, and made my education (*ta'dib*) most excellent." (Al-Ghazali, 1993). *Adab* includes disciplining the mind and soul. It is also about achievement of good abilities and qualities of the mind and soul, so that individual can distinguish between: good and bad; right and wrong; and real and false (Al-Naquib Al-Attas, 1979). Three elements inherent in the concept of education, i.e. the method, a content, and recipient refer to "human beings" (Al-Attas, 1991). The comprehensively recognized meaning of education today is growth and development. It is a continuous and lifelong process of one's potentialities (Khan, 1988). This opinion is repeated in the Hadith—The Prophet said, "Acquiring knowledge from the cradle to the grave." In conclusion, in the context of Islam Education is the organized process of acquiring knowledge that makes a complete person, including the rational, spiritual, and social dimensions.

Acquisition of Knowledge as Highlighted by Qur'an

The Qur'an places the utmost emphasis on the importance of the acquisition of knowledge. Al Qur'an states: "Are those equal, those who know and those who do not know? It is those who are endued with understanding that receive admonition." (Qur'an 39: 9, Ali, 1989a). It is understood from this verse that the rank of the learned and their honour are much high (Al-Ghazali, 1993). It drives further to encourage believers to pray for improvement in knowledge and stresses on knowledge achievement even in times of crisis. In Islam all knowledge is reflected religious be it rooted in the social, physical sciences, professional or theological field. This is confirmed in several verses that command, advice, encourage and warn, people to detect the phenomenon of nature, to look into all in the universe, to travel, examine, explore, and understand them (Abukari, 2014). Placing Islamic education in the context of knowledge acquisition should be able to draw out the potential good in the individual, to substitute error with truth, to transfer from illiteracy and incompetence to knowledge and competence. The Qur'an says: "By the Soul, and the proportion and order given to it. And its enlightenment as to its wrong and its right—Truly he succeeds that purifies it, and he fails that corrupts it." (Qur'an 91: 7-10). The Qur'an discourage the only memorization of heavenly revelation without practice its order and such education is empty of meaning in respect of use to the individual and society in this life and the hereafter as well. In this favour the Qur'an says: "The similitude of those who were charged with the (obligations of the) Mosaic Law, but who subsequently failed in those (obligations), is that of a donkey which carries huge tomes (but understand them not)."(Qur'an 62: 5).

Standards for Islamic Education

Numerous Islamic scholars in the arena of education contribute effort to state the standards of Islamic education, i.e. Muhib Aldin, Abu al Rahman, Dr. Saied and Dr. Mugdad Yalgin are the debaters. Muhib Aldin explains Islamic education contains the raising and development of an individual life by the colour of Islamic model together with bodily, mentally and intellectually. Abu Salih exactly shows Islamic Education considered the nurturing and preparation of the Muslim for his worldly and eternal life. The content and systems of education will closely destined by the philosophy and ideology of Islam (Abu Salih, 1982). Dr. Saied considered Islamic Education as the organized ideas and thoughts which are structured in intellectual outline itself built on an Islamic philosophical and moral framework (Abu Salih *et al.*, 1982). Abd al Rahman Al Nahlawi detects Islamic education as a set of practical and oral actions motivated by knowledge of the Qur'an and Sunnah and founded on them in matters to do with faith (Abu Salih *et al.*, 1982). Dr. Mugdad Yalgin cited Islamic education as an autonomous educational system containing its separate basic aspects, purposes and methods; all motivated by the major philosophical principles of Islam (Yalgin, 1986). The basic criteria of Islamic education are which creates human resources ensuing the Islamic teaching; particularly spirituality and morality. It is the process for an individual to achieve divine code. Islamic education arrange many subjects, i.e. Islamic theology, science, philosophy, sociology, geography, Islamic culture and civilization.

The Goal of Education in Islam

Allah declares in the Holy Qur'an, "Nor should the Believers all go forth together: if a contingent from every expedition remained behind, they could devote themselves to studies in religion, and admonish the people when they return to them,—that thus they (may learn) to guard themselves (against evil)." (Qur'an 9: 122). Al-Qurtobi, the renowned Qur'anic scholar, stated the above verse of the Holy Qur'an indicates the goal of Islamic education. The goal of that education described as understanding in religious matters (*tafaqquhfī al-dīn*). Knowledge seekers are delegated with the obligation to circulate the knowledge and skills they knew to those who do not have the chance to acquire knowledge (Yasin, Firdaus, & Jani, 2013). The aim of Islamic education is not to fill up the learner's head with particulars but to formulate them for a life of pureness and seriousness. This total pledge will build based on the models of Islamic ethics is the maximum goal of Islamic education (Al-Naquib Al-Attas, 1979). Al-Attas further mention "the comprehensive and unified approach to education in Islam is focused towards the "balanced development of the total personality...through training Man's spirit, intellect, rational self, feelings and bodily senses...such that faith is infused into the whole of his personality" (Al-Naquib Al-Attas, 1979). In Islam the purpose of education is to enlighten the human soul and improves the resources of knowledge that helps in knowing Allah SWT, the Creator of all humankind and universe. This will promote the sense of obligation to worship the Creator and obey His command at all periods and circumstances. The Qur'an says, "And I did not create the jinn and mankind except to worship Me." (Qur'an 51: 56). Al-Ghazālī narrates the aim of education with the purpose of life that is to achieve pleasure by getting close to God. Therefore, the aim of education is "to improve in man a personality that abides by the educations of religion, and is hence assured of salvation and happiness in the eternal life of the Hereafter" (Nofal, 1993). Muslim students have to be aware that the acquisition of knowledge is "not merely to satisfy an intellectual curiosity or just for material or worldly gains, but to produce rational and righteous human beings, who are able to meet the spiritual, moral and physical needs of their families, their people and mankind" (Ashraf & Hussain, 1979). A perfect personality like this is a product of education whose philosophy is founded on faith in Allah and a promise to realize God-given moral code well-entrenched in the sacred teaching of Sharīah (Ajijola, 1999). The aim of education in Islam as specified in the First World Conference on Muslim Education held in Jedda Mecca (1393 A.H.-1977 A.D.) "Education should aim at the balanced growth of the total personality of man through the training of man's sprit, intellect, his rational self, feelings and bodily senses. Education should cater, therefore, for the growth of man in all aspects: spiritual, intellectual, imaginative, physical, scientific, linguistic, both individually and collectively and motivate all aspects towards goodness and the attainment of perfection. The ultimate aim of Muslim education lies in the realization of complete submission to Allah on the level of the individual, the community and humanity at large" (Ashraf, 1985). The ultimate goal of Islamic education is certainty that knowledge without the origin in faith and religion is merely partial education. Islamic education teaches the promise towards the basic values which have been arranged in religion and scripture. It also emphasizes on the sense of accountability towards Almighty Allah so that men can pass their lives as a faithful servant (Sharif, 1964). International brotherhoods can be succeeded by the teachings from Islamic education irrespective of differences in groups, occupations and social classes amongst the persons who are knit together by a common religion and faith. The aim of Islamic education is that people be capable to live as he lived. While education does make humankind for happiness in this life, "its ultimate goal is the abode of permanence and all education points to the permanent world of eternity" (Nasr, 1984).

Islamic Views on Girls' Education as Rights

Seeking knowledge is obligatory for every Muslim man and woman in Islam. Therefore, knowledge, in general, is respected and highly appreciated in Islam. It is thus not surprising that scholars are held in high esteem and are praised in many verses from the Qur'an. The deep respect for knowledge and those who possess knowledge is evident in the following verse. Allah (SWT) says:

> *"Allah will raise to high ranks those that have faith and knowledge amongst you."* [58:11]

The Almighty (SWT) also speaks highly of the excellence of scholars and their superiority over the common people. He (SWT) says:

> *"Are the wise and the ignorant equal? Truly, none will take heed but men of understanding."* [39:9]

Allah (SWT) has linked His testimony and the testimony of the angels with that of the people of knowledge. This is indeed a privilege and proof of their superiority:

> *"Allah hears witness that there is no god but Him, and so do the angels and men of learning. He is the Executor of justice, the only God, The Mighty, The Wise."* [3: 18]

The first verses revealed to the Messenger(s) also stress the importance of knowledge:

> *"Read in the name of your Lord who created,*
> *created man from a clinging substance.*
> *Read! Your Lord is The Most Bountiful One.*
> *Who taught by the pen,*
> *taught man what he did not know''* [96:1-5]

These verses were revealed to define the outlines of a religion based on knowledge, as well as to establish the importance of this knowledge. Hence, the first word revealed, spoken by the Angel Gabriel was *"Read."* Reading is the key to knowledge and since writing complements reading, Allah (SWT) Highlights this act by saying *''Taught by the pen*". The pen was and still is the best and most useful utensil used in transmitting and preserving knowledge, and has left its impact on humanity over the centuries." By reading and writing, a human being can acquire knowledge. This knowledge is taught by his Lord since He is the one who has endowed us with intellectual capacities and the five senses which permit us to receive, learn and comprehend information.

Writing is also mentioned in Aayat "Ad-dain":

> *"O believers, when you contract a debt for a fixed period, put it in writing. Let a scribe write it down for you with fairness; no scribe should refuse to write as Allah has taught him. Therefore, let him write..."* [2:282]

The above verse emphasizes the importance of acquiring the knowledge of writing. Allah orders us to do so: *"put it in writing"*, *"let a scribe write", "therefore, let him write."* The importance of the scribe is also stressed. It is mentioned twice in the same verse: *"let a scribe write it", "no scribe should refase." The* knowledge of writing is also a blessing and a gift from Allah.

Allah has ordered us to record our debts and contracts in writing. Therefore, acquiring the knowledge of writing is a necessity and our need for people who master reading and writing is great indeed. We also learn from the autobiography of the Prophet(s) that the ransom of each of his hostages in the battle of Badr was to teach ten Muslims to read and write. He(s) used to say: "Acquiring knowledge is an obligation upon every Muslim." The word 'Muslim' in this narration refers to both Muslim men and women. The scholars have agreed that all the commandments ordained by Allah apply equally to both men and women. Hence, men and women are equal in terms of obligations. "It is obligatory for every woman to pray, fast, to pay alms-tax (*zakaat*), to perform pilgrimage, to correct her creed, to enjoin good and prohibit evil, and to compete with others in doing good deeds. In fact all the obligations enjoined upon the Muslim in the Qur'an and the Sunnahare obligatory for every woman. Therefore, it is her obligation to learn about her rights and duties and to put this knowledge into practice. Teaching others about Islam is also important. It is an established fact that Islam involves worship, conduct, politics, sociology, economics and regulations dealing with issues of everyday life, the knowledge of which is not acquired automatically.

Rather, it is acquired through studying, learning and teaching. Islam is indeed a vast, diverse, comprehensive and detailed religion. Furthermore, women represent half of society. Consequently, they share with men the burden of building this society. "They share private and public responsibilities which require good education and enough knowledge in order to fulfil the need of the individual and the growing nation of Islam." Woman's education is vital for our society since she is the one who produces future men and women. She is the primary school of our children. From her they learn the foundation of humanness and the basis of moral education. She is the one who produces either good or bad members of society. Ibrahim Haafez was indeed correct when he said:

"For he who can teach our girls,
I say: Their ignorance, in the East is the reason of our failure.
A mother is her children's kindergarten,

If well prepared, a nation of decent stock, ours would be.
A mother is a garden.
If watered, flourishing white, it would be.
I am not saying, to let the women, unveiled, wander amongst the men.
Teach our girls virtuousness;
In all situations, it is a firm righteousness."

The female companions knew and understood the importance of knowledge in Islam. They passionately competed amongst themselves and endeavoured to gain sound knowledge. The Prophet (s) encouraged their enthusiasm and allowed them to attend his study circle. How could he not after his Lord had taught him to say: *"Lord, increase my knowledge"* (20:114). When the female companions heard the Prophet saying: "When Allah wants to do good for a person, He gives him sound knowledge in religion", they understood this narration to be directed to both male and female Muslims and not exclusively to men as some people seem to believe. They sought sound knowledge and competed amongst themselves in doing good deeds.

Aisha (R) said: "How excellent are the women of the Ansaar!

They do not feel shy while learning sound knowledge in religion." The women persevered in doing so and regularly attended study circles.

There they asked the Prophet various questions, some general and some concerning women's issues. In a narration by Abu Sa'eed Al-Khudri, we learned that some women requested that the Prophet(s) even set aside a day for them because the men were taking all his time. In response to their request he promised them one day for religious lessons and commandments. Once during such a lesson the Prophet(s) said: "A woman whose three children die will be shielded by them from the Hellfire." A woman asked, "If only two die"? He replied, "Even two will shield her from the Hell-fire."

The Prophet(s) showed kindness and affection to his female companions. He encouraged them to seek knowledge and helped them in comprehending and understanding their religion. Knowledge should be sought by all men and women, whether free-born or slaves. Abu Badra's father narrated that Allah's Messenger(s) said: "Any man who has a slave girl whom he educates properly, teaches good manners, manumits and marries, will get a double reward." He also said, The man who has a slave girl whom he educates, treats kindly, manumits and marries, will get a double reward."

The female companions would gather and listen to the Prophet(s).

They would also pray with him in congregation even though they knew that it is better for a woman to offer her prayers at home. They did so because they were so eager to seek knowledge from the Prophet's(s) own lips. The books of history describe at great length the contribution of 'Aisha(R), the Prophet's wife, to the teaching and preserving of the religion. Her knowledge was vast; she memorised and related numerous narrations of the Prophet(s)." 'Ataa' bin Abi Rabaah said:

"Aisha (R) was a scholar, the most knowledgeable one, who provided the best counsel." Also, Al-Zuhri said: "The knowledge of 'Aisha exceeds the knowledge of all the mothers of the believers, (the Prophet's other wives) as well as the knowledge of all the women put together. And Hishaam Ibn 'Arwah said: "I never heard of anybody with more knowledge in Islamic jurisprudence, medicine, and poetry than 'Aisha (R)."

The female companions eagerly sought to learn writing. Al-Shaffa' Bint Abdullah taught writing to Hafsa(R), the Prophet's(s) wife with his approval." The female companions contributed to the religion by directly relating some of the sayings of the Prophet(s).

The scholars of Hadith did not stipulate that the narrator should be a man. Their criteria were based on the intellectual capabilities of the narrator, their accuracy, righteousness and commitment to Islam. If these four conditions were available, the narration would be authenticated regardless of the gender of the narrator. Therefore, the books of Hadith abound with names of female narrators amongst the companions and those who came after them *(Attaabi'iyaat).*

Some of the scholars have devoted whole sections to narrations related by women. For instance: The book of "Attabaqaat" by Ibn Sa'd, "Al-Isaabah Fee Tamyeez As-Sahaabah", and "Asadulgaabah Fee Ma'rifat As-Sahaabah." For the last centuries Muslim women have been prevented from seeking and acquiring knowledge. Consequently, illiteracy and ignorance became widespread amongst Muslim women. Only in the last twenty five years has this begun to change.

Previously, fathers had prevented their daughters from reading and writing. They were confined to household tasks. If a father wished to educate his daughter, he would only allow her to learn how to read, since writing—they believed—was forbidden for them. A father would only entrust his daughter to a teacher if the latter promised not to teach his daughter how to write. In fact, some people claimed that Islam prohibited women from seeking worldly knowledge and even religious knowledge. This misconception was based on a forged statement. It was falsely narrated that the Prophet said: "Do not lodge your women in rooms and, do not teach them how to write."

Recently the scholars have confirmed that the narration prohibiting women from reading and writing was a complete fabrication. It was proved to be invalid and can no longer be used. Men and women are equal when it comes to learning, reading and writing religious and moral books, as well as books dealing with health issues, home management, children's education, home crafts etc. This includes books of creed, explanation of the Qur'an, the biography of the Prophet(s), books of Hadith, jurisprudence, Islamic history and books describing the code of conduct of the companions (R). These readings will bring women from the darkness of ignorance to the light of knowledge. No wise person would question the positive impact of such readings on both men and women. However, women should be able to seek knowledge without compromising in any way their modesty and chastity.

The most knowledgeable women were undoubtedly the female companions of the Prophet(s) and those who came after them (At-Taabi'iyaat). Amongst them were relaters and narrators of Hadith.

The scholars have mentioned that many scientific skills were mastered by some. There are many texts of the Noble Qur'an whose calligraphy comes from women from Damascus and Iraq. Some of these women have been described as "Geniuses with natural eloquence." Nevertheless, scholars are divided into two groups regarding the type of knowledge a woman should seek.

One group limits her education to religious issues, as well as home management and motherhood skills. They believe that she does not need to learn sciences like chemistry, physics, maths, architecture etc. This opinion prevailed in Egypt and was advocated by many. For instance, Haashim Ibrahim used to say: "The place of a woman is at home. Therefore, she should not seek any knowledge which would take her away from her family. She should only seek an education which will help her to grow into a perfect wife and a perfect mother."

Another group of scholars believe that women's education ought to be comprehensive. A woman should seek all types of knowledge without exception, even if the subject is contrary to her nature, her physiological constitution and her primary role in society. This group includes advocators of the so-called women's liberation movement. At the head of the list we find Qaasim Ameen.

Both opinions are pertinent to a certain extent. However, commenting on the first opinion, we say that a woman should acquire the foundations of all different sciences so that she can understand the mechanisms of everyday life. With this knowledge in hand, she will be able to help her children in their studies. This is especially important as it is the mother who is in charge of her children's education at home.

As far as the second opinion is concerned, we say that undertaking a study without careful planning and thinking, like for instance a study of sciences which are not compatible with women's physiology and natural role in society is a waste of time and energy. It is of no use to the woman herself, nor to her family. It will lead her to neglect her responsibilities towards her family and her Creator. The Prophet(s) said: "A woman is a steward of her husband's house and his children and she is accountable for those who are placed under her care."

The answer lies in between these two opinions. Islam has not forbidden any knowledge of any science. On the contrary, it gave women the right to seek unlimited knowledge. It gave her the freedom to choose, select and decide. It is up to her to make the correct choice which would suit her inherent instincts and agree with her physical constitution as well as her natural role in society. This choice, however, should not lead her to overlook her most important role as a mother and wife. Consequently, two different educational programmes should be designed, one for each sex. Each programme would take into account the different and separate specialisation of each sex and help it to fulfil and perfectly achieve its role in society.

The scholars have divided the knowledge that a woman should seek into two types of obligations:

1. **Individual obligation:** This includes correcting her creed, strengthening her faith, improving her manners, perfecting her home management skills, providing good education for her children and attending to her children.
2. **Collective Obligation:** When the nation is in need of female doctors, gynaecologists, nurses and teachers to teach in girls' schools, then the nation should ensure that adequate numbers of female doctors, nurses and teachers are produced. At this stage, seeking the knowledge of such sciences becomes an obligation upon Muslim women. Unfortunately, some people exceed the limits and take part in activities that contradict the values and principles of Islam. This of course should be

avoided by every Muslim woman, as well as every Muslim man. The purpose of gaining knowledge is to acquire the skills necessary to become a good Muslim member of society. Therefore, careful thought and planning is required by the Muslim woman regarding this issue.

Barriers of Girls' Education in India

India is the developing Muslim minority country. The ratio of girls' education gradually increased in the recent decades but this is not satisfactory standard. Several dimensions of barriers are playing vital role to prevent girls' education. The following common barriers to girls' education:

(1) **Poverty in India:** Poverty of family is a prominent factor disturbing girls' education. In case of financial adversity the poor families cannot meet the costs of education, e.g. school fees, clothing, shoes and books.
(2) **Cultural environment:** In the society established belief that girls' are naturally inferior to boys in psychological ability and aptitude, and hence are less worthy of investment for education, is still very pervasive (USAID, 2002). The commonness of child marriage is another hampering factor (Raynor & Wesson, 2006).
(3) **Inadequate State strategies and policies:** Inadequate legal outline is absent in the areas, e.g. compulsory education, child labour and re-entry into school with deficient national budgetary apportionments to education.
(4) **School atmosphere:** Schools in India offer a miscellaneous atmosphere of learning for girls' depending upon where they are situated, who are involved the management committees are. School atmosphere, for example a separate toilet for girls and potable water is much less favourable in rural areas than in urban areas. Girls' are highly vulnerable outside the home.
(5) Lack of proper religious knowledge.
(6) Lack of political will.

Recommendations: The following recommendations may be considered for the promotion of well start of girls' education in India.

(1) Increase the budgetary allocation and actual expenditure to the education sector especially for girls' education.
(2) Grow awareness programmes with proper direction of religion towards education.
(3) Take particular actions to eradicate poverty, socio-cultural barriers and horror among girls' and parents both on the way to school and within school.
(4) Formulate the policies related to gender education and provide effective mechanism to the proper implementation of girls education in India.
(5) The state apparently prevents the child from leaving school in early. If all children leave schooling for engaged work, then society will suffer irreparable loss in the long run as highly educated and highly skilful people will not be available. This ultimately will lead to the collapse of society (Munir, 2014).

Conclusion

The first human being has honoured for knowledge over all creations and the maiden direction of last religion of Islam is read (*Iqra*). Education is an organized method through which a child or an adult obtains knowledge, skill experience and sound attitude. It creates an individual civilized, cultured, refined and educated. In Islam the concept of education must take into consideration of all the dimensions consist of *tarbiyyah, ta'līmandta'dīb*. Education of girls not only goes to advance the socio-economic status as individuals but also increases the general standard of living of society. Islam perfectly emphasizes about acquiring knowledge without gender discrimination between boys and girls for harmonious development of body mind and soul. However, the reason why Muslim nations are far behind compared to the developed countries is the fact that the Muslims have failed to understand and society and Qur'an pertaining to seeking knowledge and learning. They have marginalized women when it comes to learning and this marginalization of women is that has caused them to be far behind in the race of progress and prosperity. If Muslims properly understand and implement this message of Islam, there is no denying the fact that Islam can take back the same glory which it had in its prime.

References

Abu Salih, M.Y., & Nahlawi, A.R. (1982). *Dirasatfi'l-tarbiyya al-Islamiyya.* Riyad: Muhammad Saud Islamic University.

Abukari, A. (2014). Education of Women in Islam: A Critical Islamic Interpretation of the Qur'an. *Religious Education,* 109, 4-23. http://dx.doi.org/10.1080/00344087.2014.868203

Afshar, B. (2013). Islam and Rights of Children. *International Research Journal of Applied and Basic Sciences*, 7, 750-756.

Ahmed, A.S. (2002). *Discovering Islam: Making Sense of Muslim History and Society.* London: Routledge.

Ajijola, A.A. (1999). Re-Structuring of Islamic Education. New Delhi: Adam Publishers.

Alam, K.U.A., & Muzahid, M.A.U. (2006). Informal Islamic Education and Its Role in Human Resource Development in Society: A Theoretical Evaluation. *IIUC Studies,* 3, 83-92.

Alamgeer, P.M. (2010). *An Analytical Look into Modern & Islamic Education.* Dhaka: Ahsan Publication.

Al-Attas, M.N. (1978). *Islam and secularism.* Malaysia: Muslim Youth Movement of Malaysia.

Al-Attas, M.N. (1991). *The Concept of Education in Islam a Framework for an Islamic Philosophy of Education.* International Institute of Islamic Thought and Civilization, International Islamic University

Al-Attas, N. (1980). *The Concept of Education in Islam.* Malaysia: Muslim Youth Movement of Malaysia.

Al-Bukhari, M. (1987). Sahih al-Bukhari. Hamdaan Publications. Al-Ghazali, I. (1993) Ihya'Ulumuddin Juz III. Beirut: Dar ihya al-Kutub al-Ilmiyah, t. th), hlm, 48, 12.

Ali, A.Y. (1989a). *The Holy Qur'an: Text, Translation and Commentary.* Benton Harbor, MI: Amana Corporation.

Ali, Y. (1989b). *Abdullah, the Holy Qur'an: Text, Translation and Commentary.* USA: Amana Corporation.

Al-Naquib Al-Attas, S. (1979). *Aims and Objectives of Islamic Education.* Sevenoaks [etc.]: Hodder and Stoughton [etc.].

Al-Qaradawi, Y. (1985). The *Lawful and the Prohibited in Islam.* London: Shorouk International.

Al-Sijistani, A.D. u. S. a. A. a., & Hasan, A. (1993). *Sunan Abu Dawud.* Lahore: Sh. M. Ashraf. Ashraf, S.A. (1985). *New Horizons in Muslim Education.* London: Hodder & Stoughton.

Ashraf, S., & Hussain, S. (1979). *Crisis in Muslim Education.* Jeddah: Hodder and Stoughton.

Asif, M., & Khan, M.M. (2010). Comparative Study of Analytical and Synthetic Methods of Teaching Mathematics. *Journal of International Academic Research,* 10, 7.

Badshah, S.N. (2012). Concept of Education in the Light of Qur'an and Sunnah. *International Journal of Education and Social Science*, 3, 487.

Daud, W.M.N.W. (1998). *The Educational Philosophy and Practice of Syed Muhammad Naquib al-Attas: An Exposition of the Original Concept of Islamization. Kuala Lumpur*: International Institute of Islamic Thought and Civilization.

Ibn Sina (1929). *Tadabir al-Manazil aw al-Siyasah al-Ahliyyah*. Baghdad: Maktba'at al-Falah. Imaillah, L. (1999). *Pathway to Paradise: A Guide of Islam*. Carlisle, PA: *Ahmadiyya Movement in Islam*, Time & Time Again.

Islam, M.S. (2015). Fundamental Human Rights towards Childhood: Islamic Guidelines Are Unique to Protect the Child. *Journal of Alternative Perspective in the Social Sciences*, 7, 65-75.

Khamis, M.H., & Salleh, M.J. (2010). The Philosophy and Objectives of Education in Islam. *Proceedings of the Regional Conference on Islamic Education*, Shah Alam, 24-25 July 2010, 1-14.

Khan, M.F. (1988). *The Quraanic Principles of Education*. Dhaka: Islamic Foundation, Bangladesh.

Khan, M.W. (1981). *Education and Society in the Muslim World*. Jeddah: Hodder and Stoughton.

Majah, I. (1952). *Sunan Ibn Majah*. Beirut: Darul Kutub Al Ilmiyyah.

Malaekah, M. (2000). *What Is the Purpose of Life?* Mecca: Islamic Education Foundation.

Munir, M. (2014). *Rights of the Child: An Islamic Perspective on Preventing Violence, Abuse, and Exploitation of Children and Pakistani* Law. (December 14, 2014).

Muslim, I. (1971). Sahih Muslim. Nasr, S.H. (1984). The Islamic Philosophers' Views on Education. *Muslim Education Quarterly*, 2, 5-16.

Nik, R., & Yaacob, N. (2013). An Islamic Perspective on the Role of Education in Responding to Social Issues among Students in Malaysia. Online Submission, 3, 439-446.

Parankimalil, J. (2012). *Meaning, Nature and Aims of Education.* https://johnparankimalil.wordpress.com/.../meaning-nature-and-aims-of Rahman.

F. (1980). *Major Themes of the Qur'an*. Chicago, IL: Bibliotheca Islamica. Rayan, S. (2012). Islamic Philosophy of Education. *International Journal of Humanities and Social Science*, 2, 151-156.

Raynor, J., & Wesson, K. (2006). The Girls' Stipend Programme in Bangladesh. *Journal of Education for International Development*, 2, 1-12.

Sarwar, G. (2001). *Islāmic Education: Its Meaning, Problems & Prospects*. London: Muslim Educational Trust.

Sharif, M.M. (1964). *Islamic and Educational Studies* (Volume 2). Lahore: Institute of Islamic Culture.

Tirmizi, A.I.M. (1980). *Sunan al-Tirmizi. Beirut: Dar al-Fikr*. USAID (2002). https://www.usaid.gov/. Wan Daud, M. (2010). *Al-Attas' concept of ta'dib as true and comprehensive education in Islam.*

Wehr, H., & Cowan, J.M. (1979). *A Dictionary of Modern Written Arabic*: (Arabic-English). Otto: Harrassowitz Verlag.

WORLD-COME (1977). Paper Presented at the First World Conference on Muslim Education, Mecca.

Yalgin, M. (1986). *Al-jawanib al-asasiyyafi'l-tarbiyyaal—Islamiyya*. Beirut: Muassassat al-Rayhani.

Yasin, F., Firdaus, R., & Jani, M. (2013). Islamic Education: The Philosophy, Aim, and Main Features. *International Journal of Education and Research*, 1, 1-18.

14
Human Rights in the Light of Islam

Usma Nazir

Introduction

All human beings are possessed with some basic rights, whose denial or violation is identical to a negation or degradation of which makes us human, because they are so deeply rooted in our humanness. From the perspective of the Qur'an, these rights came into existence when we were created by God in order that all our human potential could be actualized. Rights created or given by God cannot be abolished by any temporal ruler or human agency. Eternal and immutable, they ought to be exercised since everything that God does is for a just purpose. These rights describe certain moral standards of human behaviour and are commonly understood as inalienable fundamental rights or Human Rights; to which every human being is inherently entitled with, and which are inherent in all human beings regardless of their nation, location, language, religion, ethnic origin or any other status. They are applicable everywhere and at every time in the sense of being universal, and they are egalitarian in the sense of being the same for everyone. They are regarded as requiring empathy and the rule of law and imposing an obligation on persons to respect the human rights of others, and it is generally considered that they should not be taken away except as a result of due process based on specific circumstances.

Qur'an is the Magna Carta of human rights and a large part of its concern is to free human beings from the bondage of traditionalism, authoritarianism (religious, political, economic, or any other), tribalism, racism, sexism, slavery or anything else that prohibits or inhibits human beings from actualizing the Qur'anic vision of human destiny embodied in the classic proclamation: *"Towards Allah is thy limit"* (Surah 53: An-Najm: 42). The first thing that we find in Islam in this connection is that it lays down some rights for human beings. In other words it means that every human whether he belongs to this country or that, whether he is a believer or unbeliever, whether he lives in some forest or is found in some desert, whatever be the case, he has some basic human rights simply because he is a human being, which should be recognized by every Muslim. In fact it will be his duty to fulfil these obligations.

The Right to Life

The first and the foremost basic right is the right to live and respect human life. The Holy Qur'an lays down "*Whosoever kills a human being without (any reason like) man slaughter, or corruption on earth, it is as though he had killed all mankind.*" (5:32)

As far as the question of taking life in retaliation for murder or the question of punishment for spreading corruption on this earth is concerned, it can be decided only by a proper and competent court of law. If there is any war with any nation or country, it can be decided only by a properly established government. In any case, no human being has any right by himself to take human life in retaliation or for causing mischief on this earth. Therefore, it is incumbent on every human being that under no circumstances should he be guilty of taking a human life. If anyone has murdered a human being, it is as if he has slain the entire human race. These instructions have been repeated in the Holy Qur'an in another place saying:

Do not kill a soul which Allah has made sacred except through the due process of law (6:151). Here also homicide has been distinguished from destruction of life carried out in pursuit of justice. Only a proper and competent court will be able to decide whether or not an individual has forfeited his right to life by disregarding the right to life and peace of other human beings. The Prophet, may God's blessings be on him, has declared homicide as the greatest sin only next to polytheism. The Tradition of the Prophet reads: "*The greatest sins are to associate something with God and to kill human beings.*" In all these verses of the Qur'an and the Traditions of the Prophet the word 'soul' (*nafs*) has been used in general terms without any distinction or particularization which might have lent itself to the elucidation that the persons belonging to one's nation, the citizens of one's country, the people of a particular race or religion should not be killed. The injunction applies to all human beings and the destruction of human life in itself has been prohibited.

The Right to the Safety of Life

Immediately after the verse of the Holy Qur'an which has been mentioned in connection with the right to life, God has said: "*And whoever saves a life it is as though he had saved the lives of all mankind*" (5:32). There can be several forms of saving man from death. A man may be ill or wounded, irrespective of his nationality, race or colour. If you know that he is in need of your help, then it is your duty that you should arrange for his treatment for disease or wound. If he is dying of starvation, then it is your duty to feed him so that he can ward off death. If he is drowning or his life is at stake, then it is your duty to save him.

Respect for the Chastity of Women

The third important thing that we find in the Charter of Human Rights granted by Islam is that a woman's chastity has to be respected and protected under all circumstances, whether she belongs to our own nation or to the nation of an enemy, whether we find her in the wild forest or in a conquered city; whether she is our co-religionist or belongs to some other religion or has no religion at all. A Muslim cannot outrage her under any circumstances. All promiscuous relationship has been forbidden to him, irrespective of the status or position of the woman, whether the woman is a willing or an unwilling partner to the act. The words of the Holy Qur'an in this respect are: "*Do not approach (the bounds of) adultery*" (17 : 32). Heavy punishment has been prescribed for this crime, and the order has not been qualified by any conditions. Since the violation of chastity of a woman is forbidden in Islam, a Muslim who perpetrates this crime cannot escape punishment whether he receives it in this world or in the Hereafter. This concept of sanctity of chastity and protection of women can be found nowhere else except in Islam.

The Right to a Basic Standard of Life

Speaking about the economic rights the Holy Qur'an enjoins upon its followers: And in their wealth there is acknowledged right for the needy and destitute (51:19).

The words of this injunction show that it is a categorical and unqualified order. Furthermore this injunction was given in

Makkah where there was no Muslim society in existence and where generally the Muslims had to come in contact with the population of the disbelievers. Therefore, the clear meaning of this verse is that anyone who asks for help and anyone who is suffering from deprivation has a right in the property and wealth of the Muslims; irrespective of the fact whether he belongs to this nation or to that nation, to this country or to that country, to this race or to that race. If you are in a position to help and a needy person asks you for help or if you come to know that he is in need, then it is your duty to help him. God has established his right over you, which you have to honour as a Muslim.

Individual's Right to Freedom

Islam has clearly and categorically forbidden the primitive practice of capturing a free man, to make him a slave or to sell him into slavery. On this point the clear and unequivocal words of the Prophet: "*There are three categories of people against whom I shall myself be a plaintiff on the Day of Judgement. Of these three, one is he who enslaves a free man, then sells him and eats this money*" (Al-Bukhari and Ibn Majjah).

The words of this Tradition of the Prophet are also general, they have not been qualified or made applicable to a particular nation, race, country or followers of a particular religion. The Europeans take great pride in claiming that they abolished slavery from the world, though they had the decency to do so only in the middle of the last century. Before this, these Western powers had been raiding Africa on a very large scale, capturing their free men, putting them in bondage and transporting them to their new colonies. The treatment which they have meted out to these unfortunate people has been worse than the treatment given to animals. The books written by the Western people themselves bear testimony to this fact.

The Right to Justice

This is a very important and valuable right which Islam has given to man as a human being. The Holy Qur'an has laid down: *"Do not let your hatred of a people incite you to aggression"* (5:2). "*And do not let ill-will towards any folk incite you so that you swerve from dealing justly. Be just; that is nearest to heedfulness*" (5:8). *Stressing this point the Qur'an again says: "You who believe stand steadfast before God as witness for (truth and) fair play*" (4:135). This makes the point clear that Muslims have to be just not only with ordinary human beings but even with their enemies. In other words, the justice to which Islam invites her followers is not limited only to the citizens of their own country, or the people of their own tribe, nation or race, or the Muslim community as a whole, but it is meant for all the human beings of the world. Muslims, therefore, cannot be unjust to anyone. Their permanent habit and character should be such that no man should ever fear injustice at their hands, and they should treat every human being everywhere with justice and fairness.

Equality of Human Beings

Islam not only recognizes absolute equality between men irrespective of any distinction of colour, race or nationality, but makes it an important and significant principle, a reality. The Almighty God has laid down in the Holy Qur'an: "*O mankind, we have created you from a male and female.*" In other words all human beings are brothers to one another. They all are the descendants from one father and one mother. *"And we set you up as nations and tribes so that you may be able to recognize each other"* (49:13).

This means that the division of human beings into nations, races, groups and tribes is for the sake of distinction, so that people of one race or tribe may meet and be acquainted with the people belonging to another race or tribe and cooperate with one another. This division of the human race is neither meant for one nation to take pride in its superiority over others nor is it meant for one nation to treat another with contempt or disgrace, or regard them as a mean and degraded race and usurp their rights. *"Indeed, the noblest among you before God are the most heedful of you"* (49:13).

In other words the superiority of one man over another is only on the basis of God-consciousness, purity of character and high morals, and not on the basis of colour, race, language or nationality, and even this superiority based on piety and pure conduct does not justify that such people should play lord or assume airs of superiority over other human beings. Assuming airs of superiority is in itself a reprehensible vice which no God-fearing and pious man can ever dream of perpetrating. Nor does the righteous have more privileged rights over others, because this runs counter to human equality, which has been laid down in the beginning of this verse as a general principle. From the moral point of view, goodness and virtue is in all cases better than vice and evil. *This has been exemplified by the Prophet in one of his sayings thus: "No Arab has any superiority over a non-Arab, nor does a non-Arab have any superiority over an Arab. Nor does a white man have any superiority over a black man, or the black man any superiority over the white man. You are all the children of Adam, and Adam was created from clay"* (Al-Bayhaqi and Al-Bazzaz).

In this manner Islam established equality for the entire human race and struck at the very root of all distinctions based on colour, race, language or nationality. According to Islam, God has given man this right of equality as a birth right. Therefore, no man should be discriminated against on the ground of the colour of his skin, his place of birth, the race or the nation in which he was born.

The Right to Co-operate and Not to Co-operate

Islam has prescribed a general principle of paramount importance and universal application saying: "Co-operate with one another for virtue and heedfulness and do not co-operate with one another for the purpose of vice and aggression" (5:2). This means that the man who undertakes a noble and righteous work, irrespective of the fact whether he is living at the North Pole or the South Pole, has the right to expect support and active co-operation from the Muslims. On the contrary he who perpetrates deeds of vice and aggression, even if he is our closest relation or neighbour, does not have the right to win our support and help in the name of race, country, language or nationality, nor should he have the expectation that Muslims will co-operate with him or support him. Nor is it permissible for Muslims to co-operate with him. The wicked and vicious person may be our own brother, but he is not of us, and he can have no help or support from us as long as he does not repent and reform his ways. On the other hand the man who is doing deeds of virtue and righteousness may have no kinship with Muslims, but Muslims will be his companions and supporters or at least his well-wishers.

To conclude we can say that human rights are those basic or fundamental rights, which are granted by Allah and cannot be withdrawn from any race, party or individual. No one has the right to abrogate or withdraw them. They are not simple basic rights only to be conferred on paper for the sake of show and exhibition and not to be enacted upon. These laws are Universal and for all mankind. Every administrator who claims to be a Muslim has to accept these laws. If he denies them or does not enforce them he is a disbeliever, as the Qur'an states: "And those who do not judge by what Allah has laid down they are surely disbelievers." (Holy Qur'an 5: 44)

References

Al-Bayhaqi and Al-Bazzaz cited from All are equal under Islam (2003).

Al-Bukhari and Ibn Majjah cited in *Human Rights in Islam* (1995). Islamic Publications Lahore.

Allamah Abu al-'A'laMawdudi (1407) Human Rights in Islam. *Al Tawhid Journal*, Vol. IV No. 3.

Al-Qur'an Surah 17. Al-Israa, Ayah 32, Juz 15.

Al-Qur'an Surah 4. An-Nisaa, Ayah 135, Juz 6.

Al-Qur'an Surah 49. Al-Hujurat, Ayah 1, Juz 26.

Al-Qur'an Surah 5. Al-Maida, Ayah 2, Juz 7.

Al-Qur'an Surah 5. Al-Maida, Ayah 32, Juz 7.

Al-Qur'an Surah 5. Al-Maida, Ayah 44, Juz 7.

Al-Qur'an Surah 5. Al-Maida, Ayah 8, Juz 7.

Al-Qur'an Surah 51. Az-Zariyat, Ayah 19, Juz 27.

Al-Qur'an Surah 53. An-Najm, Ayah 42.

Al-Qur'an Surah 6. Al-An'am, Ayah 151 Juz 8.

15

Tajdid (Islamic Revival) of Shah Wali Allah Dehlawi: Political Dimension

Thanveer T.

Introduction

The political condition of India during Shah Wali Allah's lifetime was characterized by instability and insecurity. Violence and conflicts, looting and pillage were prevalent everywhere. The stability of the Mughal reign was shaken during the last years of Emperor Aurangzeb, but the situation was kept under control due to the firmness and determination of the emperor.[1] By the death of Aurangazeb the era of great Mughals was ended.

Mughal Empire in the Post-Aurangazeb Era

As the weakened Mughal authority was not able to militarily enforce rules and regulations in all parts of the empire, many regional governors and kingdoms which had been subjugated by the early Mughals rejected their central authority and claimed independence. Some regional groups emerged like the Marathas, Jats, Sikhs and Rajputs etc. and consolidated their political power. Due to the disintegration of the Mughal Empire, people had to suffer much at their hands.

The empire remained united but the conflicts in the nobility reached their height in Bahadur Shah's reign (r.1707-1712). After his short rule, the Mughal Empire entered a period of rapid decline attributable both to his sudden death and the empire's geographical overreach.

From Shah Wali Allah's (1703-1762) childhood the period of supreme authority of the Mughal ruler came to an end and a new era of the supremacy of kingmakers began. With Bahadur Shah's death in February 1712, the rulers began to be confined to the role of puppets. The posts of *wazir* and *bakhshi al-mamalik* were shared by either one leader or between close relatives. The main concern of the *wazir* was to post his own kinsmen or favourites in the governorship of prominent areas and provide them with high privileges. *Farmans* (royal edicts) to governors and local officials were sent by the nobles in the emperor's name, but were meant to serve their own interests.

The individual failure of the later Mughals caused the disintegration of the imperial power. Jahandar Shah (r.1712-1713) lacked control over the empire, Farrukhsiyar (r.1713-1719) was fickle-minded, and Muhammad Shah Rangila (1720-1748) was a pleasure-seeker and a drunkard.

The gradual disintegration of the central authority caused the emergence of many regional kingdoms. Many talented nobles established independent kingdoms for themselves. Then the main focus of the central authority was to preserve its image by ensuring the flow of revenue from different regions.[2]

Many ethnic and sectarian groups such as the Jats, Marathas and Sikhs emerged in this period but their mutual rivalries prevented them from consolidating their power. Thus they failed to become an effective challenge to the Mughals.

The biggest power that emerged in the Mughal reign was that of the Marathas. They gathered tribute from the Mughal territories under the title of *sardeshmukhi* and *chauth* (one-tenth and one-fourth of land revenue respectively).

Nadir Shah's Invasion and its Impact

Nadir Shah attacked Delhi in 1739 with a well-trained army, expert in guerrilla tactics. They mercilessly slaughtered the inhabitants of Delhi and looted and plundered their property. Around twenty thousand people, including women, children and old men, were killed in the massacre.[3]

Nadir Shah's invasion of Delhi speeded up the disintegration of the empire. Many small dynasties were established in different parts of the country. Sa'adat Khan established his independent reign in Awadh, 'Ali Wardi Khan established his rule in Bengal, and Nizam al-Mulk in Hyderabad. Punjab was conquered by the Sikhs, while the south-Western realms were captured by the Marathas. Bihar, Orissa and

Bengal were almost destroyed by the Maratha campaigns. Delhi was totally disturbed by Irani-Turani conflicts. The Marathas could establish their hold in Delhi through the princes who sought their help to defeat their Irani and Turani enemies.[4]

The Marathas sought help from the Jats and attacked Delhi in August 1757. They advanced into Punjab, captured Lahore in April 1758 and turned to Rohelkhand. Instead of attacking Mughal soldiers, the Marathas massacred common Muslims throughout the campaign, whereas the Mughal soldiers didn't target the Hindu people.[5]

The Third Battle of Panipat and its Impact

Ahmad Shah Abdali, the Afghan ruler, attacked India in 1759. He captured Punjab and re-established Muslim rule there. Then he moved towards Delhi and defeated and killed Data Sindhia. A combined army of Janko Ji Sindhia and Milhar Rao tried to stop Ahmad Shah Abdali but they were also defeated. Ahmad Shah Abdali captured Delhi on 30 August 1760. Shiv Rao Bhao, who had defeated Nizam al-Mulk in the Deccan, came with his Maratha troops to fight against Abdali. The Afghans and Marathas met at Panipat and the battle continued for a few months. On 14 January, 1761 Afghan troops defeated the Marathas and killed Shiv Rao Bhao and Viswas Rao.

The third battle of Panipat indirectly determined the fate of India. The Sikhs lost in Punjab. The Rajputs who tried to recover their lost lands were prevented by Nizam al-Mulk. The supremacy of the *Peshwa* (chief minister) was no longer recognized in the Maratha confederacy and the clans of Holkar, Bhosle, Sindhia, and Gaikwad, became virtually independent. The British used the defeat of the Marathas as an opportunity to consolidate their power in India.

The eighteenth century was not lacking in talent and efforts. Many leaders such as Dawud Khan, Muhammad Khan Bangash, 'Ali Muhammad Khan, Sa'adat Khan Burhan al-Mulk, Dost Muhammad Khan, Murshid Quli Khan, Haydar 'Ali and Najib al-Dawla, rose from very humble origins. But the inability of the Mughals to utilize their talent, efforts, initiative, qualities of leadership, dynamism and farsightedness led them to establish independent kingdoms in different parts of the country.

Shah Wali Allah's *tajdid* in the Prevalent Political Situation

The Arabic word *tajdid* implies renewal. In the context of Islam *tajdid* refers to revival, i.e. "cleansing Islam of all un-Godly elements and presenting it and making it flourish more or less in its original pure form. Islamic revival is neither striking compromises with un-Islam, nor preparing new blends of Islam and un-Islam."[6] One who undertakes *tajdid* is a *mujaddid.* He "is a most un-compromising person with regard to un-Islam and one least tolerant as to the presence of even a tinge of un-Islam in the Islamic system."[7] Shah Wali Allah is regarded as the *mujaddid* of the eighteenth century so that his revivalism on the prevalent conditions of India is very significant.

Although Shah Wali Allah Dehlawi was extremely disturbed by the condition, yet he did not let despair; rather he determined to eradicate evils and to strengthen Islam in the society. The two major objectives of his revival were the restoration of peace in the empire and the reformation and reconstruction of law according *shari'ah.*[8] In order to fulfil these objectives he sought contact with the contemporary Muslim rulers, scholars and officials through meetings and letters which suggested eradicating evils and saving India. He also tried to familiarize the teachings of Islam among the rulers and ruled, so that they could easily understand and rely on it.

Shah Wali Allah pondered that how Islam to be strengthened in India and how regain the former glory of Muslims. He found that the only solution is returning to the early Muslim caliphate adopting their peculiar characters.[9] He was aware that the Muslims were unable to get rid of the malaise of kingship, so that instead of presenting a utopian model state, he sought both the ruler and ruled to reabsorb the faith and spirit. He believed that Islam was a universal religion which cannot be occurred in one cultural pattern. Analysing its history one could see that its spirit and faith were always same, but its body was always evolved with changing times and contexts.

In order to strengthen Islam in the reign Shah Wali Allah Dehlawi boldly criticised corruption, misdeeds, luxury, indolence of the contemporary rulers and their officials. He advised them to leave the evils and to repent for their past. Similarly, he advised the soldiers to adopt true Islamic practices. He sought them to leave their hostile approach towards common people and their addiction intoxicants. According to Shah Wali Allah the ruler was obliged to make arrangements for the proper training of the army. The superintendents were obliged to be brave, kind hearted to their colleagues and subordinates, and loyal to the ruler. Each and every official of the state was to be regularly paid because due to the delay in getting salaries they had to borrow money on interest which would ruin not only them, but also the entire system.[10]

According to Shah Wali Allah only those who adopted orthodox beliefs and had never been charged with bribery was to be appointed as judges and regulators of public business. The leaders of prayers were to be well-paid. It is the duty of the ruler to instruct them to lead the daily prayers punctually.[11]

Shah Wali Allah suggested that the territory whose revenues accrued directly to the royal treasury (*khalisah*) was required to be extended because the major sources of weak administration was decrease in *khalisah* land and the consequent shortage in treasury.[12]

Shah Wali Allah's letters served as the instrument to bring about the third battle of Panipat. Through letters and meetings, he pleaded and encouraged Nizam al-mulk, the ruler of Hyderabad, Najid al-Dawla, the Rohilla chief and Ahmad Shah 'Abdali, the Afghan ruler to end the exploitations of Jats, Sikhs and Marathas and to restore peace.[13]

Conclusion

The meetings and letters of Shah Wali Allah Dehlawi with the leaders of his time was the practical way of his *tajdid* (revival). Besides that he interpreted the political teachings of Islam. *Al-Budur al Bazigha*, *Izalat al Khifa 'anKhilafat al Khulafa'*, *Hujjat Allah al-Baligha* and the *Political Epistles of Shah Wali Allah Dehlawi* are the writings of Shah Wali Allah which provide his political ideas.

The process of Islamic revival (*tajdid)* requires a new mode of *ijtihad* as Shah Wali Allah Dehlavi had done with an insight and independent mind.

Acknowledgement: This paper is a part of my Ph.D. research, being pursued under the supervision of Dr. Safia Amir, Department of Islamic Studies, Hamdard University, New Delhi.

Notes

1. Sayyid Athar Abbas Rizvi, *Shah Wali Allah and His Times*, Australia, 1980, p. 6.

2. http://download.nos.org/srsec315new/History%20Book_L15.pdf, p. 252 (Retrieved on 20/09/2014)
3. Rizvi op.cit., p. 144.
4. Khaliq Ahmad Nizami, *Shah Wali Allah Dehlavi ki Siyasi Maktubat*, Delhi, 1969, pp. 42-43.
5. *Ibid.* pp. 43-44.
6. Sayyid Abu al A'la Maududi & Al-Ash'ari, *A Short History of Revivalist Movement in Islam* (*Tajdid WaIhya' al-Din*), Delhi, 2010, p. 37.
7. *Ibid.*
8. Abdur Rashid Bhat, *Political Thought of Shah Wali-u-Allah, an analytical study*, Delhi, 1996, p. 87
9. Shah Wali Allah, and Hujjat al-Islam Maulana Abd al-Shukur Sahib Faruqi, *Izālat al-Khifā' 'anKhilāfat al-Khulafā'*. Deoband, pp. 31-50.
10. Abdur Rashid Bhat, *Political Thought of Shah Wali-u-Allah, An analytical study*, 1996, pp. 85-87.
11. K.A. Nizami, "Shah Wali Allah: His Work in the Political Field", *A History of Freedom Movement*, vol. 1, Karachi, 1957, pp. 522-24.
12. *Ibid.*
13. *Ibid.*, p. 88; J.N. Jalbani, *Life of Shah Wali Allah*, p. 47.

References

English

1. Al-Ghazali, Muhammad. *The Socio-Political Thought of Shah Wali Allah*. Delhi: Adam Publishers and Distributers, 2009.
2. Bhat, A.R. *Political Thought of Shah Wali-u-Allah*. Delhi: Adam Publishers, 1996.
3. Bhatia, Harbans Singh. *Mughal Empire in India: Their Political, Legal, Social, Cultural, Religious and Military Systems*. New Delhi: Elegant Printers, 2001.
4. Chandra, Satish. *Parties and Politics at the Mughal Court: 1707-1740*. New Delhi: Oxford University Press, 2002.
5. Cheema, G.S. *The Forgotten Mughals: A History of the Later Emperors of the House of Babar, 1707-1857*. Delhi: Manohar Publishers and Distributers, 2002.
6. Jalbani, G.N. *Life of Shah Waliyullah*. Delhi: Idarah-i Adabiyyat-i Dilli, 2009.
7. K.A. Nizami, *"Shah Wali Allah: His Work in the Political Field", A History of Freedom Movement*, Vol. 1, Karachi: Pakistan Historical Society, 1957.
8. Keene, Henry George. *The Fall of the Moghul Empire*. Delhi: Atlantic Publishers and Distributers, 2000.
9. Maududi, Sayyid Abu al-A'la. *A Short History of Revivalist Movement in Islam*. New Delhi: Markazi Maktaba Islami Publishers, 2010.

10. Rizvi, Sayyid Athar Abbas. *Shah Wali-Allah and His Times, A Study of Eighteenth Century Politics and Society in India.* Australia: Ma'rifat Publishing House, 1980.

Urdu

1. 'Abd al-'Aziz, Shah., *Malfuzat Shah 'Abd al-'Aziz,* Meerut, 1897.
2. Dehlavi, Shah Wali Allah, and Hujjat al-Islam Maulana Abd al-Shukur Sahib Faruqi, *Izālat al-Khifā' 'an Khilāfat al-Khulafā'*. Deoband: Hafzi Book Depot, 1995.
3. Nizami, K.A., *Shah Wali Allah Dehlawike Siyasi Maktubat*, Delhi. 1146 A.H. (1822 A.D).

Index